THE STRESSES OF
COUNSELLING
IN

COUNSELLING · IN ACTION ·

Series editor: Windy Dryden

Counselling in Action is a series of books developed especially for counsellors and students of counselling which provides clear and explicit guidelines for counselling practice. A special feature of the series is the emphasis it places on the *process* of counselling.

Titles include:

Standards and Ethics for Counselling in Action
Tim Bond

Feminist Counselling in Action
Jocelyn Chaplin

Gestalt Counselling in Action
Petrūska Clarkson

Hard-Earned Lessons from Counselling in Action
Edited by Windy Dryden

Questions and Answers on Counselling in Action
Edited by Windy Dryden

Training and Supervision for Counselling in Action
Edited by Windy Dryden and Brian Thorne

Psychodynamic Counselling in Action
Michael Jacobs

Person-Centred Counselling in Action
Dave Mearns and Brian Thorne

Transactional Analysis Counselling in Action
Ian Stewart

Cognitive-Behavioural Counselling in Action
Peter Trower, Andrew Casey and Windy Dryden

Psychosynthesis Counselling in Action
Diana Whitmore

THE STRESSES OF
COUNSELLING

IN *Action*

EDITED BY
WINDY DRYDEN

SAGE Publications
London · Thousand Oaks · New Delhi

First published 1995

 SAGE Publications Ltd
6 Bonhill Street
London EC2A 4PU

SAGE Publications Inc
2455 Teller Road
Thousand Oaks, California 91320

SAGE Publications India Pvt Ltd
32, M-Block Market
Greater Kailash – I
New Delhi 110 048

British Library Cataloguing in Publication data

A catalogue record for this book is available from the British
Library.

ISBN 0 8039 8995 4
ISBN 0 8039 8996 2 pbk

Library of Congress catalog card number 94-69048

Typeset by Mayhew Typesetting, Rhayader, Powys
Printed in Great Britain by Biddles Ltd, Guildford

Contents

Preface

Counsellors frequently work with people who are under stress or who are distressed. To counsel effectively, counsellors need to be able to give all their attention to their clients and to do this they need to be relatively free from stress themselves. However, we are increasingly becoming aware that counselling itself can be a stressful activity for the counsellor. Such stress can emerge in the work that counsellors do with specific client groups (see Part 1), in the contexts in which counselling takes place (see Part 2) and in the educational process both for counsellor educators and for counsellors in training (see Part 3).

In this book these themes are explored by workers with first-hand experience of dealing with stress in counsellors. First, though, their contributions are put into context by Brady *et al.* in the opening chapter, who review the relevant research that has been carried out on counsellor stress. Contributors were asked to use a common chapter structure in which they were to introduce their topic, describe the nature of the stresses that counsellors experience in the relevant area, detail the typical responses (healthy and unhealthy) that counsellors make to the stresses described, and suggest methods for improved coping.

Editing a book can also be a stressful experience! However, I would like to thank all the contributors for helping to make the compilation of this book relatively stress free and an important addition to the Counselling in Action series.

1 Stress in Counsellors: An Integrative Research Review

Joan L. Brady, Francis C. Healy, John C. Norcross and James D. Guy

Few professions provide the variety, challenge and satisfaction found in a counselling career. The array of extrinsic and intrinsic rewards continues to draw talented, caring individuals into this type of work. However, with the potential rewards come serious hazards that must be addressed throughout the career of psychotherapists. To thrive in this role it is necessary to be cognizant of and prepared for the pitfalls inherent in a counselling practice.

In this introductory chapter we have set for ourselves the ambitious task of overviewing the vast literature on counsellor stress and extracting its recurrent themes. We can properly be criticized for favouring breadth over depth; length restrictions did not afford a more comprehensive review or consideration of coping with these stressors, the latter a focus of our forthcoming book (Norcross and Guy, 1995) and the 'Suggestions for improved coping' which conclude the subsequent chapters in this book. Our integrative literature review yielded seven broad, overlapping burdens of practising counselling: patient behaviours, working conditions, emotional depletion, physical isolation, psychic isolation, therapeutic relationships and personal disruptions. We have drawn from our own clinical experiences, the relevant literature published in English (and largely in the United States), and the following chapters in this volume to describe and amplify these seven ubiquitous stressors experienced by mental health professionals.[1]

It is our sincere hope that the discussion contained in this chapter (and, indeed, the entire book) will assist readers in obtaining the conceptual and experiential tools required for a long, satisfying career as a mental health professional. The resulting satisfactions and pleasures are worth every bit of effort at identifying and managing the liabilities that accompany this endeavour.

Patient behaviours

Probably the largest amount of empirical research on the stressors of psychotherapy practice has been conducted on client behaviours. In general studies, both Deutsch (1984) and Farber (1983a) found similar results concerning the most distressing patient presentations as perceived by mental health professionals. Deutsch (1984) listed suicidal statements, anger toward the therapist, severely depressed patients, apathy or lack of motivation, and premature termination as most stressful, in that order. Farber (1983a) found suicidal statements, aggression and hostility, premature termination, agitated anxiety, and apathy and depression as the most stressful. Let us consider these behaviours in turn.

Of all the patients who test our patience, those who are suicidal top the list (Chemtob *et al.*, 1989). Kottler (1986) describes the challenge of treating suicidal patients on four levels. First, therapists may feel terrified at the knowledge of being so close to someone so desperate that nothingness seems a viable option. Second, clinicians can experience immense responsibility to help a suicidal patient. The moral and professional obligations are extraordinary, and any mistake may prove to be lethal. Third, once a patient is assessed as suicidal, the entire therapeutic process is altered. Extra precautions on the part of the staff must be made, and everything must be done 'by the book'. Kottler (1986: 74) states that 'the margin for error is small, and the pressure on the therapist is profound'. Fourth, being able to leave the problems of dealing with a suicidal patient at the office constitutes an additional challenge. Bringing the pressure into one's personal life will only compound the stress for all involved. It is easy to understand why suicidal statements lead the lists of stressful client behaviours.

Should the tragedy of a patient suicide ensue, the psychotherapists involved will probably experience substantial disruptions in their personal and professional lives. Approximately one-quarter of psychologists and one-half of psychiatrists will experience a patient's suicide (Chemtob *et al.*, 1989). What places a therapist at higher risk of experiencing the suicide of a patient? Age, experience, gender and theoretical orientation appear to have relatively insignificant bearings, but practice characteristics, such as work settings and the types of disorders treated, are significant predictors (Chemtob *et al.*, 1989). Patient suicide may represent the ultimate failure for a psychotherapist, who is left to deal with the sadness, anger, self-doubt, confusion and fear of it happening again.

Not far behind on the lists of stressful client behaviours is aggression, including physical violence. Approximately 40 per cent of clinical psychologists have been attacked by a patient at least once during their professional career (Guy *et al.*, 1992b). The most frequent negative effects of actual physical attacks are an increase in the personal sense of vulnerability, escalation of fearfulness, decrease in emotional well-being, increase in a loved one's concern for the clinician's personal safety, and a decrease in feelings of competency (Guy *et al.*, 1990, 1991). Intense anxiety, fatigue, headaches, ruminations, hyperactivity, nightmares, flashbacks and intermittent anger are also common consequences of patient violence (Guy *et al.*, 1990; Wykes and Whittington, 1991).

Patient violence and aggression manifest themselves beyond overt physical attacks, of course. Unwanted phone calls to the home or office, verbal threats against one's personal safety and that of the family, and threats of destruction to the office contents or home all represent violence (Guy *et al.*, 1992a). Having experienced these violations, clinicians acknowledge ongoing concern for their safety and well-being, which extends beyond physical attacks to emotional wellness.

Severely apathetic and depressed clients are bound to evoke anxiety in a psychotherapist. A continuous string of 'Uh', 'Um', 'Yes' and 'No' can elicit frustration in the best of therapists. The withdrawn and silent patient can make a single hour seem endless; time stands still. Eventually, therapists may begin to suspect themselves and their competency. Sometimes they even begin talking and answering for the client, and the whole process breaks down. When this happens, the therapist runs into tremendous pressure to 'get' the client to speak and make the treatment 'work' (Corey and Corey, 1989).

The threat of malpractice or ethical complaint is omnipresent in helping professions, and psychotherapy is no exception. Over a 13-year period, about 1 per cent of American psychologists have been sued – a rate that has remained stable in recent years (Dorken, 1990). Approximately one-quarter of psychologists report being in a situation – suicide, homicide, child custody evaluations and fee disputes, for example – which caused them to fear an ethical complaint or a malpractice suit (Knapp *et al.*, 1993). However, the determination of guilt or innocence due to malpractice or an ethics infraction is only part of the story. A year-long investigation may eventually bring out the truth, but not before the therapist has had to fight for her reputation, defend herself to her peers, and survive the mental anguish of the harassment involved (Kottler, 1986).

Although it is impossible to fault them directly, terminally ill patients will also probably provoke distress. Our life experiences and professional training are usually inadequate to prepare us for the dilemmas involved when working with dying patients (Bennett, 1991). The death of patients elicits old feelings and memories associated with loss, death and dying, which prompt the clinician to confront mortality. In the case of AIDS victims, these distressing reactions are often amplified in the therapist. These clients may displace their feelings of anger, betrayal and hope-lessness on to the therapist. Sexually explicit topics may be encountered with discomfort and, far more disconcertingly, the therapist is likely to encounter the death of relatively young clients.

Virtually all patients experiencing interpersonal difficulties will bring those problematic relationship patterns into the consulting room with them. Perhaps the most difficult to manage are those suffering from personality disorders.

Passive-aggressive and covertly resistant behaviours are special challenges. The notorious signs of passive-aggressive behaviour include late arrival, minimal disclosure and hollow assurance that all is well. Although appearing bored, these patients constantly inform the therapist that they are managing nicely. Accentuating the distress is the fact that these behaviours are so hard to deal with directly – an 'elusive' quality, not always amenable to firm evidence or a confident interpretation. Corey and Corey (1989: 105) state, 'You don't know what hit you ... however, you will certainly have reactions to clients who make hostile remarks, who offer sarcasm, and who seem to engage in hit and run behavior.' Monitoring, controlling and expressing these reactions contribute mightily to therapist distress.

A common passive-aggressive manifestation in psychotherapy is premature termination, which frequently results in relatively high degrees of stress for the counsellor (Farber, 1983b). This under-scores the reality that therapists are not simply detached observers of the psychotherapeutic process; we do not consider our patients to be replaceable parts. Clinicians are personally as well as professionally invested in the emotional growth and welfare of patients, and they experience feelings of rejection and regret when treatment is terminated prematurely.

Clients suffering from dependent personality disorders desire to make someone else responsible for their reactions. Such patients must check with their therapists first before making even a minor decision. Their fragile sense of self often manifests itself in seeking continual reassurance of their therapist's love and appreciation. Dependent clients want their therapist to tell them what to do, how to do it, and when to do it (Corey and Corey, 1989).

Seductive and histrionic clients can stretch a counsellor's power of restraint to the limit. For these patients, such behaviour satisfies their desire to flirt with the forbidden but frustrates the therapist in much the same way that treatment frustrates the patient (Kottler, 1986). For the therapist, the pressures of temptation are sometimes overwhelming and may interfere with the therapy itself. If the practitioner is unable to address the situation effectively, the relationship is lost and the treatment is unsuccessful.

The ultimate test of stress management may well be patients suffering from borderline personality disorder. In one person, the therapist encounters many of the distressing patient behaviours previously discussed: recurrent suicidal threats, self-mutilating acts, intense anger alternating with chronic dysphoria and loneliness, identity disturbance, and the worst elements of histrionic and passive-aggressive disorders. These behaviours can be so over-whelming that it is hard to know where to begin. The therapist is so busy extinguishing weekly brush fires caused by 'acting out' behaviour that it becomes difficult to attend to the underlying forest fire in the patient's identity.

The range of stressful patient behaviours seems infinite at times. Our core is touched again and again, as Coppenhall writes in Chapter 2 of this book, describing therapists working with sexually abused clients and hearing their unspeakable horrors. In Chapter 3 Bond addresses the 'death sentence' of HIV/AIDS patients and the consequences of counsellors getting caught up in these patients' secrecy, uncertainty and loss. Working with physically disabled patients, according to Segal in Chapter 4, can activate nightmares of our own old age or dying and terrors of being confined to a wheelchair. And those conducting family therapy will invariably confront physical violence and emotional abuse in the families before them as well as residual pain from their own family of origin. Independent of the demographics and disorders of the particular client, the core of the therapist as a person is indeed touched again and again.

Working conditions

Ideally, a practitioner's workplace is a 'holding environment' or a 'safe haven' for the therapist perpetually confronted with this litany of conflict-ridden patient behaviours. But realistically, the workplace often represents an additional source of stress.

Any one of a wide range of employment conditions contributes to therapist distress. Organizational politics, excessive paperwork, demanding workloads and professional conflicts head the list of complaints of experienced practitioners (Farber and Heifetz, 1981). Students who enter the helping professions identify the slowness of the system, resistance to new ideas and unrealistic expectations as major sources of their stress (Corey and Corey, 1989).

Stillson, White and Harris (1986) describe two types of work-related stress: episodic and chronic. Episodic work stress encompasses events that occur sporadically and produce changes in the psychotherapist's life, such as an increase in caseload or a promotion from practitioner to supervisor. Chronic work stress, by contrast, develops over a period of time from constant pressures, such as too much work given the time constraints or being excluded from administrative decisions.

As House observes in Chapter 6, virtually all healing contexts are dominated by a sense of damage, despair and disease. And that's only the clients! Throw in bureaucratic nonsense, colleague misbehaviour, inadequate resources, onerous paperwork and assorted other organizational and peer problems and one begins to recognize the potential damage of 'working conditions' in the helping professions.

To be sure, different contexts bring different patterns of stress, as is amply demonstrated in Part 3. The type of practice setting also emerges in the research literature as a significant determinant of the work-related stress encountered. Hellman and Morrison (1987) found that psychotherapists in an institutional setting, as opposed to private practice, reported more stress in the form of personal depletion and overinvolvement in their work. However, psychotherapists in private practice found patient behaviours more stressful, particularly negative affect, patient resistances, suicidal threats and passive-aggressive behaviour. The type of stress, but not the amount, differed by practice location.

Several studies have been conducted to explicate the stress encountered in private practice. In one study, the major stresses of independent practice were, in descending order, time pressures, economic uncertainty, caseload uncertainty, business aspects and excessive workload (Nash *et al.*, 1984). Negligible sources of stress were professional conflicts, monotony of the work, and loss of authenticity in relating to patients. Recurrent themes distinctive to private practitioners include frustrations with insurance companies and third-party reimbursers, and unrealistic demands for superhuman feats from clients, insurers and the court system (Nash *et al.*, 1984). According to Guy (1987: 247):

> The financial instability and risk associated with full- or part-time private practice, engaged in by as many as 90% of those psychotherapists surveyed, was found to be another source of difficulty. Also, the tendency towards overwork and overcommitment can have a detrimental impact on the life and relationships of some therapists.

The moral is that each work setting comes equipped with generic stressors as well as its unique pressures.

In an agency, a counsellor is often expected to meet unrealistic demands, especially insistence that problems be solved quickly and efficiently. A helper in an institution may be under pressure to see that behavioural changes take place in a specified time, so that more people are provided with service and increased income is generated. If staff are unable to meet regulations, policies and procedures, they may experience feelings of frustration, anger, guilt and disillusionment. When there is an absence of criteria for client success, therapists are left to define their own terms, which often prove to be unrealistic or idealistic (Raider, 1989).

Cooper (1986) asserts that the psychotherapist is greatly hindered by the general absence of outcome data. Most counsellors have little objective means for confirming their long-range effectiveness with clients. The lack of such knowledge fuels the counsellor's feelings of self-doubt and may lead to guilt and self-recriminations for their supposed incompetence. This cynicism may extend even further, causing the clinician to begin questioning the efficacy of psychotherapy in general. Self-esteem is lost when practising a profession that has no perceived merit.

Even those mental health professionals at the upper end of institutions encounter their own forms of stress from working conditions. Residency directors experience unique pressures and difficulties – picking residents, struggling to ensure that the faculty provides adequate care, contending with bureaucratic details, being overloaded with tasks, and warily watching residents released to function independently, to name a few (Yager and Borus, 1990). Clinical supervisors, likewise, must attend to multiple and occasionally conflicting constituencies: student learning, client welfare, programme requirements and so forth (Carroll in Chapter 11).

Several studies have examined the covariation of work stress among counsellors. First, clinical experience makes a difference: older, more experienced therapists generally report less stress associated with work-related factors, including scheduling and overinvolvement, than less experienced therapists (Hellman *et al.*, 1987). Second, size of the practitioner's caseload obviously matters: counsellors with heavy caseloads (more than 32 hours per week) report more work stress concerning their relationships, scheduling and doubt than those therapists with average caseloads. Third is the type of caseload: therapists with primarily psychotic or character-disordered patients report more stress from work-related factors than those with primarily neurotic patients (Hellman and Morrison, 1987). This result is consistent with previous findings of less satisfaction and poorer relationships among therapists at institutions with more difficult and chronic patients.

Emotional depletion

As the above discussions have illustrated, the field of counselling is riddled with a plethora of occupational stressors. However, the impact these stressors exert on the counsellor varies from person to person. While some therapists are challenged and even invigorated by increased stress, others become emotionally depleted, run down, or 'burnt out' by the same pressure. House, in Chapter 6, laments the dearth of discussion on the *psychodynamics* of stress: the failure to link stress symptoms to underlying personality vulnerabilities. Characteristics of patients and settings will obviously affect therapists differently, largely depending on their predisposing personality characteristics. These are the clients or issues that 'ring our bells', 'push our buttons' and 'activate our neuroses'. One person's stressor is another's invigorator. But however individualized, it is the unmediated, unrelenting stress and resultant dissatisfaction that breeds burnout.

While burnout has been defined in a variety of ways (Freudenberger and Richelson, 1980; Perlman and Hartman, 1982; Guy, 1987), Pines and Maslach (1978: 233) directly link emotional depletion to burnout. These authors define burnout as 'physical and emotional exhaustion, involving the development of negative self-concept, negative job attitudes, and loss of concern and feelings for clients'. When the emotional drain from work-related factors is so great that it hinders personal and professional functioning, the therapist is likely to be suffering from burnout.

According to Farber (1990), approximately 2–6 per cent of psychotherapists are experiencing burnout at any one time. However, in a survey by Wood, Klein, Cross, Lammers and Elliot (1985), psychotherapists estimated that 26 per cent of their colleagues suffered from symptoms related to burnout and depression and over 32 per cent of the respondents reported experiencing burnout and depression to a degree serious enough to interfere with their work. Thus, while exact numbers are difficult to obtain, burnout in the helping professions is prevalent.

What are the typical clinical consequences of burnout? Therapists suffering from burnout may exhibit more rigid, narrow-minded thinking with a decreased capacity to handle ambiguity (Freudenberger, 1975). They may also become more detached, critical and suspicious, making tolerance and acceptance of clients more difficult. Farber (1990) notes that emotional changes such as increased anxiety, sadness and irritability may be observed. Such cognitive and affective changes mean that therapists may be less caring and giving to their patients. Physically, the therapist is likely to be exhausted and have difficulty relaxing and sleeping (Guy, 1987). Psychosomatic symptoms – headaches, muscle tension and hypertension – may increase (Farber, 1990). Behavioural changes occur as well, such as decreased work productivity and increased use of alcohol and drugs. The burnt-out therapist may become more argumentative, leading to increased conflict with family and friends (Farber, 1990). This, along with many of the changes mentioned, puts a great strain on inter-personal relationships, heightening communication problems and feelings of isolation (Freudenberger, 1975).

In general, burnout stems from a wide range of factors including therapist and patient characteristics, work conditions and societal attitudes (Guy and Brown, 1992). One recent longitudinal study found that high job stress, inadequate supervisor support, inadequate organizational resources, dissatisfaction with clientele, low self-esteem and high number of hours worked all significantly predict burnout among social workers (Poulin and Walter, 1993). As one might expect, therapists who tend to be overly idealistic, high achievers, socially isolated or controlling are more susceptible to burnout (Freudenberger, 1975; Deutsch, 1984; Freudenberger and Robbins, 1979). Farber (1990) summarizes his research on therapist burnout by concluding that therapists become burnt out when their work does not, ultimately, 'pay off'. While therapists expect a fair amount of stress in their daily work they also expect to reap benefits that compensate for their efforts. Farber found that lack of therapeutic success was the most stressful part of counsellors' work and that lack of mutual giving and responsibility in the therapeutic relationships was deemed most responsible for burnout. Constantly giving to patients, without the satisfaction of success, leads to discontent and eventual burnout.

Women may be especially vulnerable to burnout and career dissatisfaction. Female psychotherapists have chosen two histori-cally non-traditional roles: psychotherapist and professional woman (Rasmussen and Guy, 1989). Societal pressure to conform to a more standard female role can be quite stressful, especially when coupled with one's own self-doubt about career choice and competence. Married women and those who have children are under even more pressure. A woman therapist with a family is often pulled in many directions as she attempts to relate and respond to the needs of her patients, her family and her self alike (Gadzella *et al.*, 1991; Freudenberger and Robbins, 1979).

Constant juggling depletes the emotional reservoir already tapped by clinical responsibilities.

The increased number of dual career families calls for a reorganization of household roles and a rethinking of sex role stereotypes and duties for successful adaptation (Freudenberger, 1984). It appears that married women psychotherapists still hold more responsibility for household and family affairs than do their spouses (Rasmussen and Guy, 1989). Wahl *et al.* (in press) found that female therapists in their study reported that their biggest stressor was trying to manage a home while maintaining a professional career.

Physical isolation

Despite the expectations of many counsellors entering the field, psychotherapeutic practice often does not provide a deep sense of interpersonal intimacy and connection. In fact, one of the most common stressors that result from conducting psychotherapy is intense isolation and aloneness (Deutsch, 1984; Hellman *et al.*, 1986). This isolation emanates from both physical and psychological factors inherent in the practice of psychotherapy.

Few anticipate the physical isolation that stems from conducting psychotherapy in the same small room, hour after hour. With clients often scheduled back to back, there is little opportunity to emerge from the consulting room for an extended period of time. Few, if any, interruptions are permitted. The usual 50-minute hour is guarded closely; phone calls or interruptions are permitted only for urgent matters. The therapist is hidden away, with little exposure to the daily happenings of life outside the therapy room walls. While some therapists may find this withdrawal comforting to a degree, the isolation eventually becomes a great strain (Cooper, 1986).

The physical seclusion endemic to psychotherapeutic work also extends to the outside world. The counsellor is often oblivious to the outside surroundings, unaware of changes in weather or environment. Therapists with large client loads or who work long hours may begin and end their days in darkness. Local, national or international events may also occur without the therapist's knowledge. While clients may be the only contact with the outside world, most therapists would consider it inappropriate to quiz clients on world events when they are paying for therapeutic services.

Isolation from colleagues is often the tension most keenly felt by counsellors. Whereas most other professions have a fair degree of social give and take in their work settings, psychotherapy affords limited interaction among peers (Freudenberger and Kurtz, 1990). While there is much interpersonal contact with clients, it cannot be compared to the mutuality and sharing that can occur between colleagues. Clinicians in group practices or clinics may interact with colleagues in meetings, but there is generally little opportunity in these settings to consult with peers on professional or personal matters (Guy, 1987). Therapists in independent practice tend to be even more isolated from colleagues. The tight scheduling of clients may prevent meeting peers for lunch or even conveniently telephoning colleagues. Many counsellors go for days or weeks without significant contact with peers.

Therapists who lack such interaction are more vulnerable to stress since emotional support and practical help are needed to deal with issues related to working in the mental health field (Lewis *et al.*, 1988). Freudenberger (1990) suggests that isolation is exacerbated when minimal feedback is received from colleagues, causing counsellors to retreat even more and to become more withdrawn.

Psychotherapists are also isolated from the typical cross-section of the population. Therapists usually interact with people who are emotionally distressed and in need of help to resolve their conflicts. As a result, unlike many other professions, those working in the field of mental health rarely see people 'at their best' (Guy, 1987). Exclusively dealing with this population can colour therapists' perceptions of society and humanity. A clinician who works with sexual abuse victims day after day, for instance, may form a skewed perspective of the world. Consistent immersion in a world replete with psychopathology and dysfunction isolates the clinician and constitutes an occupational hazard (Freudenberger and Robbins, 1979).

Friends and family are isolated from the practising psychotherapist. The rigid framework of the 50-minute hour and the inherent privacy of the work make the counsellor substantially unavailable. While in other professions spouses or children may feel free to call the workplace regarding minor illnesses, car problems or dinner arrangements, therapists cannot welcome or even allow such interruptions. This becomes especially problematic for clinicians who are single parents or primary caretakers of young children. Working mothers, already experiencing societal pressure to stay at home with their children, may feel even more tension in the psychotherapist role, knowing their children's access to them is limited.

Psychotherapists may also suffer a form of physical isolation that Greben (1975) describes as 'environmental deprivation'. While conducting psychotherapy is a complex task, it can also be limiting since it involves only the functions of talking and listening. Counsellors are thereby excluded from the wide range of possible human behaviours (Guy, 1987). Experienced therapists may find that their clients present with common themes and complaints; they may begin to treat clients in similar ways using similar techniques and similar words. Eventually, the authenticity and creativity of the therapist become circumscribed (Freudenberger and Robbins, 1979). The result is a counsellor who mechanically fulfils her role, producing a sense of boredom and isolation.

Conducting a therapy session involves relatively little physical activity. Many therapists sit for eight or more hours a day in the same chair and room, rendering them physically exhausted from immobilization (Will, 1979). The practice of psychotherapy affords little opportunity for walking, stretching or other mild forms of activity. Such sedentary days do not allow for the physical release of stress often necessary after continued exposure to emotional pain and psychic conflict. Those in the field who do not take time out from their busy schedules to exercise or participate in outside activities are more likely to suffer from fatigue and emotional exhaustion. Findings indicate that satisfaction with leisure activities significantly decreases therapists' feelings of burnout (Hoeksma *et al.*, in press). Physical inactivity probably plays a role in physical isolation.

Psychic isolation

Unfortunately, therapists' experience of isolation is not limited to the physical realm. This isolation also pervades the psyche, impacting on emotional well-being, relational intimacy and inter-personal style. Despite the intense relational contact in the therapeutic role, many practitioners experience a sense of emotional aloneness. One survey (Thoreson *et al.*, 1989) revealed that 8 per cent of the psychologists reported significant distress in the past year due to recurrent feelings of loneliness. This psychic isolation is due to several aspects of the counselling relationship.

The very nature of the therapeutic encounter mandates that the therapist's own needs and interests be secondary to those of the client. According to Greben (1975), the primary characteristic of psychotherapy is two people exploring the thoughts and feelings of just one. This requires the counsellor to limit the amount of self-disclosure she imparts in the relationship. Varying degrees of personal information will be withheld according to the therapist's particular style and theoretical orientation, but it is usually deemed inappropriate to share in depth with a client one's more private material. This holding back causes the therapist to be a stranger of sorts. While the client's background and current situation are known in detail, the practitioner is only vaguely understood. Hellman and colleagues (1986) found that withholding personal information was, indeed, a major source of work-related stress for the psychotherapist.

Along these same lines, not only does personal data need to be withheld, but personal concerns as well. Despite the intensity of a counsellor's current problems, the emphasis of the session is to focus on the client's needs and concerns. While maintaining these boundaries may reduce some professional stress by preventing the blurring of roles (Hellman *et al.*, 1987), it can also elicit feelings of loneliness within the therapist. The practitioner's continual concealment of personal problems from hour to hour is naturally an emotional strain, and especially difficult when a client's conflict is a painfully similar one (Deutsch, 1984; Guy, 1987).

The therapeutic process further requires a great deal of emotional restraint on the part of the therapist. In order to provide a stable environment a counsellor must monitor her emotional reactivity closely. Disproportionate emotional reactions are to be examined outside the treatment context with the goal of providing uncontaminated reactions and greater objectivity for the client (Deutsch, 1985). However, findings indicate that psychotherapists do have many strong emotions in regard to their therapeutic relationships. Pope and Tabachnick (1993) found that approximately 80 per cent of therapists surveyed experienced fear, anger and sexual feelings in the context of their work. The constant emotional regulation that these reactions require isolates the therapist from others, and possibly from her own feelings. The isolation becomes especially problematic if the emotional restraint is generalized to other, non-therapeutic, relationships.

Detachment and distance are appropriate at times for the therapist; however, they may also hinder the therapist from responding in a genuine, spontaneous way, leading to artificial interactions with the client (Freudenberger and Robbins, 1979; Guy, 1987). This pattern may generalize to outside relationships as well, limiting the ability to be comfortable and forthright with friends (Farber, 1983c). The therapist, trained to listen, may listen too well in her various relationships, forgetting to attune to her own person and eventually losing a clear sense of self (Freudenberger and Robbins, 1979).

The therapist's professional obligation to maintain confidentiality also promotes psychic isolation. While many professionals find that seeking emotional support from family and friends can help alleviate feelings of alienation, the confidentiality requirement may stand in the way of utilizing this coping mechanism (Tamura *et al.*, in press). Therapists must monitor closely any self-disclosure of their workday so as not to breach a client's confidentiality, making the venting of frustration or the sharing of a therapeutic success a complicated matter (Spiegel, 1990). Kaslow and Schulman (1987) contend that such secrecy conflicts with the need for open communication among family members. The family may perceive confidentiality as a rule that shuts them out from the therapist's world, engendering jealousy and resentment from those who might otherwise help ease the isolation. Is there a psychotherapist alive who has not, along with Feltham (in Chapter 7), experienced the disheartening duplicity of one moment being the attentive, empathic psychotherapist and the next moment the tired, preoccupied family member?

All these factors converge and contribute to the 'one-way' intimacy experienced by the therapist and client (Guy, 1987). The client is asked to share herself in great detail while the counsellor responds with correspondingly little disclosure. Thus, the therapist experiences a sense of intimacy with many people but with little personal risk or expressed vulnerability; true mutuality is lacking. The practitioner is given only a glimpse of intimacy, which is eventually found to be insufficient. It has been suggested that the personality of some therapists may lead them to choose a career where their loneliness and fear of isolation can be overcome (Guy and Liaboe, 1986). Henry, Sims and Spray (1973) found that 60 per cent of psychotherapists surveyed reported having few friends in high school and felt somewhat isolated. The one-way intimacy found in the profession of psychotherapy may then only compound these pre-existing feelings of isolation.

Isolation can inflate one's judgement, leading the therapist to become grandiose and arrogant to compensate for losing touch with her intrapersonal and interpersonal relationships (Freudenberger and Kurtz, 1990). This self-imposed omnipotence is further heightened by some patients who idolize the therapist. While such exaltation and admiration may be enjoyable in the moment, they may compound isolation by begetting secrecy and hiding faults so as not to destroy the perfect image (Guy, 1987). Desire to live up to these superhuman expectations hinders the therapist's ability to show her neediness and be fully human.

Of course, therapists are not always idealized. Clients may

devalue their counsellors due to negative transference or to bolster their feelings of security and competence. This often leaves the therapist feeling alone in her goal of helping the client. Public perception can be negative as well. While some in our society may view psychotherapists as saints, many others will see them as voyeurs, capitalizing on the misery of others (Guy and Liaboe, 1986). Some see psychotherapists as the professionals to whom they turn as a last resort, or as the professionals with extrasensory powers that strip down defences against the client's will. These suspicious and hostile attitudes make it difficult for counsellors to relax and be spontaneous. Female psychotherapists' isolation may be exacerbated since the public's non-acceptance of psychotherapists is often coupled with the public's non-acceptance of women in a professional role (Rasmussen and Guy, 1989).

Finally, competition between colleagues fosters psychic isolation in several ways (Guy, 1987). As professionals vie for referrals, they may become reticent about exposing their limitations or seeking help for their own impairment. Those eager to establish themselves in positions of prestige among colleagues may present themselves as infallible and omnipotent. The pervasive notion that competent therapists are free of personal problems encourages the concealment of difficulties. Isolation can also stem from rival theoretical orientations and therapy formats. In Chapter 5 of this book, Street discusses the problem of professionals with a systemic orientation working in an agency embracing a contrasting ideology. Similar divisions between, say, psychoanalysts and behaviourists, psychopharmacologists and psychotherapists, generate the ironic feeling of being alone among colleagues.

Brooks (1990) suggests that males may have even more difficulty cultivating relationships with peers since men are socialized to inhibit expression of most emotions and to interact competitively with other men, thereby avoiding emotional closeness with male colleagues. Their disinclination for emotional support and honest communication may perpetuate relationships between men characterized by competition and homophobia. All told, silence and secrecy inhibit meaningful sharing among colleagues and breed loneliness.

Therapeutic relationships

The therapeutic relationship is the agony and the ecstasy of our work. It is, at once, the most significant source of pleasure and displeasure in psychotherapy. We alternate between sleepless nights fraught with recollections of hostility and anxiety incurred from characterologically impaired patients and fleeting moments of realization that we have genuinely assisted a fellow human being.

Among the most widely reported stressors associated with the therapeutic relationship are the responsibility for the patients' lives, the difficulty in working with disturbed patients, and the lack of gratitude from patients (Farber and Heifetz, 1981). The very process of working intimately with human suffering presents the practitioner with real, painful psychic discomfort (Goldberg, 1986a). The inability to relieve a person's suffering immediately can be excruciating for people entering a profession 'to help others'. Guy (1987) reported that recurring doubts about the efficacy of treatment and the difficulty associated with evaluating and treating patients were found to be sources of considerable distress for psychotherapists.

Perhaps the most stressful agent associated with the relationship is countertransference. Ever since Freud identified the phenomenon, overidentification and overinvolvement with the patient manifested through countertransference has plagued psychotherapists. Countertransference is often invoked when the practitioner recognizes within herself the patient's experience and is caught in the dilemma of trying to empathize with the client's feelings while, at the same time, trying to avoid being adversely affected by them (Goldberg, 1986a). As a result, the therapist may lose her ability to communicate her understanding to the client, diminishing therapeutic effectiveness. Therapist and patient alike then begin to doubt the efficacy of the treatment.

Countertransference reactions are intensified when treating difficult clients. These reactions include the arousal of guilt from unresolved personal struggles, inaccurate interpretations of the client's feelings due to therapist identification and projection, therapist feelings of being blocked, helpless and frustrated with a client, and evidence of boredom or impatience during work with a client. If the therapist closely identifies with the suffering of a particular client instead of following a scientific framework for treatment, she may find herself thwarted by not being helpful enough (Goldberg, 1986b). Of course, not all patients incur these feelings; only certain clients evoke such stressful reactions. As psychotherapists, we still struggle with distortions, unconscious reactions, unresolved conflicts, misperceptions and antagonism in relation to particular clients (Kottler, 1986). Each client rubs the therapist a different way, bringing about different reactions.

Although specific patient behaviours were discussed earlier in this chapter, they deserve mention here. According to Goldberg

(1986b), sometimes a less fortunate therapist encounters those 'obnoxious' and 'boring' clients who never provide the proper recognition, gratitude or admiration needed by the therapist. When the relationship is the cause of unsuccessful treatment, it proves a major source of distress for the therapist. Moreover, difficult clients prompt the therapist to try more unfamiliar treatment methods since the typical strategies and stances of the therapist are not effective.

Distress may also result from the intense emotional reactions of being so closely involved with patients. Feelings including anger, disgust, fear and revulsion experienced in the therapeutic relationship may cause distress for the practitioner, which in turn may affect his personal life as well as his clinical style (Greenfeld, 1985). Which of us has not been repulsed by the actions and attitudes of a child molester, rapist, thief or murderer? On the other hand, the feelings of intense connection and caring engendered by a therapeutic relationship are likely to precipitate equally strong feelings of distress. Which of us has not been deeply touched by the loss of a treasured client by termination of treatment or life?

Clinical interactions are typically characterized by constant emotional arousal (Raider, 1989). This arousal is simultaneously a curative agent for the client and a damaging one for the counsellor. Coppenhall addresses in Chapter 2 the paradox of empathy with the client's distress deepening the therapist's pain. The therapeutic relationship demands a delicate balance of remaining open to anguished feelings while retaining a modicum of self-preserving distance.

Lastly, fear of psychopathology as a result of intense contact with behavioural disorders may cause a psychotherapist, particularly a trainee, continual fear and intermittent symptoms (Greenfeld, 1985). Examining and concentrating on the psychological disorders of others fosters morbid self-examination by the therapist and infinite amounts of distress. Not only must the practitioner attend to the treatment of the patient, she must also deal with the emotional problems in her own mind. Identifying with the psychopathology of the patient and then trying to develop the psychological-mindedness necessary to practise are proverbial challenges to our mental health (Doyle, 1987).

Personal disruptions

Despite attempts by counsellors to remain consistent and caring in their therapeutic relationships, events in their personal lives may significantly interfere with this steadfast stance. Life events can cause considerable distress in the therapist's own inner world. While this distress is personal in nature it often impacts on the therapist's professional life as well. In several studies (e.g. Guy *et al.*, 1989; Norcross and Prochaska, 1986; Prochaska and Norcross, 1983), between 75 per cent and 82 per cent of responding psychotherapists reported that they had experienced a distressing episode within the past three years. More than a third of these respondents indicated that these personal problems decreased the quality of patient care they provided. In another study by Pope, Tabachnick and Keith-Spiegel (1987), 62 per cent of psychotherapists surveyed admitted to working when too distressed to be effective at frequencies ranging from 'rarely' to 'very often'. The most common precipitating events of psychotherapist distress are disruptions in their own lives – dysfunctional marriages, serious illnesses and other interpersonal losses, to name the most frequent – as opposed to client problems (Norcross and Aboyoun, 1994).

For the psychotherapist, a change in marital status brings unique stresses relative to her therapeutic relationships. Since marital status influences how clients perceive their therapists and their expectations regarding their therapists' world, a change in marital status can be quite unsettling to the treatment relationship. The therapist may struggle over whether to disclose an upcoming marriage to her clients and, if so, exactly what to disclose and how. The struggle to objectively evaluate the personal needs of the therapist and the needs of the client can cause a great deal of tension. Further stress is likely to be felt as the therapist must manage the myriad feelings each client has regarding the marriage while also sorting through her own intense feelings about such a significant life event.

Just as a change of marital status can provoke distress, so too can maintaining a marital relationship. While a spouse can be a counsellor's best source of support and nurturance, much time and energy are needed to keep this relationship intact. Freudenberger (1990) asserts that the emotionally taxing profession of the psychotherapist has negative consequences for the marital relationship. The psychological-mindedness of the clinician may cause her to respond to a spouse in a 'therapeutic' manner, leaving the spouse feeling estranged and misunderstood. In Deutsch's (1985) survey of therapists' personal problems, over 75 per cent of respondents reported having experienced relationship difficulties. Many described marital difficulties related to the practice of psychotherapy, such as a spouse refusing to enter marital therapy out of fear that their marriage counsellor would side with the therapist spouse. Thoreson, Miller and Krauskopf (1989) also found that over 10 per cent of psychologists surveyed had experienced high levels of distress due to marital or relational dissatisfaction. Wahl, Guy and Brown (in press) found a correlation between psychotherapist stress and marital dissatisfaction, suggesting that increased work stress may be related to decreased marital satisfaction.

Marital stress is probably both a cause and a result of psychotherapeutic work stress. The counsellor must seek to provide emotional stability for her clients despite considerable conflict at home. Discord in the therapist's marriage may affect the therapist's ability to be helpful in the professional setting, especially when a client's conflicts centre on marital disruptions.

Pregnancy is another significant life event that has ramifications for both male and female mental health professionals. The first pregnancy brings especially profound changes in roles and lifestyles as well as the therapist–patient relationship (Guy *et al.*, 1986). For female therapists, Paluszny and Pozanski (1971) point out that pregnancy is a non-verbal communication to patients, destroying any desired anonymity. It becomes obvious that the therapist has a personal life which involves sexual activity and family ties (Ashway, 1984). The myriad patient reactions can add to the therapist's already increasing apprehension regarding impending motherhood.

Pregnant female therapists are likely to experience a wide variety of reactions to being a therapist during this time. Many fear being less attentive to patients and becoming increasingly self-absorbed with thoughts and fantasies about the baby (Balsam and Balsam, 1974; Fenster *et al.*, 1986). Bienen (1990) notes that some may feel guilty for becoming pregnant and abandoning their patients to care for the newborn. During her own pregnancy, Bienen felt a tendency to distance herself from intense affect in treatment and to collude with patients' denial of the pregnancy's effect on the therapeutic process. The growing physical vulnerability, hormonal changes and fatigue are also likely to reduce the female therapist's effectiveness (Guy *et al.*, 1986). Even the kicking of the foetus provides a constant reminder of the many changes that await her (Ashway, 1984).

Though little research or discussion has focused on the effects of pregnancy on the male therapist, Guy *et al.* (1986) suggest that men experience many of the same role changes, conflicts and emotions as the female therapist. The male therapist may become increasingly preoccupied with concerns for the mother and baby, and with his own ability to be an adequate father. Increased financial concerns may heighten his sensitivity to premature terminations and cancelled sessions. He may also find himself more reactive to patient material involving pregnancy, parenting or abortion. Such factors imply that counsellors would be wrong to assume that pregnancy has no effect on the male practitioner.

Parenthood supplies a variety of disruptions in the therapist's professional relationships with clients. Children become ill, break limbs, and need their parents in emergencies. These realities of parenting cause a bit more complexity for psychotherapist parents. Most find themselves in a precarious balancing act as they attempt to meet the ever-changing needs of both their children and their patients. Freudenberger and Robbins (1979) suggest that therapists must continually evaluate their capacity to integrate such complex roles and pressures. These authors also recommend that therapists carefully discuss their professional and parental commitments within the marriage as well as talk candidly with patients regarding their family priorities. Certainly this may cause some intense feelings in clients, potentially creating more stress for the counsellor if only in the short term.

Psychotherapists who are also parents may allow their therapeutic role to impinge upon their family life by overanalysing and overinterpreting their children's behaviour (Freudenberger and Kurtz, 1990). Such intrusiveness can cause children to feel emotionally invaded and intimidated. Counsellors as parents may also put pressure on their children to appear emotionally healthy at all times (Japenga, 1989). Many psychotherapists find that they are too tired and emotionally drained to engage in family relationships after a full day's work (Piercy and Wetchler, 1987; Kaslow and Schulman, 1987). In fact, Farber and Heifetz (1981) found that 75 per cent of therapists complained that work issues spilled over into their family affairs. Research on family therapists by Piercy and Wetchler (1987) revealed that the most frequent stressor experienced was that too little time and energy were left for the therapists' own families. The therapist's family may come to resent the energy and caring that seems more available to patients. Enjoining clients to devote more time and energy to nurturing their own family has an empty, if not hypocritical, ring to many therapists who are neglecting their own.

Personal disruption frequently takes the form of loss – divorce and the empty nest being just two of many examples. Divorce may precipitate therapists' anxiety: they may worry about its possible discovery by patients, or doubt their personal and professional competency since their marriage has failed (Guy, 1987). Children 'moving out' may precipitate feelings of abandonment, despair and depletion as the therapist is left behind by offspring in whom she has invested so much love. Therapists who experience these losses may find terminations especially difficult; having experienced so many partings, letting clients go may be increasingly painful (Kaslow and Schulman, 1987). In a study of terminations, Guy, French, Poelstra and Brown (in press) found that therapists significantly affected by recent departure of children from the home reported a desire for longer terminations with their clients. The study also found that those therapists substantially affected by divorce were more likely to maintain social contact with clients after termination. The therapeutic relationship may be used, to some degree, to compensate for losses in therapists' personal lives.

Ageing and serious illness often go hand in hand for the psychotherapist in later adulthood. King (1983) states that the ageing process, often accompanied by a deterioration in skills, is further complicated by illnesses which exacerbate the depletion of the therapist's abilities. The ageing or ailing psychotherapist often experiences a host of feelings as well as professional complications. Many feel anxiety as they confront, perhaps for the first time, the reality of their own mortality (Guy and Souder, 1987). Schwartz (1987) indicates that some therapists feel guilty about becoming ill and having to 'abandon' their patients temporarily. Some counsellors' feelings of vulnerability and helplessness increase their desire to be cared for by their clients. This sense of weakness may be quite disturbing to the therapist who typically perceives herself to be strong and competent (Dewald, 1982).

Professional complications are numerous when serious illness occurs. Appointments must be cancelled or rescheduled, temporary or permanent termination of clients must be considered, referrals to other therapists must be discussed, and the daily office tasks of paying bills and answering phones must be managed (Guy and Souder, 1986). Serious illness will severely damage any practice. The pressure of handling all of these practical considerations, coupled with the emotional strain and the physical illness itself, can cause intense distress for the psychotherapist. Moreover, if the illness is incapacitating or directly related to the ageing process, the therapist may be forced to consider retirement, causing further upheaval in future role and identity.

Concluding reflections

Freud aptly characterized psychotherapy as an 'impossible profession'. Mental health professionals are regularly engulfed by their clients' pain and disability, are routinely confronted by conscious and unconscious hostility, and are ethically bound to secrecy concerning the most troubling confessions and occasionally the most heinous of crimes. All of this is accomplished under unremitting pressure in frequently less than humane working conditions with interpersonally disturbed patients. Emotional depletion, physical isolation and psychic withdrawal seem only too natural responses. Throw in the inescapable disruptions of our personal lives and one is tempted to accept Kottler's (1986: 8) dramatic assertion that: 'If we ever really considered the possible risks in getting involved with a client, we would not do so for any price. Never mind that we will catch their colds and flus, what about their pessimism, negativity, and psychopathology?'

While it is obvious that ordinary counsellors face trials and tribulations encountered by their clients, this is no less true of the talented contributors to this book or of 'master clinicians' surveyed for a previous book (see Norcross and Guy, 1989). Their autobiographical accounts make it painfully clear that they have experienced many of the same personal tragedies, failures and stressors as the rest of us. Despite our secret fantasy that prominent counsellors may have discovered a way to inoculate themselves against the ravages of distress, a careful reading of the following chapters proves otherwise. It appears to us that the contributors to this volume are just as vulnerable to the exigencies of counselling as those with less talent and experience.

In Chapter 10, John McLeod observes that 'perhaps the most significant benefit' to be achieved from reflecting on stresses in counselling is the realization that similar kinds of pressure are experienced by virtually all mental health professionals. Confidentiality, isolation, shame and a host of additional considerations lead us to overpersonalize our own sources of stress, when in reality they are part and parcel of the 'common world' of counselling. Disconfirming our individual feelings of unique wretchedness and affirming the universality of stresses related to patient behaviours, working conditions and emotional depletion, as well as physical and psychic isolation, are in and of themselves therapeutic. Moreover, appreciating the universality and accepting some of the inevitable distress associated with conducting psychotherapy contribute to the creation of corrective actions.

The counsellor who denies that clinical work is gruelling and demanding is, in Thorne's (1989) words, mendacious, deluded or incompetent. We concur wholeheartedly, but would add that the counsellor who claims not to have personally benefited from this gruelling and demanding work is also likely to be mendacious, deluded or incompetent. Without trivializing the enormous strains of this 'impossible profession', we would conclude on this positive note: the vast majority of mental health professionals, including the contributors to this book, are satisfied with their career choice and are planning to remain in the field (see, for example, Norcross *et al.*, 1993). Most of us feel enriched, nourished and privileged in conducting counselling, but these benefits come at a significant cost. Understanding and alleviating the distress of conducting psychotherapy enhances our personal functioning and our clinical effectiveness, and thereby the health of those we are privileged to assist through their distress.

Note

1   Throughout this chapter we employ the terms *client* and *patient* as well as *counsellor* and *psychotherapist* interchangeably.

References

Ashway, J.A. (1984) 'A therapist's pregnancy: an opportunity for conflict resolution and growth in the treatment of children', *Clinical Social Work Journal*, 121: 3–17.

Balsam, A. and Balsam, R. (1974) 'The pregnant therapist', in A. Balsam and R. Balsam (eds), *On Becoming a Psychotherapist*. Boston: Little Brown. pp. 265–88.

Bennett, S. (1991) 'Issues confronting occupational therapists working with terminally ill patients', *British Journal of Occupational Therapy*, 54: 8–10.

Bienen, M. (1990) 'The pregnant therapist: countertransference dilemmas and willingness to explore transference material', *Psychotherapy*, 27: 607–12.

Brooks, G.R. (1990) 'The inexpressive male and vulnerability to therapist–patient sexual exploitation', *Psychotherapy*, 27: 344–9.

Chemtob, C.N., Bauer, G.B., Hamada, R.S., Pelowski, S.R. and Muraoka, M.Y. (1989) 'Patient suicide: occupational hazard for psychologists and psychiatrists', *Professional Psychology: Research and Practice*, 20: 294–300.

Cooper, A.M. (1986) 'Some limitations on therapeutic effectiveness: the "burnout syndrome" in psychoanalysts', *Psychoanalytic Quarterly*, 55: 576–98.

Corey, M.S. and Corey, G. (1989) *Becoming a Helper*. Pacific Grove, CA: Brooks/Cole.

Deutsch, C.J. (1984) 'Self-reported sources of stress among psychotherapists', *Professional Psychology: Research and Practice*, 15: 833–45.

Deutsch, C.J. (1985) 'A survey of therapists' personal problems and treatment', *Professional Psychology: Research and Practice*, 16: 305–15.

Dewald, P.A. (1982) 'Serious illness in the analyst: transference, countertransference, and reality responses', *Journal of the American Psychoanalytic Association*, 30: 347–63.

Dorken, H. (1990) 'Malpractice claims experience of psychologists: policy issues, cost comparisons with psychiatrists, and prescription privilege applications', *Professional Psychology: Research and Practice*, 21: 150–2.

Doyle, B.B. (1987) 'The impaired psychiatrist', *Psychiatric Annals*, 17: 760–3.

Dryden, W. and Spurling, L. (eds) (1989) *On Becoming a Psychotherapist*. London: Tavistock/Routledge.

Farber, B.A. (1983a) 'Psychotherapists' perceptions of stressful patient behavior', *Professional Psychology: Research and Practice*, 14: 697–705.

Farber, B.A. (1983b) 'Dysfunctional aspects of the psychotherapeutic role', in B.A. Farber (ed.), *Stress and Burnout in the Human Service Professions*. New York: Pergamon. pp. 97–118.

Farber, B.A. (1983c) 'The effects of psychotherapeutic practice upon psychotherapists', *Psychotherapy*, 14: 697–705.

Farber, B.A. (1990) 'Burnout in psychotherapists: incidence, types, and trends', *Psychotherapy in Private Practice*, 8: 35–44.

Farber, B.A. and Heifetz, L.J. (1981) 'The satisfactions and stresses of psychotherapeutic work: a factor analytic study', *Professional Psychology*, 12: 621–30.

Fenster, S., Phillips, S. and Rapoport, E. (1986) *The Therapist's Pregnancy: Intrusion in the Analytic Space*. Hillsdale, NJ: Analytic Press.

Freudenberger, H.J. (1975) 'The staff burn-out syndrome in alternative institutions', *Psychotherapy*, 12: 73–82.

Freudenberger, H.J. (1984) 'Burnout and job dissatisfaction: impact on the family', in J.C. Hansen and S.H. Cramer (eds), *Perspectives on Work and the Family*. Rockville, MD: Aspen. pp. 95–105.

Freudenberger, H.J. (1990) 'Hazards of psychotherapeutic practice', *Psychotherapy in Private Practice*, 8: 31–4.

Freudenberger, H.J. and Kurtz, T. (1990) 'Risks and rewards of independent practice', in E.A. Margenau (ed.), *The Encyclopedic Handbook of Private Practice*. New York: Gardner. pp. 461–72.

Freudenberger, H.J. and Richelson, G. (1980) *Burnout: The High Cost of High Achievement*. Garden City, NY: Anchor.

Freudenberger, H.J. and Robbins, A. (1979) 'The hazards of being a psychoanalyst', *Psychoanalytic Review*, 66: 275–95.

Gadzella, B.M., Ginther, D.W., Tomcala, M. and Bryant, G.W. (1991) 'Educators' appraisal of their stressors and coping strategies', *Psychological Reports*, 68: 995–8.

Goldberg, C. (1986a) 'Understanding the impaired practitioner', *Psychotherapy in Private Practice*, 4: 25–34.

Goldberg, C. (1986b) *On Being a Psychotherapist*. New York: Gardner.

Greben, S.E. (1975) 'Some difficulties and satisfactions inherent in the practice of psychoanalysis', *International Journal of Psychoanalysis*, 56: 427–34.

Greenfeld, D. (1985) 'Stresses of the psychotherapeutic role', *Hillside Journal of Clinical Psychiatry*, 7: 165–82.

Guy, J.D. (1987) *The Personal Life of the Psychotherapist*. New York: Wiley.

Guy, J.D. and Brown, C.K. (1992) 'How to benefit emotionally from private practice', *Psychotherapy in Private Practice*, 10: 27–39.

Guy, J.D. and Liaboe, G.P. (1986) 'The impact of conducting psychotherapy on psychotherapists' interpersonal functioning', *Professional Psychology: Research and Practice*, 17: 111–14.

Guy, J.D. and Souder, J.K. (1986) 'Impact of therapists' illness or accident on psychotherapeutic practice: review and discussion', *Professional Psychology: Research and Practice*, 17: 509–13.

Guy, J.D. and Souder, J.K. (1987) 'The aging psychotherapist', paper presented at the Annual Convention of the American Psychological Association, Washington, DC (August).

Guy, J.D., Guy, M.P. and Liaboe, G.P. (1986) 'First pregnancy: therapeutic issues for both female and male psychotherapists', *Psychotherapy*, 23: 297–302.

Guy, J.D., Poelstra, P.L. and Stark, M.J. (1989) 'Personal distress and therapeutic effectiveness: national survey of psychologists practicing psychotherapy', *Professional Psychology: Research and Practice*, 20: 48–50.

Guy, J.D., Brown, C.K. and Poelstra, P.L. (1990) 'Psychotherapist as victim: a discussion of patient violence', *The California Psychologist*, 22: 20–2.

Guy, J.D., Brown, C.K. and Poelstra, P.L. (1991) 'Living with the aftermath: a national survey of the consequences of patient violence directed at psychotherapists', *Psychotherapy in Private Practice*, 9: 35–9.

Guy, J.D., Brown, C.K. and Poelstra, P.L. (1992a) 'Safety concerns and protective measures used by psychotherapists', *Professional Psychology: Research and Practice*, 23: 421–3.

Guy, J.D., Brown, C.K., Poelstra, P.L. and French, R.J. (1992b) 'Protecting self and loved ones from patient violence', *The California Psychologist*, 25: 15–24.

Guy, J.D., French, R.J., Poelstra, P.L. and Brown, C.K. (in press) 'Therapeutic terminations: how psychotherapists say good-bye', *Psychotherapy in Private Practice*.

Hellman, I.D. and Morrison, T.L. (1987) 'Practice setting and type of caseload as factors in psychotherapist stress', *Psychotherapy*, 24: 427–33.

Hellman, I.D., Morrison, T.L. and Abramowitz, S.I. (1986) 'The stresses of psychotherapeutic work: a replication and extension', *Journal of Clinical Psychology*, 42: 197–204.

Hellman, I.D., Morrison, T.L. and Abramowitz, S.I. (1987) 'Therapist experience and the stresses of psychotherapeutic work', *Psychotherapy*, 24: 171–7.

Henry, W.E., Sims, J.H. and Spray, S.L. (1973) *Public and Private Lives of Psychotherapists*. San Francisco: Jossey-Bass.

Hoeksma, J.H., Guy, J.D., Brown, C.K. and Brady, J.L. (in press) 'The relationship between psychotherapist burnout and satisfaction with leisure activities', *Psychotherapy in Private Practice*.

Japenga, A. (1989) 'Analyzing psychiatrists' kids', *Los Angeles Times*, 9 April: 1, 14.

Kaslow, F.W. and Schulman, N. (1987) 'How to be sane and happy as a family therapist', *Journal of Psychotherapy and the Family*, 3: 79–96.

King, P. (1983) 'Identity crises: splits or compromise – adaptive or maladaptive', in E.D. Joseph and D. Widlocher (eds), *The Identity of the Psychoanalyst*. New York: International Universities Press.

Knapp, S., VandeCreek, L. and Phillips, A. (1993) 'Psychologists' worries about malpractice', *Psychotherapy Bulletin*, 28 (4): 46–7.

Kottler, J.A. (1986) *On Being a Therapist*. San Francisco: Jossey-Bass.

Lewis, G.J., Greenburg, S.L. and Hatch, D.B. (1988) 'Peer consultation groups for psychologists in private practice: a national survey', *Professional Psychology: Research and Practice*, 19: 81–6.

Nash, J., Norcross, J.C. and Prochaska, J.O. (1984) 'Satisfactions and stresses of independent practice', *Psychotherapy in Private Practice*, 2: 39–48.

Norcross, J.C. and Aboyoun, D.C. (1994) 'Self-change experiences of psychotherapists', in T.M. Brinthaupt and R.P. Lipka (eds), *Changing the Self*. Albany, NY: State University of New York Press.

Norcross, J.C. and Guy, J.D. (1989) 'Ten therapists: the process of becoming and being', in W. Dryden and L. Spurling (eds), *On Becoming a Psychotherapist*. London: Tavistock/Routledge.

Norcross, J.C. and Guy, J.D. (1995) *Leaving it at the Office: Understanding and Alleviating the Distress of Conducting Psychotherapy*. New York: Guilford.

Norcross, J.C. and Prochaska, J.O. (1986) 'Psychotherapist heal thyself I: the psychological distress and self-change of psychologists, counselors, and laypersons', *Psychotherapy*, 23: 102–14.

Norcross, J.C., Prochaska J.O. and Farber, J.A. (1993) 'Psychologists conducting psychotherapy: new findings and historical comparisons on the Psychotherapy Division membership', *Psychotherapy*, 30: 692–7.

Paluszny, M. and Pozanski, E. (1971) 'Reactions of patients during pregnancy of the psychotherapist', *Psychiatric Opinion*, 13: 20–5.

Perlman, B. and Hartman, E.A. (1982) 'Burnout: summary and future research', *Human Relations*, 35: 283–305.

Piercy, F.P. and Wetchler, J.L. (1987) 'Family–work interfaces of psychotherapists', *Journal of Psychotherapy and the Family*, 3: 17–32.

Pines, A.M. and Maslach, C. (1978) 'Characteristics of staff burnout in mental health settings', *Hospital and Community Psychiatry*, 29: 233–7.

Pope, K.S. and Tabachnick, B.G. (1993) 'Therapists' anger, hate, fear, and sexual feelings: national survey of therapist responses, client characteristics, critical events, formal complaints, and training', *Professional Psychology: Research and Practice*, 24: 142–52.

Pope, K.S., Tabachnick, B.G. and Keith-Spiegel, P. (1987) 'Ethics of practice: the beliefs and behaviors of psychologists as therapists', *American Psychologist*, 42: 993–1006.

Poulin, J. and Walter, C. (1993) 'Social worker burnout: a longitudinal study', *Social Work Research and Abstracts*, 29: 5–11.

Prochaska, J.O. and Norcross, J.C. (1983) 'Psychotherapists' perspective on treating themselves and their clients for psychic distress', *Psychotherapy*, 20: 161–73.

Raider, M.C. (1989) 'Burnout in children's agencies: a clinician's perspective', *Residential Treatment for Children and Youth*, 6: 43–51.

Rasmussen, J.C. and Guy, J.D. (1989) 'Married female psychotherapists: intrapsychic conflicts and external stressors', *Journal of Training and Practice in Professional Psychology*, 3: 29–43.

Schwartz, H.J. (1987) 'Illness in the doctor: implications for the psychoanalytic process', *Journal of the American Psychoanalytic Association*, 35: 657–92.

Spiegel, P.B. (1990) 'Confidentiality endangered under some circumstances without special management', *Psychotherapy*, 27: 636–43.

Stillson, K., White, J. and Harris, E.F. (1986) 'Helping the helper: stress management for alcoholism treatment personnel', *Alcoholism Treatment Quarterly*, 3: 107–23.

Tamura, L.J., Guy, J.D., Brady, J.L. and Grace, C. (in press) 'Maintaining confidentiality, avoiding burnout and psychotherapists' needs for inclusion: a national survey', *Psychotherapy in Private Practice*.

Thoreson, R.W., Miller M. and Krauskopf, C.J. (1989) 'The distressed psychologist: prevalence and treatment considerations', *Professional Psychology: Research and Practice*, 20: 153–8.

Thorne, B. (1989) 'The blessing and the curse of empathy', in W. Dryden and L. Spurling (eds), *On Becoming a Psychotherapist*. London: Tavistock/Routledge. pp. 53–68.

Wahl, W.K., Guy, J.D. and Brown, C.K. (in press) 'Conducting psychotherapy: impact upon the therapist's marital relationship', *Psychotherapy in Private Practice*.

Will, O.A. (1979) 'Comments on the professional life of the psychotherapist', *Contemporary Psychoanalysis*, 15: 560–75.

Wood, B., Klein, S., Cross, H.J., Lammers, C.J. and Elliot, J.K. (1985) 'Impaired practitioners: psychologists' opinions about prevalence, and proposals for intervention', *Professional Psychology: Research and Practice*, 16: 843–50.

Wykes, T. and Whittington, R. (1991) 'Coping strategies used by staff following assault by a patient: an exploratory study', *Work and Stress*, 5: 37–48.

Yager, J. and Borus, J.F. (1990) 'A survival guide for psychiatric residency training dictators', *Academic Psychiatry*, 14: 180–7.

PART 1

THE STRESSES OF WORKING WITH SPECIFIC CLIENT GROUPS

2   The Stresses of Working with Clients Who Have Been Sexually Abused

Kate Coppenhall

The material for this chapter comes from my own experiences in working with survivors of childhood sexual abuse for the past five and a half years, and the experiences of others who responded to a questionnaire detailing the stresses they encountered within this field. The range and depth of experience, theoretical training and backgrounds of my respondents vary enormously. The counsellors work within the public, private and voluntary sectors, some in agencies whose sole focus is working with survivors of sexual abuse, for example Rape Crisis and SURVIVORS. Not surprisingly, the setting in which the counsellors work, combined with the degree and intensity of contact, have a direct effect upon the counsellor in either promoting or dissipating her stress.

I have chosen the broadest definition of sexual abuse to reflect the diversity of the clients' experiences and consequently that of the counsellor. The client may, therefore, be an adult or a child, and may have been abused by member/s of their family, friend/s or stranger/s. The sexual abuse involved may range from the possibility of exposure through fondling to penetration with violence, with or without ritual, once or over a long period of time. Fortune (1983) offers a multidimensional definition of sexual violence which embraces not only the physical assault on the victim but also the impact upon the community.

Sexual violence is seen as:

an offence against the victim, in that it denies and violates the personhood of the victim;
an offence against self, in that it is a destruction of relationship with another and a distortion of one's own sexuality;
an offence against the community, in that it creates a hostile, alien environment which diminishes the possibility of meaningful relationships;
an offence against God, in that it is a violation of God's most sacred creation, 'a human being'.
(Fortune, 1983, in Bagley and King, 1991: 54)

Anomalies within the data-gathering process were suggestive of the degree of stress. Two counsellors chose not to fill in the questionnaires, saying that the act of putting pen to paper and words to their experience would mean their having to acknowledge their own levels of burnout. One counsellor was unwilling to commit himself to paper, feeling unable to trust me. Seen in the light of the third statement in Fortune's (1983) definition of sexual violence and the concomitant destruction of trust which takes place within sexual abuse, this attitude appears not only realistic but also reflects how hard and contaminating is the impact of the work upon the counsellor. Finally, two respondents were actively taking time out of work because of their levels of stress.

Similarities common to all therapeutic relationships are present in this area of focused counselling. These include the clients' narration of their stories, the therapists' responses and interventions in keeping with their theoretical perspectives; and the process of narration leading to the clients making sense of their painful and difficult experiences. In these encounters the therapists are essentially enabling and empowering their clients.

When considering what it is about this work which makes it different from other counselling, common themes emerge. A major theme is the role of gender and sexuality. Sexuality is experienced as a core part of our identity. When working with survivors of sexual abuse our core is touched time and again. Perhaps more than in any other field, counsellors of survivors have to have a greater honesty about their own sexuality and be clearer about their own boundaries when working with clients whose boundaries have been destroyed by abuse (cf. the second of Fortune's statements). In reflecting the issue of sexuality and working within one counsellor's own theoretical orientation, one therapist described experiencing 'a greater need to analyse the erotic countertransference' when working with survivors.

When responding to the questionnaire, male counsellors were hyper-aware of their gender and were fearful of being perceived or experienced as oppressive or abusive. The potential for being identified with the abuser was ever present, in the knowledge that the incidence of males as abusers is 96 per cent (Russell, 1983). It was apparent from their responses that male counsellors felt a greater need to explore their motives and justify their presence within this field of counselling, not only to themselves but also to others.

Working in the murkier side of society's taboos means that counsellors not only lose a belief in a safe world, but are also confronting sexual mores and prejudices within themselves, colleagues and friends. The counsellors described and experienced feelings of isolation and a sense of stigmatization as direct consequences of this work. One counsellor said she felt like 'the pariah of the counselling world'. The counsellors' experience appears to be a reflection of those dynamics described by Finkelhor (1987) and found within the survivors themselves: stigmatization, sexualization, powerlessness and betrayal.

One dynamic present to a lesser degree within all therapeutic relationships is trust, more specifically the promotion of trust within the therapeutic alliance. When a client has experienced the betrayal of trust that occurs when she or he has been sexually abused, how can trust be engendered within the therapeutic relationship? From the client's point of view, perhaps it is the hope and desire of healing the wounds of abuse that enables them to permit trust. The following remarks from one counsellor, in answer to the question as to how this work differs from other types of counselling, demonstrates both the difficulty in gaining trust and the needy client's desire to trust: 'I try to get someone to trust me, yet know they are entitled not to . . . [and also] I see how easy it is to get a needy child to trust me.'

The nature of the stresses

Stresses occur when the environment imposes demands beyond the individual's ability to cope with them. Kafry and Pines (1980) describe such demands in terms of 'capacity (ability) and alacrity (willingness)'. The converse is also true, with stresses arising from 'demands below one's perceived resources' and the rewards for work being below one's expectations.

In the arena of working with survivors of sexual abuse stresses appear to arise totally from excessive demands placed upon the resources of the counsellor. Two kinds of pressure named by counsellors who responded to my questionnaire have been described by Kafry and Pines (1980) as: '(1) pressures imposed on the cognitive capacity and decision-making mechanism by excessive demands', and '(2) those imposed by one's sense of meaningfulness and achievement by lack of feelings of self-actualisation and success'. In considering the first pressure upon cognitive capacity, the counsellor experiences the stresses arising from the relationship between the complexity of the work with survivors and his or her perceived or actual levels of knowledge and skill. Counsellors expressed this stress in terms of 'not knowing enough' and in some cases, despite extensive training, 'feeling de-skilled in the face of the obduracy of clients who have survived appalling abuse'.

The counsellors' sense of meaningfulness is gained from assessing their effectiveness with clients and by judging the results of their efforts. Evidence for this is collected through feedback from colleagues and clients, combined with the counsellors' own self-assessment of their significance and achievements. Within this area counsellors expressed feelings of omnipotence ('wanting to save clients', 'to stop all the abuse and suffering' and 'feeling responsible for their [the clients'] healing') and impotence ('not being able to offer enough in the face of my clients' needs', with the experience of 'trying to get it right and feeling like failing most of the time', all the while 'knowing that the client's childhood can never be redeemed'). These feelings increase the demands and stresses of this work.

Spensley and Blacker (1976: 543) write that 'the very process of psychotherapy presents to the therapist real and painful psychological discomfort'. In empathizing, counsellors are caught in a double bind: they have to recognize both emotionally and intellectually the feelings of the client. At the same time, paradoxically, they have to avoid being caught up in those same feelings. This may lead to a reduction in their ability to understand the client's world and to communicate their understanding to the client. The essence of Spensley and Blacker's paper is that empathy with the client deepens the therapist's pain.

How can the counsellor remain open to the strength of feelings of the client who has been sexually abused while retaining some form of therapeutic distance, when one stress, which might be described as the client's story and its contents, has such an awful impact? Solely to suggest that the client's story of abuse is stressful would minimize the impact of the daily toll of hearing horrendous stories. The counsellor has to struggle to 'keep in emotional touch with the horror' without switching off from the uniqueness of each client's story. A counsellor described having to live with the anger of realizing that children are tortured and 'feeling sickened by what adults do to children'. The trouble with this kind of work appears to be that the counsellor gets lulled into a false sense of security: 'just when I think I have heard it all, a new horror emerges, for example ritualistic, institutional abuse'.

One counsellor stated that 'the experiences of working with sexual abuse can damage your sexual health'. Listening to descriptions of sexually abusive experiences suffered by clients caused considerable stress upon the counsellor's sexuality generally, more specifically sexual expression within their own intimate adult consenting relationships. Appropriate acts of normal sexual behaviour became contaminated by the client's story.

Tensions within the therapeutic relationship itself impose additional stresses and arise from either the fear of somehow re-abusing the client, or 'feeling like a perpetrator when processing the story of the abuse'. For the counsellor, there exists a tightrope between 'balancing the client's need to tell and be heard whilst not compounding the abuse'. Counsellors suggest that it is only in this type of work that they are confronted by the abuser within themselves and the latent potential that role holds. This factor causes additional stress, given the powerful dynamics of the therapeutic relationship, where at any time there may be experienced a mirroring of the original trauma, with the client taking either the victim or the abuser role, and the counsellor feeling either victimized or abusive in response. As one counsellor wrote: 'sometimes I allow myself to be victimized because I identify too much with the victim and feel revulsion towards the abuser'.

This dynamic can be compounded when counsellors have an additional source of stress related to their role within their employing organization. Maslach (1987) considers role ambiguity (where there is a lack of clarity about the work role) and role conflict (when the worker is caught between competing demands or faced with demands to do things he or she does not want to do) to be related to job burnout. These role-related stresses are more likely to be present within voluntary organizations and self-help groups. Here, the counsellor may also hold an administrative role (for example as committee member), may supervise the work of other counsellors and helpers and may act in some sort of training capacity. In whatever setting, an additional stress may be the strong possibility that some counsellors are themselves survivors of sexual abuse. Freudenberger (1975) points out that a very real stress within the voluntary sector is simply the number of hours one person devotes to the work. Offering voluntary time in addition to regular life, 'literally means that he is holding down two jobs, and most likely giving more than full measure to both' (Freudenberger, 1975: 78).

An external stress for those working with children is the knowledge that a child is being sexually abused yet that there is not enough evidence either to prosecute or to act. In addition, there is the knowledge that this one client may be just the tip of the iceberg. This was described by one counsellor as follows: 'sometimes I groan as yet another survivor lands at my door, because the size of the problem seems so enormous'. Hopkins (1992: 149), in exploring 'the interrelationship between the experiences of the workers and those of the child', calls the effects of this work upon the child protection worker 'secondary abuse'. In the light of the experiences described by counsellors, it seems legitimate to recognize the validity of the term 'secondary abuse'.

Stress is caused by organizational factors, such as too little funding, inadequate supervision and not enough trained counsellors. Counsellors describe such stresses as being compounded by the fact that they are invested with specialist skills, 'being viewed as the local expert', and feel pressurized by the organization to be a 'valuable internal local resource to train and supervise others'. Thus they end with a caseload made up solely of survivors. Maslach (1976: 19) points out that 'burnout becomes inevitable when the professional is forced to provide care for too many people'. She goes on to say that:

> As the ratio increases the result is higher and higher emotional overload until, like a wire that has too much electricity flowing through it, the worker just burns out and emotionally disconnects. (Maslach, 1976: 19)

Another consequence she suggests is that 'a high ratio of clients to staff was one of the factors forcing a dehumanized view of clients' (1976: 19). The fear of this was expressed most poignantly by one counsellor as 'the fear of getting used to horror stories, a sort of "is that all?" phenomenon', and 'losing sight of the uniqueness of the client in front of me'.

Finally, even if the counsellors, in their ordinary lives, have resisted contamination by their work experiences there are social dilemmas. This is not the sort of work for light dinner-party conversation. Counsellors are constrained as much by confidentiality as by people's responses to the nature of their work. Even when they allude to their work in the most general of terms counsellors meet with varied reactions: the ghoulish, the voyeuristic, the sympathetic, the disbelieving; none is conducive to a relaxing evening away from work. The tendency would be to stay at home and avoid those uncomfortable meetings, only deepening the gulf between normal existence and the world of sexual abuse.

Counsellors' responses to the stresses

Edelwich and Brodsky (1980) suggest that 'the belief in magic dies hard'; in this statement they allude to the energy and enthusiasm of new and idealistic workers. They describe the experiences of those same workers, within the helping professions, whose loss of original expectations contributes to their levels of stress and burnout. Expectations which are present when starting in their chosen field include: those of being in control; of there being simple solutions to clients' problems; and of universal success, along with the new worker's enthusiastic idealism and unlimited commitment. To a greater or lesser degree, the responses of the counsellors that I surveyed showed those stages of disillusionment detailed by Edelwich and Brodsky (1980: 28) in defining the insidious process and progress towards burnout:

Enthusiasm: the 'initial period of high hopes, high energy and unrealistic expectations when one does not know what the job is all about'. Major hazards at this stage are the 'over-identification with the clients and excessive and inefficient expenditure of one's own energy'.

Stagnation: the stage where the job no longer holds the thrills; 'one is still doing the job' but reality has crept in: 'issues of money, working hours and career development are important'.

Frustration: in this stage the workers question their effectiveness in the job and its value. Here the 'limitations of the job situation are now viewed as not simply detracting from one's personal satisfaction and status, but as threatening to defeat the purpose of what one is doing'.

Apathy, described as 'the typical and natural defence mechanism against frustration', occurs when the person needs the job to survive yet is chronically frustrated by it; apathy is the attitude that 'a job is a job is a job'.

Intervention, the final stage, will be considered later in this chapter. It is the stage which breaks the cycle and, on a hopeful note, the cycle can be 'interrupted by a decisive intervention at any point'.

Whilst many may blame their employing organization for increased stress, the nature of this work gives rise to strong feelings in counsellors of inadequacy, failure and powerlessness. There is the powerlessness to influence clients' more self-destructive tendencies, for example self-mutilation or anorexia. There is inadequacy in the face of the reality of sexual abuse, its devastation and consequences. There is the failure to rescue the child within the adult from abuse and the final admission 'that some clients are beyond my skills'.

Two ways of defending against the feelings of powerlessness were described by counsellors. The first was through the process of denial: for one counsellor this meant he had to acknowledge 'feeling overwhelmed', rather than trying to prove that he was not. The second was in the experience and expression of anger. One counsellor described herself as 'getting angry at the wrong times or being over-aggressive' and another found herself 'being inappropriately angry with powerful people'. Anger deriving from the powerlessness to influence a bureaucratic public sector system was used as constructive energy to establish a local survivors' organization, able to meet the clients' needs in a way denied to them within the existing system.

Some counsellors reported experiencing nightmares and flashbacks connected to the client's story, the vicarious experience of the trauma akin to the secondary PTSD experienced by jurors involved in horrific criminal hearings. In the words of one responder, 'I get intrusive images from sessions which leave me shaken and low.' One defence against the horror of the stories was to become desensitized, to assume that they have heard it all before. This technique of detachment from the client's pain and the consequent reduction of emotional involvement 'makes the client seem less human, more like an object', and has been described by Maslach (1976) as part of withdrawal in response to the stress of intensely emotional work.

The stress of this experience is magnified when the counsellors are also survivors of sexual abuse; in such cases they find themselves resonating with the client's story, leading to overidentification, stimulation of unresolved areas within their history, role confusion and loss of boundaries. Examples of these phenomena were described by one counsellor as 'not knowing who I am in relation to my client', whilst another suggested this happened when 'I get in touch with my own history in the present and have to struggle to shut it out'. One counsellor found himself minimizing his own abusive experiences by 'having my own life coloured by abuse work and thinking "I got off lightly".' As many self-help and voluntary agencies are staffed by survivors who have trained as helpers or counsellors, it can be assumed that this type and level of stress is experienced frequently.

Counsellors in my sample noted loss of trust in day-to-day encounters, which they attributed to contamination from their work. This was described as follows:

Looking at men and wondering if they are sexually abusing their children, mistrust of men.

Loss of trust in relationships and people's motives, especially those who work with children and disabilities.

Hyper-awareness – observing people very carefully, listening for particular attitudes and responses.

Over-protection of my own children, not wanting my young son to go into men's loos.

Looking at the world through abuse-coloured specs.

The response of one counsellor was to give her own children 'permission to be more assertive – even though the consequences may be unreasonable or give offence'.

Returning to the issues of gender and sexuality, the responses to the questionnaire revealed that male counsellors feared being perceived as abusers. This led one counsellor to become over-cautious: he selected different therapeutic interventions, stating that 'the fear of being inadvertently abusive constrains and disempowers me'. Another counsellor was left with feelings of 'guilt for being a man' and even 'denied being a man'. In describing the ways the sexualized content of the work affected their lives, and in response to the stresses on their sexual health, counsellors noted a 'loss of pleasure in life and sex for certain periods'; or even 'not wanting to do certain things within a sexual relationship because of the connections with the client's story'.

For some, increasing use of alcohol to blot out the images and to 'help' with relaxing was a reality. Turning to tranquillizers, drugs or alcohol as 'solutions' to stress has been noted by researchers in this field (Freudenberger, 1987); naturally there is the potential for abuse and addiction through overuse. Healthier responses included learning to recognize when there was 'a need for more support – when feeling really isolated', with writing and art playing a part in helping to discharge the images and the feelings of responsibility.

Suggestions for improved coping

Intervention may be self-initiated or may occur in response to an immediate frustration or threat. It may be fuelled in part by one's own strength and in part by support and guidance (sometimes misguidance) from peers, supervisors, family and friends or whoever else is important in one's life. It may be a temporary stopgap or a real change. (Edelwich and Brodsky, 1980: 191)

The question of how stressful phenomena might be prevented or minimized is being answered in part by this book. Greber (in Farber and Heifetz, 1982: 299) suggested that the problem be made more public. He contended that 'the only way to prevent demoralisation among therapists is by the continual insistence upon seeing and describing conditions of [therapeutic] work as they really are'.

Albert Ellis (1984), in his paper 'How to deal with your most difficult client – you', continues the theme of realistic assessment of the work, by offering 15 techniques to dispute and surrender irrational beliefs held by a counsellor. In his inimitable style he demonstrates how an idealized, perfectionist and unobtainable image serves to increase stress; not unnaturally the answer is to confront the irrational beliefs promoting this image. In his conclusion, he suggests that the counsellor should 'ferret out the absolutistic philosophies and perfectionist demands that seem to underlie your difficulties' (Ellis, 1984: 33). An additional and connected phenomenon to this theme was demonstrated by Hellman *et al.* (1987), who showed that more rigid therapists reported greater levels of stress than their flexible counterparts. This was specifically the case in the therapeutic relationship and through self-doubt. To combat these stresses, two important strategies for the counsellors were to adopt the roles of personal counselling and supervision, which gave them essential and realistic feedback. If counsellors recognize their own wounds and become involved in their own self-healing, the risks to their clients are minimized. This latter aspect is in keeping with the effects of personal counselling identified by Groesbeck and Taylor (1977).

The counsellors in my survey identified the part that personal counselling played for them on many levels, in offering them support and the opportunity to sort out their story from that of the client. I would suggest that personal therapy is not only necessary for counsellors who are survivors but also for others who have had different experiences of being a victim and so may be less aware of the possibility of identification with their client. One counsellor suggested that women in this work may be reminded of times in their own socialization process when they thought themselves 'to be abnormal for not wanting or liking unsolicited touching'. The memory of having difficulties extricating themselves, even with minimal damage, from sexually threatening situations left a nasty taste in the mouth and the thought 'there but for the grace of God go us all'.

An important aspect to emerge from personal counselling was self-acceptance, described as 'feeling deeply accepted – to forgive, accept and care for myself – ceasing hating and punishing myself'.

Counsellors also found that it was important to accept their own limitations and stop blaming themselves for the lack of progress, and to accept that the work is difficult; this is in keeping with Ellis's ideas.

Farber and Heifetz in their study of therapist burnout state that:

> most therapists found the role of support systems essential. All those who could utilised supervisory relationships to help them through difficult moments; of those who were not currently being supervised, 51.1% relied on informal support of colleagues. (Farber and Heifetz, 1982: 298)

Seventy-five per cent of respondents to the questionnaire reiterated the above by stating that an important factor in coping was 'frequent, adequate supervision'. In fact there were plenty of suggestions and examples relating to the part organizations could play in improving the work arena, through supervision and other creative working practices. Supervision could appear as peer, individual or group supervision; it was clear that counsellors preferred two complementary forms of supervision, giving them a firm sustaining foundation to the therapeutic relationship.

Individual supervision allowed specific time for the individual to experience support and the opportunity to explore case material. The work in supervision could run parallel to the counsellor's journey in personal therapy, each process informing the other. Peer or group supervision served to reduce the sense of isolation, enabling the counsellors to give and receive support from each other, promoting unity and a sense of belonging. An organizational advantage must be the cost-effectiveness of such groups, although some were concerned that the introduction of a group would lead, at most, to the loss of one-to-one supervision, or at least be instrumental in reducing its frequency.

Hawkins and Shohet's (1989) process model of supervision defines six aspects to supervision: the content of the therapeutic session; strategies and interventions used by the counsellor; the process of therapy and the nature of the therapeutic relationship; the therapist's countertransference; the supervisory relationship as a mirror of the therapy relationship; and finally the supervisor's countertransference. When focusing on the dynamics at play within therapeutic relationships one respondent described two areas: the importance in the 'analysis of the countertransference to diminish or avoid unnecessary stress', and the fact that the counsellor should 'not take the transference personally – it's not me the client really hates or loves'. These areas would be formally addressed within the supervision model described.

Edelwich and Brodsky (1980) identify one of the main tasks of the supervisor in enabling improved coping as helping 'staff members experience the four stages [of burnout] with greater awareness and thus be less subject to violent swings of emotion'. There is a part to be played by internal supervision (Casement, 1991): here counsellors assess their own emotional responses during and on leaving the session, thus increasing their self-awareness and preparedness for the stresses arising from each case.

One way of diluting the impact of the work was to counsel in pairs. Hoffman *et al.* (1987) have described this dialectical therapy within the family therapy area but only in terms of efficacy for the client. They state that

> Dialectical therapy with one patient can facilitate change and growth in a relatively short period of time. The approach enables the patient to more quickly and effectively become aware and come in contact with the 'divided self' and make appropriate cognitive, perceptual, affective and behavioural changes. (Hoffman *et al.*, 1987: 215)

While not denying the value of a co-therapist as a potential strategy to reduce the counsellor's levels of stress, the client might perceive the presence of two therapists as scapegoating, or inadvertently replicating an abusive triangle of victim, persecutor and rescuer. The stress levels of the client must be considered, and the suitability of this strategy as an intervention. It may be better to increase supervision rather than to overload the client with therapeutic weight.

Other clinical and organizational responses included the counsellors actively managing their caseload by 'limiting the amount of child sexual abuse work'. This strategy liberated the counsellors to explore other alternatives for work, for example, 'supporting others as a supervisor, rather than be involved in direct one to one work with survivors'; thus valuable skills and experiences of counsellors are re-utilized to the benefit of others. It was also important for the counsellor to develop skills in assertiveness to deflect additional work commitments; this was described as 'now bowing to waiting-list pressures by taking on more clients' and 'cutting other stressful work out'.

The contemporaneous writing up of sessions, an organizational requirement of client documentation which is often perceived as a hindrance, for one counsellor acted as part of her debrief, enabling her to put distance between the acute effect of the work and her return to 'normal' life.

In reviewing the organizational aspects of improved coping, structural changes may need to be made, for example in work hours, distribution of responsibilities, patterns of authority and communication and, as Maslach (1976) found, lowering the staff–client ratio. Adequate training, increased information and updating of skills, and negotiating periods of time out from the work were viewed as paramount and a professional requirement for counsellors working within the changing field of sexual abuse. Not all coping strategies are long lasting; some serve to address surface problems, acting as sticking plaster, not taking into account deeply rooted problems and the long-term solutions necessary for change.

It is worth noting the phenomenon described by Edelwich and Brodsky (1980: 194) as 'false interventions'; they suggest that these 'are being handed out all the time'. For example, with a disgruntled and stale workforce a common solution is to run a workshop, designed to lift sagging spirits; 'the workshop high' may last a couple of months but little will have really changed. An intervention that can be very important is that of time out from the work whether through sabbatical or extended leave. This may be presented as a 'false intervention' in the form of *ad hoc* flexible local arrangements, whereby a blind eye is turned to a sort of 'legitimated malingering', odd hours or days off, where everybody knows it happens but may live with the anxiety of a 'crack-down' should more senior managers find out. They go on to state:

> What all false interventions for Burn-out have in common is the premise that a person can deal with Burn-out once and for all by one simple expedient. All of them attempt to get around the ever present reality of Burn-out as something that a person must always be aware of and be dealing with. (Edelwich and Brodsky, 1980: 204)

Allowing time for reflection, whether through meditation or visualization, was a distinctly personal coping strategy. Positive images were used by one counsellor 'to cast out intrusive images'. Farber and Heifetz (1982) found, in their survey of therapists within the general field, that for 73.7 per cent the lack of therapeutic success was the single most stressful aspect of therapeutic work. To counteract the despair engendered by lack of perceived success, some counsellors used a different form of reflection, which involved not only considering the costs of the work but also noting the rewards. Three counsellors described these as follows:

> The pleasure of seeing healing after horrific abuse; the client leaving abusive relationships.

> If the therapist can survive – it is gratifying to see the clients making improvements.

> No matter how small the step the client takes, noting it for them and me is important, otherwise I would give up.

Edelwich and Brodsky (1980) describe two processes for measuring success. The first is an awareness of subjective and idealistic criteria with the expectation that every case will show progress and the reliance on recidivism rates as the only available concrete measure. They suggest that the second and preferable process is to choose different parameters to measure success, which they describe as 'realistic interventions'. These include the setting of achievable goals; focusing on the process rather than the results; keeping a time perspective by not expecting immediate results; keeping one's own efforts in perspective when evaluating outcomes; and focusing on the successes rather than the failures. This last intervention was highlighted in the counsellors' responses quoted in the previous paragraph.

Edelwich and Brodsky describe the aims of interventions made to counteract burnout during each of the four stages (see page 34). They suggest that the best time for interventions to be made is within the *enthusiasm* stage, before the damage is done; these interventions are to encourage workers to take a more realistic approach to their work with clients. Within the *stagnation* stage, further education and other interventions designed to get a stalled career going again are especially useful, the aim being movement rather than worker paralysis. To counteract the feelings of discontent experienced within the *frustration* stage, interventions are intended to harness emotional energy to create the possibility of change and lead to feelings of satisfaction. If a person cares enough to be disappointed, interventions look for a way to turn that feeling around, so that *apathy* experienced within the fourth and final stage becomes renewed involvement.

Partners played a large part in the interpersonal strategies for coping. One counsellor suggested that 'a supportive partner and a reasonably stress-free home life' were necessary. She added, 'this isn't a strategy but perhaps if I can't have it I should stop doing the work for a while'. It was important to be explicit with partners about the general impact of the work upon the counsellor, and to let partners know just how they could give support, 'not relying on telepathy' to get the message through. The impact of this work on counsellors' sexual relationships had to be acknowledged. One counsellor suggested that it was important to 'just keep talking healthy normal sex'.

Healthy social relationships and the support that could come from friends were deemed very important; one counsellor actively engaged people to support her in explicit ways, another allowed herself to receive 'love, warmth and support from others and their validation'. One aspect of other relationships was just 'having friends not connected with the work to have "normal" conversations'.

Alongside this was the need to develop and maintain outside interests unconnected with work 'to promote a balanced lifestyle'. This, too, fits in with Farber and Heifetz's (1982: 298) assertion that 'virtually all therapists expressed the need for an activity outlet, such as hobbies or sports, that could provide relief for stored up tensions'. Effective and improved coping strategies are those which enable the person to renew his or her sense of the original purpose of helping people, at the same time learning to deal with the stresses that are intrinsic to this work, in ways which are healthy to the counsellor, his or her family, the client, organization and society, so that she or he may continue in the work for as long as she or he chooses and the work is there.

To end this review of improved coping strategies we will hear from the counsellors themselves concerning how they take care of themselves in healthy and well-considered ways. Their self-care strategies were diverse and idiosyncratic, ranging from the mundane to the esoteric, from lone occupations to social extravaganzas (see Figure 1).

PASSIVE	ACTIVE

massage, feet and face
aromatherapy baths
lots of time to self
'switching-off' exercises
CDs of water, waves, streams
tarot cards to focus for personal
  development
teddy bear to represent my
  caring part
	swimming
	reading
	social activities
	fun – picnics – children
	saying 'Help'
	walking in company,
	  countryside, hills
	walking the dog, woods,
	  space – in silence
	drawing and dancing

GIVING MYSELF PERMISSION TO STOP THE WORK COMPLETELY	

Figure 1   *Active and passive self-care strategies of counsellors of survivors*

References

Bagley, C. and King, K. (1991) *Child Sexual Abuse: The Search for Healing.* London: Routledge.

Casement, P. (1991) *On Learning from the Patient.* London: Routledge.

Edelwich, J. and Brodsky, A. (1980) *Burnout: Stages of Disillusionment in the Helping Professions.* New York: Human Sciences Press.

Ellis, A. (1984) 'How to deal with your most difficult client – you', *Psychotherapy in Private Practice*, 2 (1): 25–35.

Farber, B.A. and Heifetz, L.J. (1982) 'The process and dimensions of burnout in psychotherapists', *Professional Psychology*, 13: 293–301.

Finkelhor, D. (1987) 'The trauma of child sexual abuse: two models', *Journal of Interpersonal Violence*, 2 (4): 348–66.

Fortune, M.M. (1983) 'Sexual violence: the unmentionable sin', in C. Bagley and K. King (eds), *Child Sexual Abuse: The Search for Healing*. London: Routledge.

Freudenberger, H.J. (1975) 'The staff burn-out syndrome in alternative institutions', *Psychotherapy: Theory, Research and Practice*, 12 (1): 73–82.

Freudenberger, H.J. (1987) 'Chemical abuse amongst psychologists: symptoms, causes, and treatment issues', in R. Killburg, P. Nathan and R.W. Thoreson (eds), *Professionals in Distress: Issues, Syndromes and Solutions in Psychology*. Washington, DC: American Psychological Association.

Groesbeck, C.J. and Taylor, B. (1977) 'The psychiatrist as wounded physician', *American Journal of Psychoanalysis*, 37: 131–9.

Hawkins, P. and Shohet, R. (1989) *Supervision in the Helping Professions*. Milton Keynes: Open University Press.

Hellman, I.D., Morrisson, T.L. and Abramowitz, S.I. (1987) 'Therapist flexibility/ rigidity and work stress', *Professional Psychology*, 18 (1): 21–7.

Hoffman, S., Kohener, R. and Shapira, M. (1987) 'Two on one: dialectical psychotherapy', *Psychotherapy*, 24 (2): 212–16.

Hopkins, J. (1992) 'Secondary abuse', in A. Bannister (ed.), *From Hearing to Healing: Working with the Aftermath of Childhood Sexual Abuse*. London: Longman/NSPCC.

Kafry, A. and Pines, A. (1980) 'The experience of tedium in life and work', *Human Relations*, 33 (7): 477–503.

Maslach, C. (1976) 'Burned-out', *Human Behavior*, September: 6–22.

Maslach, C. (1987) 'Stress, burnout and workaholism', in R. Killburg, P. Nathan and R.W. Thoreson (eds), *Professionals in Distress: Issues, Syndromes and Solutions in Psychology*. Washington, DC: American Psychological Association.

Russell, D.E.H. (1983) 'The incidence and prevalence of intrafamilial and extrafamilial sexual assault of female children', *Child Abuse and Neglect*, 7: 133–46.

Spensley, J. and Blacker, K.H. (1976) 'Feelings of the psychotherapist', *American Journal of Orthopsychiatry*, 46 (3): 542–5.

3 The Stresses of Working with Clients with HIV/AIDS

Tim Bond

HIV counselling is a recent development which has occurred in two distinct phases. The first phase involved counselling people who had the symptoms of rare but often life-threatening illnesses which were included in the classification of Acquired Immune Deficiency Syndrome (AIDS). As the name suggests, these illnesses were indicative of a damaged immune system. In the early 1980s the source of the damage was unclear but was almost certainly an infection following a transmission route similar to hepatitis because of the incidence of illness in gay men, injecting drug users and haemophiliacs. This caused panic amongst medical and nursing staff, who are particularly at risk of infection from hepatitis from their patients. Simultaneously there was wider social panic based on fear of a twentieth-century plague and pandemic. In Europe and North America gloomy predictions about the spread of the disease abounded. Much of the progress made by gay men and haemophiliacs to gain a wider social acceptance was reversed by the fear of an epidemic and a sense of moral panic. Many patients undoubtedly received a great deal of kindness from some medical and nursing staff but many also told tales of the horrors of receiving treatment from staff concealed by disposable suits and face masks, being subjected to medical tests for research which might be abandoned without any explanation, and being refused treatment by frightened or prejudiced staff. Counselling was made available in a random fashion, depending on its availability and the views of the staff. The popular visual image of someone with AIDS at this time was an emaciated person in a hospital bed. This image had more than a grain of truth in the early 1980s and I mention it because the image has persisted long after the reality has substantially changed.

The stresses of providing HIV counselling changed in the mid-1980s when medical research discovered a slow-acting virus, now known as the Human Immunodeficiency Virus (HIV) which is thought to be the major cause of damage to the immune system. This discovery enabled the development of blood tests for antibodies which indicated the presence of the virus. These blood tests became widely available in the mid-1980s and gradually have become more sensitive and accurate as they have developed. The government actively promoted the use of these tests as part of an HIV prevention programme and simultaneously recommended that counselling should be offered to everyone considering being tested and everyone who received a positive result. This resulted in much larger numbers of people providing counselling in both statutory and voluntary organizations. Perhaps most importantly, it has expanded the range of people affected by HIV who sought counselling. The tests meant that it had become possible to identify someone who is infected but who has no symptoms of any illness. At first this was a mixed blessing, because HIV infection is incurable and seems likely to remain incurable for many years to come. The pressures of living with the knowledge of one's HIV status were considered by many self-help groups to outweigh any benefits in access to medical care. During the early 1990s the equation has changed as the treatments for illnesses caused by the impaired immune system have improved to a remarkable extent. People who a few years ago might have been bedbound and possibly dying are more likely to be in sufficiently good health to be able to continue working or to lead an active life in some other way. There has also been some limited success in delaying the replication of the virus by prophylactic treatments.

It is deceptive to talk about the typical counselling relationship when HIV is involved, because of the unpredictability of the associated illnesses. The progressive damage to the body's immune system may be rapid or slow. The effect is unpredictable because it is like throwing open windows and awaiting opportunistic illnesses to blow in. HIV is seldom a cause of illness by itself, although it does attack nervous tissue and can cause blindness and dementia. Nonetheless, I think it is possible to recognize a pattern in the take-up of counselling. This usually starts at the time of diagnosis and is used to make emotional adjustments and for support during the process of telling any partners and any consequent upheaval in relationships. Thereafter most people who do not have any symptoms of illness probably only seek counselling intermittently when there are major changes in relationships, occupation or other major life events. However, the virus does not discriminate between those who can cope with the knowledge of their HIV status and those who cannot. Equally, the virus does not discriminate between those who have extensive social support and those who are isolated and vulnerable.Therefore, there are some people who may want regular ongoing counselling throughout the time they remain free of symptoms. A significant uptake in counselling occurs with the first symptoms of illness, which may be eight or more years after HIV infection. Sometimes it is difficult to distinguish between the symptoms of stress and the early signs of illness so anything which helps to lower someone's stress contributes both to someone's own sense of well-being and their medical treatment. For this reason, counselling is often regarded as an essential part of providing health care, as well as providing support to people making decisions about the kind of treatment they want to receive. Often there may be a period of time of good health interspersed with periods of treatment for illness. Alternatively, some people experience a period of chronic illness, perhaps with some disability due to illness or the side effects of some drugs. At some point there may be a clear decision to change from treatment to palliative care and the counsellor may be involved alongside others in supporting people who are dying. This transition may be assisted by counselling partners, relatives, friends or professional carers. It is often beneficial to the person with HIV to offer counselling to a strategic carer, as any reduction in a carer's distress can benefit the person who is seriously ill or dying. Sometimes both partners or several members of a family may be seriously ill at the same time. This may compound the levels of distress encountered by the counsellor and may also raise problems for the counsellor about managing the boundaries between clients who are part of the same social network.

The nature of the stresses

The stresses of HIV counselling arise from several sources. Some are related to working directly with people with HIV. Others arise from the wider context of interprofessional relationships and the wider public fear of people with HIV. I will consider each of these in turn, but before I do so I would like to challenge anyone who is reading this and thinking in fixed categories of people with HIV as clients and people without HIV as counsellors. In reality, there are counsellors who know themselves to be HIV positive, those who have chosen not to be tested and therefore do not know their own status, and those who know themselves to be HIV negative, either because of being tested or because they have not been involved in activities which involve the risk of infection. There are stresses in each of these situations which will be experienced differently in terms of counsellors' own hopes and fears for themselves.

One stressor has diminished over the years. It is much clearer that the counsellor is not at risk of infection from HIV by sharing crockery, someone's tears or physical contact with the client. The transmission routes of the virus are well understood. It is a difficult virus to catch and certainly much harder to catch than the more common viruses like hepatitis. The major transmission routes all involve exchange of body fluids through penetrative sex, injection by sharing needles, during childbirth or by breast-feeding. Unbroken skin is an adequate protection against the virus and is the basis of some of the recommended safer sex practices which, for example, encourage the substitution of mutual masturbation for penetrative sex. The ethical counsellor would not engage in any of these activities with a client but some of the safer sex guidelines indicate that mere physical contact with infected fluids is not sufficient for transmission. Therefore, if the counsellor does provide some physical care for someone with HIV which requires more intimate contact, like helping someone move into a different position in bed or to get to the toilet, there are no significant risks of infection. Studies of nurses and carers at home have not established any transmission of HIV without the actual exchange of body fluids, perhaps by a needle stick injury or sexual contact. Simple hygiene has proved adequate protection. In medical settings, staff wash their hands with soap and water after examining or attending to someone with HIV, wear gloves when handling body fluids and wipe down contaminated surfaces with sodium hypochlorite (Jones, 1989). Sometimes knowing this is not sufficient reassurance. I have met a few counsellors and other providers of care for people with HIV who have become so afraid of being infected, even though they know this is irrational, that they have withdrawn from this kind of work.

In reality the risks of infection are often the other way round. The counsellor may import illnesses to someone with a damaged immune system. Colds, flu, and many childhood illnesses may be relatively unimportant to someone with a fully functioning immune system but can be extremely serious to anyone whose immune system is impaired. Monitoring one's own health for vulnerable clients and perhaps rearranging appointments can be a minor but significant stress.

Many of the stresses experienced by the counsellor are the indirect result of the stressors operating on the client. The problems of living with HIV often arise from secrecy, uncertainty and loss (Miller, 1987). The counsellor is caught up in the consequences of these three.

Anyone living with HIV is confronted with the realities of

probably the most dreaded and stigmatized medical diagnosis. HIV infection has replaced cancer as the condition which provokes most prejudice and the greatest likelihood of social rejection. The obvious way of minimizing the risks is secrecy. Someone who has just been told that she is HIV positive may want to tell everyone to ease a flood of distress and fear. This desire is often replaced by a desire to tell no one because reactions are so unpredictable, and also by a desire to cause as little disruption as possible to normal life.

The counsellor will share a sense of the difficulty and risks while helping someone decide the level of disclosure which is appropriate to them. The issue of whether or not to tell a partner illustrates some of the potential stresses to both client and counsellor. The responsibility for the decision must be the client's and most clients wish to tell their partners, sometimes with the counsellor present, or even to have the counsellor tell the partner. The counsellor will be only too aware of the number of people who are abandoned by partners after disclosing that they are HIV positive, particularly if the disclosure also involves an admission of previously secret sexual relationships or a drug habit. On the other hand, if a client postpones telling a partner indefinitely, or decides against disclosure, the counsellor may experience an ethical conflict, especially if the partner continues to be exposed to the risk of infection by, for example, unprotected sex (Bond, 1993). There may be times when a client seeks counselling about whether or not to be tested and during the course of this states that she has been involved with high-risk activities with people known to the counsellor, but not the client, as being HIV positive. All these situations challenge a counsellor's ethics and ability to respond to such sensitive issues.

Although the stress of dealing with these kinds of situation can be considerable, they usually occur infrequently. Most counsellors report that the day-to-day management of confidentiality is a constant background stress because they are aware of the consequences to the client of inappropriate disclosures. The management of confidentiality can be an immediate stressor for counsellors working in interdisciplinary settings where the concept of confidentiality as a personal contract, the counselling ethical standard, is not accepted and the counsellor is under pressure to accept a standard of confidentiality to a team or full disclosure to a manager. I have discussed some of the potential conflicts around the management of confidentiality elsewhere (Bond, 1991).

Some of the causes of uncertainty about the prognosis for anyone with HIV have already been mentioned. There are also frequent uncertainties about the best choice of treatment.

Sometimes someone will be encouraged to follow one treatment course only to be given contradictory guidance by another member of staff or by someone else with HIV. Some people try to inform themselves by reading the medical press, only to find that there are a range of opinions based on different interpretations of similar findings. There may be even greater uncertainty about whether to participate in trials for a new treatment, particularly if there is a risk of merely being given a placebo. It often seems that for every medical opinion in this rapidly evolving subject there are several alternatives which qualify or oppose it. Counsellors often come under pressure to try and resolve these uncertainties and may be subjected to anger if they try to insist on their role of helping a client to come to a personal decision. It is stressful to be working with someone who appears desperate for certainties when a high degree of uncertainty is the reality for both client and counsellor.

Coping with loss pervades counselling around HIV. I am being careful to distinguish between 'living' and 'dying' with HIV. As many people with HIV have pointed out, being diagnosed HIV positive is not the end of life; there may be many years of good-quality living ahead. Indeed some lives are enriched by a new sense of meaning. The choice of the name Body Positive for the largest self-help group for people with HIV is a public declaration that people with HIV are not victims living passively with HIV but can actively and positively do much to help themselves and contribute to the rest of the community. This is undoubtedly true. Nonetheless, the process of personal adjustment to being HIV positive involves coming to terms with the loss of a previous concept of self and future health. Adjustments in relationships and sexual behaviour may also involve loss. There may be many losses during the progression of HIV infection and for most people there is the ultimate loss of dying. The counsellor is working in a situation where loss is a recurrent feature of the work and inevitably this can at times seem overwhelming. In addition, the counsellor has to come to terms with her own sense of loss of people she may have got to know intimately. I sometimes think this is perhaps the most stressful aspect of loss for a counsellor working with clients with serious HIV-related illnesses. The counsellor has to find ways of managing her own sense of actual loss of earlier clients and her anticipated loss of the present client in order to work with the client's own sense of loss, which may be experienced very differently. The counsellor's sense of loss may be intensified by her own heightened awareness of death and her own inevitable death, whether from HIV or other causes.

Some stress arises from the context in which the counselling is provided. HIV counsellors who work in statutory service, usually health care but sometimes social services or education, report that their role is frequently misunderstood. For example, it may be assumed by colleagues and clients that the counsellor's role is primarily directed towards HIV prevention by telling people what they should not do or giving unequivocal advice about what they should do. This confusion is inherent in the term 'counselling,' which in English has a longstanding meaning of giving expert advice (Bond, 1993). In HIV counselling the confusion between this meaning of counselling and its use by the British Association for Counselling is enhanced because counselling posts may be funded as part of an HIV prevention programme. Role confusion and role conflict has been reported to be a major source of stress and frustration by HIV counsellors (Bond, 1991; Coyle and Goodwin, 1992).

The wider social context or prejudice and fear makes caring for people with HIV much harder for all carers, including counsellors. It can deprive them of support from their own partners and social contacts. I am aware of some counsellors who deliberately withhold information about the nature of their work from some members of their family and friends because of the prejudice they would be exposed to. I know some doctors and nurses who are equally cautious. The HIV counsellor, regardless of personal health status, shares some of the problems of social stigma by association with clients. These stresses of potential rejection spread out from the workplace into the counsellor's personal life. Even if the counsellor's work is understood and supported by others outside work, the need for confidentiality about individual clients limits the opportunities to obtain support from the counsellor's own social network.

Counsellors' responses to the stresses

I have yet to meet a counsellor who has not been profoundly affected by working with people with HIV. Most would say that they feel enriched and privileged, but this has been gained at a cost. My own theory, which is based on reflections about my own experience and that of a few HIV counsellors whom I have known over a considerable length of time, is that there is an identifiable process in coming to terms with providing HIV counselling. The sort of person who is likely to become involved is almost certainly reasonably aware of issues relating to sexuality, drug abuse, illness and death. Often some insight and commitment to the work will be derived from personal experience. This may make the counsellor more acceptable to clients, who often anticipate rejection by people who do not themselves identify with those sections of the community most affected by HIV infection. However, this may intensify counsellors' own fears for themselves. I remember the atmosphere of shock and alarm when I met a team of HIV counsellors who had just heard of a study suggesting that oral sex may be less safe than was previously thought. Some were clearly concerned about the implications for clients but many were also concerned for themselves. It would be an exceptional counsellor who is not periodically stressed by the possibility of HIV infection of themselves or of others who are emotionally important.

Counselling people with HIV produces intense feelings in the counsellor. Often these parallel the feelings of the client, especially if the counsellor is empathic. Nothing prepared me for the strength of these feelings, even though I had previous experience of working with clients facing life-threatening diagnoses. Other counsellors have made similar observations to me. The client's vulnerability to rejection by others often gives the relationship a particular intensity, which seems to become comparable to other counselling relationships only if the client feels supported by people other than the counsellor. I think an observation about the care-givers of cancer patients applies equally to counsellors of people with HIV. There is no reaction among patients which cannot also occur in the care-givers (Weisman, 1981). Mark Winiarski (1991) argues that it is important that the counsellor recognizes the significance and therapeutic usefulness of her own feelings, which often parallel the HIV-positive client's experience. However the process of making personal adjustments to strong and overwhelming feelings is stressful. Elizabeth Kubler Ross (1987) suggests that these feelings can be understood in a wider context; that the care-giver goes through a process which parallels that of the patient – denial and isolation, anger, bargaining, depression and acceptance. I will talk more about this in the next section, but for the moment I would like to describe some of the inappropriate ways of lowering stress that I have observed in HIV counsellors, and consider healthier alternatives.

Some counsellors respond to the difficulties of managing confidentiality by spreading a veil of secrecy over all their work. This deprives colleagues of insight into the nature and benefits of HIV counselling. Sometimes a tendency towards secrecy is reinforced if the counsellor is feeling vulnerable about having too few clients or has doubts about the value of what he is doing. In these circumstances it is all too easy for the counsellor and other staff to become alienated from each other in an atmosphere of paranoid fantasy. A healthier response is to establish a policy which takes into account the client's wishes about what should remain confidential and which distinguishes between personally identifiable information and general information about the take-up services and the typical kinds of counselling provided. The management of confidentiality requires the active fostering of mutual trust and respect between service providers in order to minimize the pressures towards inappropriate disclosure. Establishing this climate of trust is not always easy and may create short-term stress for the counsellor, but it has long-term benefits. In contrast, total secrecy often lowers stress in the short term but the stresses of resisting all disclosures, both appropriate and inappropriate, is likely to accumulate.

Occasionally I have met counsellors who have adopted a position of denial of the losses that are involved in being infected with HIV. This is most likely to occur when the counsellor is working exclusively with people who have not developed HIV-related illness. The counselling is directed towards helping people live their lives as fully as possible. For some people, there is a substantial improvement in quality of life as each moment is intensified by the knowledge of the diagnosis and life takes a new meaning. A counsellor can be carried away by such positiveness out of an empathic resonance with the client. However, the counsellor's positive attitude can become a form of detachment, and therefore problematic, if it results in the counsellor denying the emotional pain of working with people who are often young and may be facing disfigurement, disability and death. Sometimes this can result in premature disengagement from a client whose health is declining in order to protect the counsellor from a sense of loss. It is much healthier for the counsellor to seek counselling himself to help him face up to the losses experienced by the client.

The uncertainties about an individual's prognosis and the best forms of treatment weigh heavily on client and counsellor alike. One inappropriate way of avoiding this stress is to create artificial certainties. For example, a counsellor may be unjustifiably positive about the usefulness of a particular medical treatment or counselling method and seek to impose this on a client. But, counselling methods are no more certain in their effects than the rapidly dating medical information upon which people with HIV base important decisions. A much healthier response to the uncertainties is to respond with realistic strategies, without exaggerated claims for their effectiveness, in a spirit of realistic optimism as to their value. Counsellors who insist that a narrow range of methods assist all clients, or who require clients to progress according to a fixed timetable, may be driven by their own need to minimize the stresses of uncertainty rather than responding to their clients. An alternative response may be helplessness and a retreat to doing nothing but listen passively to clients. Active listening and responding to individual clients' needs is preferable and less stressful than remaining helpless in the face of an emotionally vulnerable client.

So far I have been commenting on some of the responses to the stresses of working directly with clients. The stresses caused by role ambiguity, role confusion and perhaps having multiple roles, for example as health adviser and counsellor, can be just as debilitating. Some counsellors who manage the stresses of work with clients appear overwhelmed by these issues. Inappropriate responses included retreat into secrecy and helplessness. Alternatively, some counsellors enter into combat perhaps fuelled by aggression and anger associated with the losses involved in HIV work. Neither response is helpful. It may be better to create situations in which it is possible to disseminate literature and other information to colleagues about counselling. Personal assertiveness in negotiating the counsellor's role may also be required.

The stresses experienced as a result of the HIV counsellor being stigmatized by association with a client group can produce a variety of responses. There is a risk of inappropriate disclosures which compromise confidentiality when the counsellor feels overburdened. These disclosures may occur out of relief when a sympathetic person is encountered unexpectedly or may take the form of saying too much in a burst of anger in an encounter with someone who is prejudiced.

The potential for HIV counsellors to become overwhelmed by several different stressors operating simultaneously is obviously greater than for other counsellors. The isolated nature of a counsellor's work required by privacy means that the counsellor may not obtain the support of others as readily as some of the other care-giving professions who are working in teams.

Suggestions for improved coping

The major strategy for reducing stress is to be forewarned that the counsellor has a personal process of adjustment to go through, and to facilitate this rather than hold back. The stressors of caring for people with HIV are shared by all the caring professions, but counsellors in particular are confronted with the emotional experience of HIV infection and as a consequence experience a particularly intense parallel process to the person with HIV.

The start of the process is often marked by a dream. Mark Winiarski (1991) drew my attention to what appears to be an almost ubiquitous phenomenon. After the first encounter with someone diagnosed HIV positive, almost all counsellors report having a dream about being diagnosed HIV positive or about someone close to the counsellor being infected. The dream is usually accompanied by strong feelings of dread, anxiety, panic and other feelings which may be too profound to be described easily. This dream can be left to fade and treated as ephemeral. However, letting the dream fade without considering its implications misses an opportunity to address some fundamental issues which may become stressors. The counsellor's personal fear of HIV may lead to overidentification with clients and leave both counsellor and client lost in overwhelming emotions. Alternatively, the counsellor may be self-protective by excessively disengaging from the client in ways which prevent empathy and inhibit the client. Most HIV counsellors can recognize a tendency towards one of these extremes. My own tendency is towards overidentification. I found it useful to receive counselling to help establish the basis of this tendency and to establish boundaries between my personal issues and those of my clients. Whether or not a counsellor responds to personal anxiety by overidentifying or disengaging, I would encourage every counsellor to have counselling when they first start working with people with HIV whether or not they experience the 'AIDS dream'. Personal counselling is in addition to counselling supervision. I will consider the function of each separately.

One of the first tasks of the counselling is to help the HIV counsellor to examine the reality behind the fears. Many counsellors are themselves sexually active or may be at risk of infection for other reasons. These risks need evaluating and the HIV counsellor needs to be helped to decide how she wishes to proceed. She may prefer to know her status and be tested. She may prefer to remain in ignorance rather than risk the periods of anxiety and depression which often follow a positive diagnosis. She may already know that she is HIV negative or positive. Whatever the situation, it is important to help acknowledge the reality of her situation and how she wants to manage it. Any personal anxieties will be firmly rooted in the counsellor's reality. The alternative is to risk free-floating anxieties which could be re-stimulated by every anxiety of her clients. This process also represents the first step from denial and isolation towards acceptance of the reality which will often entail moving through the emotional process described by Kubler Ross (1987).

Regardless of the counsellor's health status, there are likely to be moments of anger, bargaining and depression. For the counsellor who is HIV negative, these emotions may be directed at the unfairness of the suffering of her clients. Unlike the general public, who can feel relief and return to a state of denial at receiving a negative test result, the counsellor has to reconcile personal feelings of relief with coming to terms with the reality of HIV infection for others. This can produce considerable internal conflict including guilt, fear of infection, a powerful sense of exclusion and many other surprising and powerful responses. The extent to which these can be resolved may help the counsellor to establish a clear separation between her own experience and that of her clients.

The counsellor will also need to decide how she plans to protect her health status in future. This may require emotional adjustment, as any changes towards safer behaviour are often accompanied by the loss of previous freedoms. This counselling provides a model which the counsellor can replicate when helping others and which develops insight into the experience of receiving counselling. The counselling also complements and expedites counselling supervision by consolidating and clarifying the counsellor's personal experience as a starting point from which she can understand the diversity of her client's responses to HIV infection. The diversity of these responses and their intensity will probably be less stressful to the counsellor because they are less likely to become confused with her own anxieties for herself and those close to her.

Counselling supervision can reinforce the distinction between the counsellor's personal responses and those of her clients, which will enable the counsellor to work more effectively. Without this distinction, empathic responses which can be so supportive of clients can change into overidentification, with both counsellor and client becoming increasingly lost and experiencing heightened and unduly prolonged periods of stress. (Emotional distancing is usually an over-reaction to defend against the stresses of over-identification by the counsellor.) Empathic resonance is least stressful to the counsellor if she is reasonably confident of her own state of adjustment and is moving ahead of the client in that process. This confidence will often instil hope in the client that it is possible to move on to a more comfortable emotional state. Most importantly, it changes the perspective of the counsellor when she is confronted by intense feelings of anger and anxiety, which may be directed at her. A client may be extremely angry at being let down by all his carers, especially the counsellor, because no one can cure him. This could be experienced as undermining the counsellor's sense of purpose and belief that it is possible for the client to achieve a greater sense of personal acceptance of his situation. Instead, the counsellor's role is to acknowledge that she cannot cure the client but she can help the client to come to terms with his situation, and that is the purpose of the counselling. Often counsellors are knocked sideways by the strength of expression of the client's hopelessness and respond with inappropriate self-doubt. The supervisor's role is to help the counsellor understand what is happening and by doing so, to reinforce the counsellor's sense of purpose and therefore lower stress. If a client deteriorates physically, becomes disfigured or demented, the counsellor may avoid the client as a way of escaping personal stress. Again counselling supervision can help the counsellor to identify the real issues and decide on a more appropriate response, which may also involve the HIV counsellor in receiving counselling.

When I was researching my report on HIV counselling (Bond, 1991) I was left with the strong impression that the counselling services offered by the best of the voluntary sector had developed better strategies for using counselling supervision than many equally busy statutory services. Since the report was completed, anecdotal evidence suggests that there has been some movement towards enabling better counselling supervision (that is, non-managerial) in the statutory sector. However, many agencies do not fully appreciate that the provision of good supervision has developed into a highly skilled role, and settle for interdisciplinary staff support groups as an alternative. There is a strong case for providing both counselling supervision and staff support as separate activities (Smith, 1992). Counselling supervision is almost always supportive but the focus is primarily on the client's interests. In contrast, staff support validates the importance of giving time to the counsellor's and colleagues' personal needs arising from their work. Both are necessary.

Inadequate training is a major source of stress (Coyle and Goodwin, 1992). Training needs to be extensive and appropriate to the role. Participants in the consultations to the report on HIV counselling made many recommendations about what good training might consist of (Bond, 1991). Again voluntary organizations would emphasize the importance of the counsellor being adequately trained in one model of counselling with an alternative secondary model. Additional training in issues relating to sexuality, illness, loss and dying are also recommended. But good training will not be sufficient by itself. The lowering of the stress of HIV counsellors requires a combination of strategies, of which adequate supervision and support are the most important. What lowers stress in HIV counsellors also improves the quality of service provided to clients. The case seems irresistible but progress is painfully slow, especially in the statutory sector.

References

Bond, Tim (1991) *HIV Counselling – Report on National Survey and Consultation.* Rugby: British Association for Counselling.

Bond, Tim (1993) *Standards and Ethics for Counselling in Action.* London: Sage.

Coyle, Adrian and Goodwin, M. (1992) 'Training, workload and stress among HIV counsellors', *AIDS Care,* 4 (2): 217–21.

Jones, Peter (1989) 'The counselling of HIV antibody positive haemophiliacs', in John Green and Alana McCreamer (eds), *Counselling in HIV Injection and AIDS.* Oxford: Blackwell Scientific Publications.

Kubler Ross, Elizabeth (1987) *AIDS – The Ultimate Challenge.* New York: Macmillan.

Miller, David (1987) *Living with AIDS and HIV.* London: Macmillan.

Smith, Norah (1992) 'Organisational support for helpers', in Charles Anderson and Patricia Wilkie (eds), *Reflective Helping in HIV and AIDS.* Buckingham: Open University Press.

Weisman, A.D. (1981) 'Understanding the cancer patient: the syndrome of caregiver's plight', *Psychiatry,* 44: 161–8.

Winiarski, Mark G. (1991) *AIDS-related Psychotherapy.* New York: Pergamon Press.

4 The Stresses of Working with Clients with Disabilities

Julia Segal

Disabilities affect people who do not have them as well as people who do. Whatever their own state of health, counsellors may be shocked at their emotional reactions to others' disabilities. They may have no experience of working or living with other people with the particular disability, and be unsure how to behave as a counsellor with a disabled client. Vague ideas of 'treat people with disabilities as you would treat anyone else' or 'behave as you would normally' do not really work. Disability is often linked with illness, either in reality or in fantasy, and it is not normal to expect an ill person to think intelligently about painful issues. It is hardly normal not to try to avoid someone with a disturbing disability. Though socially it may in some situations be correct behaviour to pretend to ignore a disability or disfiguring condition, it is not normal for a counsellor to pretend. Without good training and support counsellors may distance themselves from the client, both failing to understand and failing to make emotional contact.

The question is how to behave appropriately as a counsellor in an abnormal situation; working this out from scratch, with the client in the room, can be very stressful indeed for the counsellor. Good preparation can enable counsellors to sort out their own reactions and to distinguish them from the clients'. Some idea of the range of feelings and thoughts to expect of clients can help counsellors to avoid the common trap of assuming that 'everyone' in the client's situation would feel as the counsellors think they would themselves. Some idea of the range of feelings which may be evoked in the counsellor may also help the counsellor cope with these feelings without splitting them off or feeling overwhelmingly guilty about them. Properly understood, these feelings can be used in the counselling, if only to provide some idea of the difficulties the client may be having with the rest of the world.

Working with people who are disabled, there may be many pressures – from the client, the counsellor and from other people around – to behave differently in some way from the counsellor's normal practice. Home visits, physical contact, additional practical help or advocacy may all be asked for in such a way that it is difficult to refuse them. It may be hard to remember that the reasons why the counsellor does not normally provide these services remain valid for people with disabilities. Of even more importance perhaps, a feeling that the client cannot cope with ordinary emotions may make the counsellor want to tread more warily than usual and may even prevent 'normal' counselling from taking place. The disturbing nature of the disability may create not only stress but also paralysis in the counsellor: the counselling process itself may be disabled.

The nature of the stresses

Clients' disabilities affect counsellors in many ways, whatever the counsellors' own state of health. As children, our natural reaction to people who looked different, especially in a way which seemed ugly, was probably to recoil in fear or horror. Historically this may have been of advantage in preventing contagious conditions from being passed on; but now that we can distinguish in theory at least between conditions which are to be avoided and those which are not, we have to struggle against such primitive survival reactions. Counselling disabled people may, like nursing, be considered a worthy thing to do because it implies we have in some sense overcome a natural revulsion.

However, disturbing feelings may still remain and leave their mark. We may not know what caused a disability, and fear it could be contagious. We do not know how the person feels about their condition and we may imagine they envy us enormously. We may see nightmares of our own old age or death reflected in a client whose condition is deteriorating. We may be reminded of a relative's death. Some people have a keen desire to behave in a politically correct fashion – in order to placate people with disabilities imagined as threatening. Pity towards someone who is disabled often appears on examination to cover up far more robust feelings of dislike, rejection or resentment. Whatever the counsellor's own feelings towards an affected client and their disability, some guilt, anxiety and fear are likely to be around, influencing their first reactions – and probably later ones too (Segal, 1991).

Lack of experience increases these difficulties. Policies of segregating disabled children have created a society which lacks the skill of knowing how to behave in the presence of disabled adults. Both counsellors and clients have limited experience from which to generalize, and their generalizations are often very idiosyncratic. Expectations which are unrealistically optimistic or pessimistic are common.

> A counsellor was concerned about seeing people with disabilities herself because she had once witnessed someone having a fit and had been so terrified she had been unable to move.

> One young professional was secretly afraid she had supernatural powers of life or death over clients because of a series of fatal accidents she had been involved in as a child and young person.

> A trainee counsellor was certain that the disabilities of multiple sclerosis could be prevented by counselling because her own physical illness had been cured by psychotherapy.

> Two counsellors said they would be terrified of being in a wheelchair. One said she would be trapped; on thinking about it she realized she meant she would be trapped in her marriage – which is how she felt at that moment. Another said she would hate to be pushed around, which also turned out to have a symbolic meaning in the present.

Clients give their condition meaning in just the same way: counsellors may not be able to seek and discover the clients' meaning if their own is too significant for them. In this situation the client is likely to feel misunderstood and pressured by the counsellor, thus increasing the counsellor's difficulties.

A particular problem which arises with clients who have chronic disabling conditions is the feeling that such people have to be protected from the normal stresses of daily life (Morris, 1989). In the counselling setting it means that the counsellor may be tempted to avoid challenging the client, or even pointing out to them how they are behaving, perhaps in the mistaken belief that bad behaviour of one kind or another is to be expected from someone who is disabled, especially if their condition is deteriorating. This can have disastrous effects on the counselling. Daring to challenge such clients (and ultimately to find out that it is possible and valuable) may be extremely stressful for the counsellor as it offends their natural inclination to protect a client perceived as vulnerable and weak.

The idea that a disability disqualifies someone from feelings and experiences such as love, sexuality, marriage, anger, power and creativity and leaves them prey to feelings such as envy, destructiveness and revenge on the able-bodied world is part of our basic heritage: Shakespeare's *Richard III* illustrates this idea in detail. Unfortunately it can underlie counsellors' or clients' beliefs as well (Greengross, 1976; Segal, 1989). The idea that intelligence, emotional strength and the ability to take responsibility for the self or others are also lost with a disability is also common. A counsellor who believes such ideas may be very anxious about counselling someone with a disability, afraid of the damage they can do emotionally as well as perhaps physically, and scared to use their counselling skills to the full. The counsellor may have serious difficulty sorting out whether their own or the clients' expectations, hope or lack of hope are realistic or unrealistic. The counsellor's expectations will affect the decision to offer or to continue with counselling, and the direction in which it moves, however much the counsellor tries to follow the client rather than impose their own ideas.

It can sometimes be hard for a counsellor to remember that a disabled person has an adult role such as being a partner, a lover or a parent (Segal and Simkins, 1993). Dealing with the situation where a client has fallen in love with the counsellor, for example, may be much harder and very painful if the client is severely disabled and the counsellor is afraid that no one else could possibly love 'someone like that'. The counsellor may feel an increased sense of responsibility for a client misperceived as lacking the ability to take responsibility. The stress can be considerable, particularly if the client exploits the situation. Determining where the real limits of a client's abilities lie may itself be a painful and stressful activity.

Working in an unfamiliar setting can give rise to a general feeling of discomfort and insecurity. If the counsellor reacts by 'seeing the disability and not the person', even if only temporarily, it can seem that the client is more experienced than the counsellor (because he or she knows about the disability), and the counsellor's own expertise (in counselling) may be forgotten. Not knowing much about the cause or consequences of a disability can make the counsellor feel for a while useless.

In addition to this general discomfort, and sometimes influencing and being influenced by it, there may be pressures from others or from the client to step outside the counsellor's normal role. Where some of the counsellor's own rules may have to be broken, it may be difficult to say which ones do not have to be. Pressure to visit the client at home, or to become an advocate, may arise from within the counsellor or from others. If a counsellor normally interprets failure of a client to arrive at a session as some kind of failure to *want* to arrive, does this still apply if the client's transport failed to turn up? The counsellor has to become aware of the client's dependence on others and the complex interplay of social, personal and political issues involved, and perhaps to modify their own behaviour and thinking accordingly. However, if the counsellor simply goes along with the client's insistence that they really could not help missing the session, the counsellor may be left with an anxiety that they have failed to treat this client as they would anyone else, namely to draw attention convincingly to reasons they might have for not wanting to come.

It may be very hard to know when to insist that the client *can* do something for themselves, such as seek an advocate or ring the DSS, or find a partner, if the counsellor does not know what is or is not possible in their situation. In my experience (in north London in the 1980s and 1990s) 'I can't come to you because I can't get out' has never turned out to be true; many clients have benefited from my insistence that they can come to me for counselling. However, a colleague in Scotland tells me that some clients in her area really are housebound; she offers counselling at their home. Whether counsellors do or do not change their own ground rules, and whichever they choose to insist upon, they may be left with uncomfortable feelings: Am I being unreasonable? Can I really work properly if I do change? What is essential to my work and what is not? What is the effect of changes I do make? Does it mean clients are getting a worse service?

Counsellors' responses to the stresses

One of the most obvious responses is avoidance. Enthusiasm for ensuring that counselling facilities are accessible may be lukewarm. A potential client may be steered in a different direction on the grounds that the counsellor lacks experience. If the client does arrive there are more subtle methods counsellors may use to defend themselves against the uncomfortable feelings aroused.

Some counsellors are aware of their own lack of knowledge of a client's disability and can tolerate it. They greet the client in the full awareness that the client's experience is greater than their own when it comes to understanding the particular condition and its implications. They may seek information independently if this is appropriate. If they draw on their own experience they will use it tentatively, asking the client rather than making assumptions.

Other counsellors have more difficulty tolerating their own ignorance. One reaction is for the counsellor to assume that the knowledge and experience they do have is sufficient and relevant. They may make assumptions about the client's reactions to their condition which are not justified and their own anxiety may make them unable to recognize that this is happening.

When trying to understand someone else's situation it is perfectly natural to 'put ourselves in their shoes'. If counsellors are inexperienced in the disability field this may misfire. Typically, counsellors imagine themselves with the disability in question but leave out significant strengths in their own character or in their social setting. They may, for example, assume that a facial disfigurement would mean isolation when in their own situation it actually would not. An unconscious splitting process often seems to go on, whereby the counsellor splits their own life into good and bad; all the bad goes with the fantasy of having the disability and all the good is discounted. This has several consequences.

In the first place it may lead to a serious underestimation of the client's abilities and strengths. Secondly, it may lead to a fear of envy: in the counsellor's unconscious fantasy the client is seen as having nothing and the counsellor as having everything worth living for. With a client who has strong feelings about losing the ability to do paid work or to have children the counsellor may find it very hard to allow themselves to be effective out of fear of arousing the client's envy.

Splitting the client and the self in this way leaves the counsellor with a very much worse concept of the actual condition: an excessive 'how awful' response. A disabling condition which gives a 30-year life expectancy may be seen as 'taking a long time to die', for example. Not only is the client in a wheelchair, perhaps, but in the counsellor's mind they may, in addition, be bereft of love and any hope of life. For the counsellor the condition is raw and new; the client has had time to get used to it.

If the counsellor has the same condition themselves the danger of making assumptions about the client may be even greater. Just as two marriages may have very little in common, so may two people's disabling conditions, even if they have the same name. In some conditions (such as MS) the disabilities themselves vary hugely between individuals; in others the disabilities may be similar but the life situations of the individual may vary so greatly that what seems the same may be experienced as very different. Which particular disability troubles someone most varies enormously, not just for practical reasons, but also as a result of the symbolism attached. Some men, for example, feel they are no longer competent, worthy men if their penis does not work; but would not mind so much losing their sight or the use of their legs. Others feel like this about their legs but not their penis. If a counsellor has a particular anxiety about losing the use of some part of themselves they may be very disturbed by a client who faces the loss in reality.

When an idea or feeling in connection with a disability is too painful for the counsellor it may be blocked, though the client might be able to, and need to, bear it. Staying with grief over loss of some aspect of bodily or mental functioning, especially in young people, may be very difficult for counsellors who in other circumstances do not block feelings. There may be a need to allow the client a very long time to do little other than to feel and share their grief; the counsellor may get impatient and feel they are not doing enough. Again, this sense of frustration is part of the work and may be shared. The sense that nothing else will ever happen, that the grief is all there is and all there will be, may be a very important part of the emotional experience the client needs to convey.

Particularly where a client feels their disability has made them useless, a counsellor too may feel useless, and quite unable to help the client by counselling them. A more experienced counsellor would recognize such feelings as perhaps connected with the client's own sense of uselessness. A less experienced counsellor may feel a strong urge to know something, perhaps even offering a 'cure' of their own. Rather than tolerating and sharing with the client the feeling of having nothing to give, a counsellor may feel a need to be sure that they offer something. They may temporarily forget that the understanding they have to offer is unique and seek to cheer the patient up; to give them something good and positive to hold on to even if this is not appropriate.

> A therapist was working with a group of mentally handicapped young women. After several weeks the women began to verbalise ideas about what had happened to them when they were babies to damage their brains. The therapist found it too painful and suggested that the next week they talk about 'treats': things they liked best for themselves.

Where a client's condition has seriously threatened their sense of their self, forcing them to give up huge and important areas of functioning, the counsellor too may for a time feel disoriented and threatened in their sense of themselves as a counsellor.

In general, many of the feelings arising from a disabling condition are shared by client and counsellor. If the counsellor can tolerate this, the experience can be used in the counselling, helping the counsellor to gain some insight into the confused feelings of the client. If the counsellor is over anxious about getting too close to the client and perhaps 'catching' the condition this process will be impossible. The counsellor will find themselves insisting on the differences between themselves and the client, perhaps behaving in ways in which they would not normally behave such as telling the client what to do. This can also arise if the counsellor cannot bear to stay with feelings of being unable to cure the condition or remove the disability.

Ideas of the body–mind link may also be used to fend off fears of getting the condition. More than one trainee counsellor has said 'Multiple sclerosis must be like cancer. It depends on your will to live, your state of mind; if your mind is OK your body will be too.' This functions to protect the counsellor from the knowledge that she too would be helpless in the face of MS. In addition it allows the counsellor a certain superiority over the client, whose mind, clearly is not 'OK', 'or she wouldn't have MS like that, would she?' The dangers of this position are clear.

Anger with others who cannot cure the client or who ill-treat him or her can also affect counsellors, who may find themselves wanting to take up cudgels on the client's behalf. Such feelings may not normally be difficult to resist, but if the clients appear weak, physically vulnerable and in need of support, it may be harder to avoid offering to do things for them. The reasons for not stepping outside the counselling role are of course as strong if not stronger with disabled clients as they are with able-bodied clients. People who are handicapped in some way often find themselves pushed to one side by others rushing to do things for them; not allowing them to do things in their own time and their own way. Where the counsellor holds on to their desire to act for the client and suffers the frustration, they may find they have learnt something of the frustration the client suffers at their own inability to act as and when they would like to, as well as understanding something of the difficulties faced by carers or others around the client. This understanding may be far more important than the advocacy itself. Somebody else can offer advocacy if it is really needed; there may be no one else who can offer such understanding.

Counsellors may also distance themselves from a client's disability and its effects by not talking about it, or by listening with only half an ear and then 'moving the client on' to something more interesting, something with which the counsellor feels more at home. The chance for the client to really be heard, perhaps to discuss and share the feelings of boredom and having had enough of the disability, may be lost. The client may not complain because it is what they have come to expect: nobody likes listening to a catalogue of symptoms. The counsellor's stress may be temporarily reduced at the expense of the client; ultimately the counselling will not be as useful as it could be.

Suggestions for improved coping

Experience and training can help to overcome some of the difficulties and stresses involved in counselling people with disabilities. Working or playing, preferably since childhood, with people who are disabled can help to reduce some of the anxieties, though this may not be enough. Generalizing from one or two friends or acquaintances with disabilities may be as much a danger as generalizing from the counsellor's own fantasies.

Training can give counsellors a chance to discover the different meanings given to disability by other people. Simple 'Disability Awareness' training is not sufficient, though it may be useful, particularly in helping counsellors to locate and overcome some of their own fears, prejudices and false assumptions. A real belief that people who are disabled can be capable, competent and happily married is probably best obtained by meeting some.

Training and supervision directed specifically at counselling people with disabilities can help counsellors to retain a firm grip on their role and prevent it being undermined by their reaction to a client's disability. Counsellors can learn by experience, but the first clients may pay a high price. It can take a considerable time for an experienced counsellor to regain their trust in using the counselling process rather than making unnecessary and damaging modifications to their technique.

Once counsellors have learnt to use their own ignorance as much as any other feeling of their own a considerable amount of stress can be removed. Learning to say to a client 'I don't know whether (you want me) to offer help or not' rather than trying to guess brings such mutual difficulties into the counselling arena where they can be discussed. The decision never to pretend to a client, however disabled they are, brings its own stresses, but in the long run strengthens the counselling process and the counsellor's confidence.

Issues of sexuality in particular need to be thought about in advance if the counsellor is not to be taken by surprise by events or by their own assumptions. Some preparation may help the counsellor as well as the client to think of people with disabilities getting married or having sex, with partners of either sex. Courses run by SPOD (Social and Personal Relations of the Disabled) can be very useful preparation. A counsellor may also think in advance about whether they would help a client in the toilet.

Counsellors need to know where to go for help, both for information and for thinking about issues which arise during the course of counselling. Some self-help organizations have counsellors, experienced in working with people with a particular disability, who will act as consultants to other counsellors. Some supervisors are sufficiently knowledgeable and realistically confident in their ability to help the counsellor; others are not. Local disability organizations may or may not be useful.

The setting is important. Counsellors in general need a safe, secure setting and most would not normally work alone in a building. If there is a risk of a client needing physical help, for example needing help in the toilet or to be picked up after a fall, the counsellor needs to know that there are other people around who can be called. Some people assume that a man is not a threat, particularly a sexual threat, if he is disabled. This may not be true; even if it is, a man may not appreciate being treated as if he were asexual and socially impotent.

Most people with disabilities are perfectly capable of looking after themselves; however, some who are not may seek counselling. A client may pretend to themselves and others that they are not as disabled as they actually are. This may cause some problem for a counsellor; if, for example, they say they can manage steps when in fact they cannot; or if they omit to mention that they need an accessible toilet available the minute they arrive. In a setting where disabilities are fully catered for, such difficulties would not matter; if a counsellor is seeing clients at home there may be a problem.

If a client is normally not left alone it may be important to ask whether there is anything the counsellor ought to know. A counsellor should never be left in a situation where their own action or inaction can cause physical distress or danger to a client. There may be a need to spell this out to a potential client and/or other person, for example a social worker or carer.

The counsellor should know where and in what circumstances to call for practical help, and be certain that help would be available within a safe time period. It may also be useful to know when it is not necessary to call for help: if a client is liable to fits or choking it may or may not be necessary to break the session, for example. If fits do occur, it may even be appropriate to attempt to understand any meaning they have in the relationship between client and counsellor.

Sometimes counsellors do not want to confront a client with the fact that the counsellor's setting and the client's disability combine to prevent them from receiving the same service as others. They may allow themselves to be pressurized into offering counselling in a situation which is not really suitable. This is short-sighted: if the counsellor is not secure the quality of the counselling will be affected. The client may be able to find counselling elsewhere, perhaps at a later date, if it is refused for good reason; whereas a bad experience with a counsellor who is not feeling safe may prevent the client from asking for counselling again.

Clearly there are also times when counsellors would be well advised not to see certain categories of client:

> A counsellor said that a close friend of hers had been diagnosed with MS and had killed herself six months ago. She decided that she was not ready to offer her services to people with MS at present.

Disabilities, especially when they are new, can cause people to feel they are falling apart; that they have lost all control over their lives; that they have lost the person they once were and are not sure of ever becoming a person they want to be again. These feelings may approximate closely a new counsellor's own experience during training. Such feelings may also affect people suffering from bereavement or divorce, but the chances are that the counsellor's training and life experience will have fitted them better for work in these areas; the counsellor is more likely to know that the feelings are temporary and will almost certainly be overcome. Counsellors who are still in training, or are recently qualified, should not normally be expected to take on clients with new disabilities. 'New' in this context may mean several years old if the client has had no opportunity to consider the meaning of their condition before.

> An attractive young woman had suffered severe brain damage in a road accident three years previously. It seemed she had been constantly surrounded by cheering and cheery nursing staff and family who were unable to address the loss and allow her to grieve; they always encouraged her to 'think positively' and could not share their grief with her. In counselling, as she was able to begin to grieve for her losses, she evoked in the counsellor enormous feelings of hopelessness, collapse and inadequacy.

A new or inexperienced counsellor would need considerable supervisory support to withstand such feelings, and might find their own sense of themselves as a counsellor under threat.

Sometimes people come into counselling through a disability of their own: they may decide to become a counsellor after being diagnosed as having MS, for example, or being injured in an accident. For some people in this situation, counselling training may be sought as a cover for feeling useless and second class. The risk is that particularly clients with the same condition may be kept in an inferior position in order to bolster a counsellor who does not really believe that either of them is worthy to take their place in the normal world. Training and two years' experience in a 'normal' setting can allow such a counsellor to find their own real abilities, and a soundly based self-confidence which does not depend on keeping themselves or others in a ghetto.

Anyone may seek to bolster themselves through becoming a counsellor, and normally such people would not be allowed to qualify while they felt like this. Some trainee counsellors seek out disabled clients on the grounds that they feel uncertain about their own abilities and 'the disabled' ought to be grateful to get even a second-class service. Clearly, counselling people with disabilities will not solve such counsellors' problems; and it may well add to the problems of their clients.

The best recipe for overcoming many of the problems and stresses involved in counselling people with disabilities is the experience of counselling them successfully. The initial difficulties, once overcome, become a source of strength and confidence for the counsellor. To see a client's emotional state improving, in spite of their disabilities perhaps getting worse, can be a huge reassurance. Many counsellors' anxieties disappear over time.

However, some counsellors find that this is not sufficient. Some never overcome their difficulties in relating to certain groups of people who are disabled. A time working with such people may serve to convince them that this work is not for them.

References

Greengross, W. (1976) *Entitled to Love*. London: Malaby Press.

Morris, Jenny (ed.) (1989) *Able Lives: Women's Experience of Paralysis*. London: Women's Press.

Segal, J.C. (1989) 'Counselling people with disabilities/chronic illnesses', in Windy Dryden, Ray Woolfe and David Charles-Edwards (eds), *Handbook of Counselling in Britain*. London: Tavistock/Routledge. pp. 329–46.

Segal, J.C. (1991) 'Use of the concept of unconscious phantasy in understanding reactions to chronic illness', *Counselling*, 2 (4) November: 146–9.

Segal, Julia and Simkins, John (1993) *My Mum Needs Me. Helping Children with Ill or Disabled Parents*. London: Penguin Books.

5 The Stresses of Working with Couples and Families

Eddy Street

Family and marital counselling cover a wide range of activities in a variety of contexts. Indeed such is the range one must ask whether all usages of the terms 'family counselling' and 'marital counselling' cover similar activities. Merely sitting down and talking to a group of family members does not constitute family counselling any more than asking a person 'How do you get on with your partner?' is the lead into marital counselling. It is difficult to provide absolute definitions of these forms of counselling but for the sake of clarity, two important distinctions can be made. First a distinction needs to be drawn in terms of the focus for offering help. This is a distinction between an individual orientation and a family orientation. In the former, there is clearly an emphasis on the individual's experience even though attention may be given to the family context in which that individual lives. In contrast, the family focus emphasizes the family's functioning, with the individual's experience being seen as a part of the way in which that family, as a unit, operates. The second distinction is ultimately more central, involving as it does underlying models of change; on the one hand there is a systems, life-cycle perspective from which relevant practice skills known as marital and family counselling flow, whilst on the other hand there are contrasting models of change which may permit practitioners occasionally to use family and marital counselling skills within their framework. Certainly these distinctions point to different contexts for counsellors and hence, given this diversity of contexts and the range of use of the skills, specifying the particular stresses that arise when working with these clients is somewhat problematic.

Clearly nothing can be labelled as stressful unless it is perceived as such. Stress is identified only when individuals believe that any given situation will place demands on them that will tax or exceed the resources available to them (Lazarus, 1990). Even though counsellors may experience difficult feelings, stress is not something that resides within an individual, nor is it equivalent to the triggering event or the circumstances around that event. Stress is the result of an interaction between an individual, be it counsellor or client, and the circumstances in which they find themselves. Stress on family/marital counsellors will be found within the context in which they operate. Within this chapter a contextual model will be applied to counsellor stresses. This will first consider the counsellor in her personal context, secondly the context of the counselling session itself, namely the counsellor and client; thirdly the 'team' context; and finally the stresses that emanate from the counsellor and agency will be considered. This model will be applied to the nature of the stresses, counsellors' responses to these stresses and finally to activities which could improve coping with these stresses.

The nature of the stresses

The personal context

As the counsellor with a family perspective is constantly dealing with material in relation to the life cycle, it should be expected that there will be some stresses related to the interaction between the client's stage of life cycle and the stage of the counsellor. When clients face life-cycle issues that fall within the same life-cycle phase as that of the counsellor or which are reminiscent of issues and problems that the counsellor has faced him/herself then one would expect some potential personal tensions in the counselling situation. This is the family and marital counselling's example of the 'it rings bells for me' phenomenon that faces counsellors from every orientation. Such tensions can occur not just with similarities but also with differences. Fulmer (1989) has pointed out that families from different backgrounds face different life-cycle issues, with the life cycle of clients being different to that which is experienced by the middle-class helping professional. Attempting to confront and resolve such differences in the counselling context can raise many personal themes for the counsellor, which can also touch on a variety of class, race and gender issues.

The only research evidence about the ways in which family therapists and counsellors personally consider the impact of the stresses they encounter is provided by Wetchler and Piercy (1986). They surveyed a number of American subjects about the impact of their job on their own marital/family issues. They recorded that 45 per cent felt their work left them little time and energy for their own family and 37 per cent found it difficult to switch roles from therapist to family member. The item with the highest stress level was recorded by 9 per cent of the sample who found being with client families more rewarding than being with their own family. These personal effects of stress are not unique to professionals who work with family matters, pointing as they do to establishing a balance between professional and private life.

The counsellor/client context

Any form of counselling brings with it 'difficult' client groups which, by the very nature of the presenting problem, are in some way stressful to the counsellor. The particular difficulties that face marital and family counsellors tend to be those that involve violence and abuse in the family, especially marital violence or abusive situations towards children. Maintaining a systemic perspective when a child has been seriously injured or consistently ill-treated can prove difficult, particularly when the popular culture wishes for blame to be readily apportioned. Dealing with such material can lead to counsellor denial. Bentovim and Davenport (1992) have argued that the way traumatic events, such as abuse, are handled can come to organize individual and interpersonal reality. Such a 'trauma organized' system can cause a professional to avoid the realities of the abuse. The stresses of holding on to an image of 'truth' in a family system which has a multitude of truths and where society itself wishes for a particular truth to be established are indeed immense. Where these families are in contact with other agencies, it is not unusual for the counsellor to be offered a role that mirrors one element of the family dynamic. In such circumstances the counsellor, in dealing with other professionals, comes to act out interactions that follow the family pattern. Reder and Kraemer (1980) have outlined how this process of replication occurs. Such events magnify the stresses of maintaining a therapeutic outlook as the extra-sessional communication with other professionals becomes so fraught. Similarly within the session itself, families and couples nearly always offer the counsellor a position within their system that would diminish therapeutic leverage (see Street, 1985) and should this position be accepted, stressful problems arise as the counsellor is drawn more and more into the family's pattern of interaction.

Within the client context, a systemic perspective would recognize that a referrer is just as much a part of the system as the family members themselves and a referrer can often be more of a customer for change than the family members themselves. When this happens the counsellor can spend many frustrating sessions attempting to change a system that for a variety of contextual reasons is unable to change. Carr (1990) has catalogued the common mistakes that arise from not being clear who the customer is, causing the engagement process of counselling to be disrupted and hence creating unnecessary pressure on the counselling itself.

The counsellor/team context

The past decades of growth in the marital and family therapies have built up a tradition that the activity is a team approach. Co-therapy, one-way screens involving watching teams, video recording for later review and techniques which emphasize the intervention of the team are all features of the desire by systemic therapists and counsellors to be seen as being 'public' in their activity. The argument is that as the approach focuses on the publicly observable interactions of a family then the use of the observations of more than one person will be helpful (Haley, 1976). Indeed it is further argued that as it is so easy for a counsellor to be inappropriately stuck within the interactions of a couple or family it is necessary for there to be an 'external' set of observers to ensure that a therapeutic momentum is maintained (see Andersen, 1987). Despite the predominance of this view there is no empirical evidence that co-therapy is superior to lone therapy and in fact no evidence, if indeed research, on the superiority of the high-tech team approach over the lone counsellor (see Gurman *et al.*, 1985). However, because of the complex nature of family and marital interaction, team and co-therapy approaches have been constructed to aid the counsellor in dealing more effectively with the interactions in the counselling room. Paradoxically, what has been created to aid the counsellor has added a different set of stresses and problems.

The process of acquiring a co-therapist, particularly to help in marital work, is a very fine art and indeed such are the difficulties of finding a match that works for two individuals that 'divorce' amongst co-therapists is surely many times greater than amongst the marriages they were created to help. Such problems are magnified when it comes to team formation, for any team will need to address its own internal interactions in a way that does not confuse issues that may arise from other professional contexts as well as the dynamics introduced by the family. Such is the fine balance of establishing a team of this nature that many professionals who feel that to do family work one should be a member of a team also feel a considerable amount of discomfort and stress from being involved in this way. As counselling and therapy are essentially creative endeavours in which the self of the helper is very much to the fore, a number of professionals in these settings report the feeling of constriction and the need for conformity when they work with a team. Hoffman (1992) has commented on the distance this creates between clients and therapists. Still others report on what is perceived as the stress of 'performing', interviewing a family in front of an audience with the use of a one-way screen or videotape; Hoffman also reports that, probably like many therapists and counsellors faced with these stresses, she behaved one way with clients when with a team and another way when alone with a family. She even labelled her activity in these circumstances as 'corny therapy', possibly because of the secretive embarrassment that ensued. Treacher and Carpenter (1993) have argued that these stresses and activities ultimately do not provide for 'user-friendly therapy'.

The private/public nature of the therapy/counselling business is indeed curious for research does show that those who work solely in private practice and therefore do not have to contend with team and organizational issues are less likely to experience 'burnout' symptoms than colleagues who work in public agencies, even when those colleagues have similar caseloads (Hellman and Morrison, 1987; Raquepaw and Miller, 1989). Individuals may be attracted to becoming counsellors because of the perceived benefits of the private intimacy offered by the counselling session, whilst some counsellors may move toward the interactive arena of couples and families because the more public nature of that context is more appealing. It may be that not every marital or family counsellor deals with these issues in the same way and the differences in attitudes and orientation to such matters undoubtedly need to be researched further.

The counsellor/agency context

When Jay Haley wrote the article, 'Why a mental health clinic should avoid family therapy' (Haley, 1975) the tongue-in-cheek approach clearly pointed to the problem of professionals with a systems perspective working in an agency which has a contrasting ideology. In a manner similar to families and other human systems, agencies develop ideologies to help explain the phenomena they meet so that they can then communicate with the outside world. As with families, the ideology is necessary so that ongoing and future events can be dealt with in predictable ways.

There are unfortunately too few agencies which have an ideology embracing the family system view (see Street and Reimers, 1993) but it is possible for individuals and groups of individuals to have their practice informed by a systemic view. Most professionals who employ family counselling and its techniques do so from a position of being in an agency which permits and condones such practice but which does not embrace the perspective's organizational and administrative goals and structures. It is in the interface between the tasks of the workers' role in the agency and the tasks of family counselling that stresses and tensions emerge. There is a *mandate* between the professional and the agency that she will apply professional skills to meet the stated objectives of the agency within terms of its ideology. Family counselling activity is therefore permitted only as long as it corresponds with objectives which in the main are not informed by systemic thinking and do not specify and hence appropriately integrate the family systems approach. As demonstrated elsewhere (Street, 1994) this tension can lead to a variety of counsellor–client problems which have to be dealt with within the negotiations between the two in terms of the professional's agency role and the expectations of the client. Frequently, however, counsellors can find themselves in a 'stuck' position with clients: for example the client may be expecting certain activities by counsellors, the counsellor wishes to provide these but the agency role does not include counselling for this type of client in these particular circumstances. Counsellors can find themselves in open dispute with their agency about roles and priorities and the structures necessary to sustain such roles. The counsellor may wish the agency to give primacy to those issues which allow for the dispensing of counselling service, whereas the agency will have other considerations which fit in with its broad organizational goals. Conflicts then develop, with the counsellor angrily expressing feelings of being undervalued, ill-considered and even undermined by the agency. In some countries, such as the UK where practice of family counselling primarily occurs in agencies with other goals, the collective frustration of family counsellors can be considerable.

Counsellor responses to the stresses

The personal context

There has been no research into the usual responses to the stresses of professional life amongst family and marital counsellors specifically, though one would speculate that the use of alcohol, depressive moods, psychosomatic complaints and other similar stress reactions are common amongst practitioners, as they are with other groups. Interestingly, Wetchler and Piercy (1986) report that working with families is not necessarily hazardous to health in that the counsellors they sampled were able to identify factors which enhanced family living for themselves and hence mitigated other stressors. These researchers found that 87 per cent reported that being a counsellor helped with the acceptance of their own part in marital/family problems; 85 per cent reported it aided in the development of communication skills and 60 per cent in the development of parenting skills; 58 per cent reported a greater understanding of sex role issues in their family; and 52 per cent reported that it led to an increased interaction with their own family of origin. Clearly these enhancers do seem relevant to the subject matter of family counselling, but it may well be that they are also the areas of gain for counsellors of other traditions, since these issues do seem related to matters that one might term 'personal growth'. At another level it could also be that these areas of enhancement represent 'need' areas which were unconscious factors in leading a counsellor into working with families.

A finding of particular note is from research undertaken by Bergin and Jensen (1990), who were investigating the role that religion played for different groups of US helping professionals. When compared to the other groups, the marriage and family therapists had the highest proportion who regularly attended church, and who believed they based their whole approach to life on their religion. Interestingly the 'religiosity profile' of this professional group was the one that most reflected the profile of the community at large. It is difficult to identify the reasons for this finding, but given that religious feeling and practices are a potent source of dealing with life's stresses it would appear that those who work with families are better able to use this coping strategy. Much more research in this area is required so that individual responses to stress can be identified and the most effective strategies of dealing with these personal stresses outlined.

The counsellor/client context

When counsellors are struggling with particular clients there are a number of signs that indicate that the change process is not going well. Burnham (1986) lists these signs:

working harder and harder without achieving any change at all;

dreading particular family sessions (the phenomenon that Treacher and Carpenter, 1993, refer to as 'Oh no, not the Smiths again');

conducting sessions consisting of pleasant but aimless chat;

arguing with a particular family member;

devising increasingly elaborate plans for interventions with decreasing amounts of change.

Systemically, it is not appropriate to 'blame' the counsellor, as the stresses of this situation arise directly out of the context, that is, out of the counsellor/family interaction and their respective interactions with the other contexts in which they exist. Hence one should consider the family in its relationship to the world around it – its ecosystem – and, in similar vein, the ecosystem of the counsellor. Counsellors tend to deal with these stresses, however, by blaming themselves and by believing that they should be capable enough to be able to deal with these difficult cases themselves. It is at this point that family counsellors individually forsake their own perspective and rather than conceive of their own behaviour as being contextually bound they shrink back into a simple linear cause and effect way of thinking that places responsibility for the poor outcome on their own shoulders. Treacher (1989) and Lask (1989) amongst others have debated the issues related to where 'responsibility' lies with regard to change. Essentially this debate has focused on whether the practice of family therapy and counselling needs to be seen purely as the approach itself or whether the mandates given to workers by their agencies, and the ideologies of those agencies, should be considered as a point around which to organize practice. This debate, systemic though it is, tends to neglect the issue of stress felt by the counsellor as an individual. The response of family counsellors collectively via this literature is to analysis and 'systems think' about the tensions that arise within systems that deal with clients. For example Dale *et al.* (1986) consider all the stresses that arise within the context of a case of child abuse. The fact of the matter is however that, regardless of how tight one's systemic formulations are, such cases in themselves are difficult, and while it is important to appreciate the tensions, to focus exclusively on this cognitive level of analysis is not necessarily helpful to the individual practitioner, who still has to deal with all the difficult emotions engendered. Any systemic analysis must include 'the self in the system', including the self of the counsellor. One can then consider the influence of the sheer human fact that it is not easy to deal consistently with issues which dehumanize or overly focus on violence and death without feeling personally depleted.

The counsellor/team context

A typical response to stress is to seek succour and support in professional relationships and consequently many counsellors find themselves seeking to join with a co-therapist. Unfortunately if this relationship is not initially constructed in an adequate manner, as Carpenter (1993) notes, problems of a professional and personal nature, including rivalry, can continue to exist unresolved. Co-therapy relationships are quite difficult to construct. Rice and Rice (1974) report on difficulties, particularly those caused by individuals with differing levels of experience attempting to work together. Problems of sharing power and control and of status and sex role inequality can also be present. Obviously different issues dominate at different times, resulting in different tensions.

These issues become magnified when one considers team functioning. In the face of problematic clients and unhelpful bureaucrats it can only be expected that groups of like-minded workers will seek comfort in an exclusive club. In some respects the tradition of forming teams amongst systemic practitioners may be the response of a group of professionals who essentially feel different and isolated from the principal theoretical and ideological formulations of the time and agency.

On the unhelpful side, personal relationships within the team can deteriorate, with interactions becoming dysfunctional, leading to disintegration and a susceptibility to the replication of unhelpful family patterns. A frequent occurrence in such a system is that one individual in his professional role acquires the scapegoat role that replicates a role present in the family. This person is placed under a great deal of pressure to 'conform' to particular thoughts and actions while some professional goal propels that individual to act in other ways. Even though such positions can be accurately identified the stress of being confined to this role can be quite considerable. If there are some unresolved tensions in the team, the process will be exaggerated and the stress heightened.

Considering the 'team' of the family therapy and counselling field itself, as with other therapeutic 'movements', the history of this field has followed a pattern in which dogmatic trends have a period of domination. It is only after such periods that a looseness allowing for creativity emerges. On a small scale similar processes in teams follow this pattern: a team coalesces, forms an ideology which develops into a dogma, and a rigidity then emerges which diminishes only when new ideas and personal preferences emerge. In some cases the rigidity results in the team disintegrating; in other situations it can lead to productive re-evaluation. As Jenkins (1985) notes, orthodoxy in working with families can all too readily become tyranny. Lask (1987) has come to this issue from another direction by pointing out the confusing nature of much of systems theorizing, which he labels 'cybernetico-epistobabble', and ably points to the pressures to conform to an orthodoxy not only of thinking but also of doing; he identifies the pressure caused by attempting to be up with all the new fashions:

What is happening? I am expected to be a linguist, a philosopher, a quantum physicist and a philosopher of quantum physics. I am expected to be a technical wizard to operate the video and to master the incredible array of strategies and techniques. I have to be able to hold network meetings enthusiastically and actively support nuclear disarmament and feminism, as well as being a hand servant to families, for ever at their beck and call.

As if this is not enough, I must always be on my toes, because the latest fashions are all sprinting by; blink and I will miss them. I would have to be Superman to keep up, or is it Superperson? (Lask, 1987: 211)

This difficulty confronts the inexperienced family counsellor not only in the terms cast here by Lask, namely identification with the field at large, but also in terms of the 'requirements' of teams to maintain a cohesion. We can see that, just like families, teams aid in the support and development of the members but they can also give rise to many problems.

The counsellor/agency context

When an agency becomes dysfunctional, as with any system, blame and guilt arise. At some stage the counsellor will blame the clients: they are seen as unmotivated, have problems that should be dealt with elsewhere, they are resistant and dependent. The counsellor can arrive very easily at a position where it is felt that 'this would be a great job if it wasn't for the clients'. This loss of respect for families encountering difficulties erodes any rewards the counsellor had from the personal contact of the job, which then creates the downward spiral of 'bosses expect the wrong things from me – clients are difficult' and ultimately ends up with the counsellor wishing to cease work.

Some counsellors deal with this loss of respect by self-blame and doubt their own worth in doing the job. For some this is internalized into a lack of confidence, which subtly expresses itself in clinical work. Other counsellors externalize this by believing that their perceived lack of skill is a practical issue and can be remedied by attending a course – any course – and as often as possible. This is a response that the agency can all too readily reinforce, whether or not they have the sponsoring funds. Training events are essential in order to sustain the counsellor but it is not good to permanently search for the Holy Grail of 'understanding and ability'; sometimes it should be sought within the interaction of counsellor and agency.

The other possible focus for blame is the agency itself. This can lead to the acting out of the conflictual issue of orientation and agency goals in the guise of arguments about coffee money, leave allocation, fund raising and so on. The family counsellor is then perceived by the agency as perhaps somewhat idiosyncratic and a delinquent, and groups who adopt a family approach are often seen as exclusive, aloof and distant. The latter is a particular phenomenon when counsellors engage in 'clandestine' family work; the scenario for this situation is an agency which does not formally support family approaches employing a number of professionals who wish to practise, so they do so in a 'secretive' manner. Sometimes this is condoned and approved by management who give the message, 'Do it but don't let me see and don't expect us to talk about it in professional supervision.' However, even though these problems do occur it is important to remember that the growth of family approaches amongst professionals has arisen from those professionals dealing with the 'alien' environment of their agency in a gentle confrontational manner. The construction of programmes based on family systems principles which have been responsibly put to management are the means by which the approach has become accepted. In this instance the tension between the worker and the agency has been used creatively and there are numerous examples of how programmes of family approaches can be applied in different contexts (see Carpenter and Treacher, 1993).

Suggestions for improved coping

The personal context
In most forms of counselling and therapy training it is assumed that trainees will at some point in their training career seek a counsellor or therapist for themselves. On some training courses it is indeed mandatory. The general arguments for counselling the counsellors is that everyone should appreciate the client role and that many personal issues that prevent effective counselling need to be addressed directly. In the case of family counselling the question is: should the trainee receive family counselling and/or personal counselling? Further to this one should ask about the nature of counselling required for the experienced counsellor. The need and desire for personal psychotherapy has been demonstrated by Everett (1980) in a survey of family therapy supervisors in the USA – 76 per cent had participated in personal psychotherapy over a mean duration of 32 months and 94 per cent believed personal psychotherapy was useful in training. However, Guldner (1978) reported on a training course where it was found that trainees involved in personal in-depth therapy were increasingly seeing fewer clients conjointly because they felt there were too

many personal issues that needed to be worked through by the clients before they could participate in marital or total family sessions. The course therefore arranged that trainees should have a therapeutic experience consistent with their training by involving them with their own family. This involvement was on a contracting basis such that the trainees were seen with their family of origin and together with their partner at times which were suggested by the trainee's supervisor. The usual practice of training courses however is to focus the 'personal' work on family of origin issues (see Lieberman, 1987; Street, 1989) rather than conjoint sessions. Such exercises can then unfortunately emphasize the cognitive appreciation of intergenerational processes to the detriment of the trainee's personal response to her family. As we have seen, therapists and counsellors report on stressors in terms of organizing time and energy for family matters but there is no evidence that those involved in family work make use of the approach to deal with this issue. Clearly, one's own family is a resource that can be used to reduce stress and in order to use this resource effectively family counselling could be utilized. Training courses should consider methods by which the trainees can benefit from the experience of being seen in their family if only to prepare the would-be counsellor and family for occasions when some family sessions may be appropriate.

Training courses should also consider means by which trainees can deal with the fact that the life cycle of the majority of clients they will meet will be in marked contrast to the life cycle issues that they, as professional people, will face. Pilalis (1984) has commented on this theme and outlined a number of models of training that could be adopted in order to deal effectively with these differences.

The counsellor/client context
Thought should be given to the requirements of the professional context in which the counsellor works and the actual requirements of the counselling role. In his consideration of 'burnout', Friedman (1985) points out the importance of dealing with issues of expectation and role definition and what he terms 'therapeutic ambition'. In order to prevent a stressful conflict of expectations between counsellor and client, the counsellor needs to have thoroughly negotiated an appropriate mandate with the family in terms of the counsellor's personal competencies and the mandate given to him by the agency (see Street, 1994). In doing this a counsellor would also be following Friedman's other suggestion that the counsellor be clear about the responsibility for change that

he is taking and the responsibility being placed on the family. It is in this area that the counsellor needs to be clear about the different forms of supervision he will require and certainly supervision should be a feature of any good family counselling and therapy practice. There is, however, a strong tendency for supervision to focus on the systemic features of the counselling context to the neglect of the more personal issues of the therapist. The current theoretical formulations and orthodoxy in fashion within the field tend to reinforce this process of neglect. As Hawkins and Shohet (1989) note, good supervision should have a variety of foci and these should include consideration of the counselling system and the process by which the supervision system reflects elements of the counselling system. An experienced supervisor should be able to point out and address those 'personal' issues which are relevant. Supervision of this quality may provide indications of themes that can be followed up in personal therapy as well as offering an intimate opportunity to share the depletion that comes from dealing with the inhumanity, misery and distress that arise naturally in families. Counselling supervision should initially focus on the issues as they emanate from the clients' mandate and the counsellor's personal response to this: this is supervision on the process of counselling. Professional supervision will focus on the management of the tasks of the job, involving the balance between the client mandate and the agency's mandate and ideology: this is supervision on the general context in which counselling occurs. Ideally both types of supervision can be provided by one person, hopefully with a systemic background. Where this is not possible, the counsellor should be clear about the supervisory boundaries in order to use each supervision effectively.

It is often helpful for counsellors to meet in groups in order to share the difficulties they confront. As with supervision, these self-help groups are most effective when the agenda is clearly demarcated between the process and context of counselling. Self-help groups, if they do not flounder, provide a valuable means of mitigating stress.

The counsellor/team context

Family counsellors often find themselves attempting to work in teams, supposedly for theoretical/practical reasons but often in order to feel the security of companionship. Unfortunately teams and co-therapy relationships are often established without the preliminary work which ensures that such a collaboration will be profitable. Kingston and Smith (1983), in their discussion of working together, emphasize the need to discuss similarities and differences in orientation and values. They suggest that there should be a reasonable congruence in theoretical and practical bases and that to ensure this some preliminary practice via role-play may be helpful. Other issues that need to be discussed are sex and role differences, and especially hierarchical issues when individuals of different professions work together. In constructing good teamwork, Kingston and Smith point out that ground rules should be applied and that agreement on these is necessary so that an egalitarian system evolves. These rules should include:

the means of dealing with the administrative tasks of the team;

the arrangements for each team member taking responsibility at some point for each of the team roles that evolve, for example, secretary, interviewer, discussion leader;

how team members will give positive and negative feedback to each other;

what types of discussion will occur before and after sessions;

what will happen when 'no one knows' and the team is uncertain about what to do. This is important as it enshrines the right 'not to know', which is often a valuable position therapeutically and can be of great help to families. Teams therefore need to know when they collectively 'don't know';

the duration of the team contract;

the means and frequency with which the team will make use of an external consultation.

This last point is particularly important as the systemic properties of teams and co-therapy relationships, whether simple or complex, are often not fully appreciated by the team members themselves. It is always useful for any group of individuals operating in concert to have some input from an external person to help them appreciate the nature of the process they are part of. It should be noted that teams often go through cycles which for clients' sakes should be considered finite, in other words when a team or co-therapy relationship does not seem to be as effective as it initially was then it may be beneficial to stop and allow the individuals to move on.

The counsellor/agency context
It is important in maintaining an enhanced feeling of well-being that one's role definition in one's job is clear. It is essential to monitor constantly the balance between our own personal expectations and our view of the expectations that others have of us.

This balance ultimately leads to the professional action we take at any time, so being confident in that balance will ultimately prove beneficial to ourselves. However, the agency which hires us can become dysfunctional and it will then be important to seek organizational consultancy. When seeking this form of input all levels of the hierarchy within the agency must discuss and agree on the need for consultation. Consultation can prove unsuccessful if individuals feel coerced into entering into it.

Agencies should also consider their responsibilities when it comes to training individuals in systems work, for although agencies can readily agree to allow individuals to attend courses, often they are not able to deal with the 'change' that has occurred in the person who received the training. Managers and counsellors need to be clear with each other about the various benefits of training and how changes in perception and practice may result. Some courses, such as those run by the Family Institute in Cardiff, attempt to facilitate the understanding of such change by involving both trainees and their managers in discussions at various points in the training process. Trainees find this helpful in later role definition issues and managers report that it is beneficial to their understanding of issues that arise later.

Conclusion

Developments in both theory and practice continue in the field of family and marital work and these developments undoubtedly reflect the continual need for therapeutic inputs into distressing situations which arise from the relationships of day to day living. The changing nature of marriage and family life and the organizational pressures on agencies which offer assistance will always result in the need for considerable reflection on the preferred means of offering services to clients. The nature and impact of stresses on those who embark on family and marital work will in many ways change. However, some aspects of these stresses will remain the same and the need is for all counsellors and therapists to ensure that such stresses are minimized in private and professional contexts. Progress will only be achieved by counsellors considering their own needs in a balanced way; once this has been achieved, dealing with the demands and needs of clients will seem less onerous.

References

Andersen, T. (1987) 'The reflecting team: dialogue and meta-dialogue in clinical work', *Family Process*, 26: 415–28.

Bentovim, A. and Davenport, M. (1992) 'Resolving the trauma organized system of sexual abuse by confronting the abuser', *Journal of Family Therapy*, 14: 29–50.

Bergin, A.E. and Jensen, J.P. (1990) 'Religiosity of psychologists: a national survey', *Psychotherapy*, 27: 3–7.

Burnham, J. (1986) *Family Therapy*. London: Routledge.

Carpenter, J. (1993) 'Working together', in J. Carpenter and A. Treacher (eds), *Using Family Therapy in the 90s*. Oxford: Blackwell.

Carpenter, J. and Treacher, A. (eds) (1993) *Using Family Therapy in the 90s*. Oxford: Blackwell.

Carr, A. (1990) 'Failure in family therapy: a catalogue of engagement mistakes', *Journal of Family Therapy*, 12: 371–86.

Dale, P., Waters, J., Davies, M., Roberts, W. and Morrison, T. (1986) 'The towers of silence: creative and destructive issues for therapeutic teams dealing with sexual abuse', *Journal of Family Therapy*, 8: 1–26.

Everett, C.A. (1980) 'An analysis of AAMFT supervisors: the identities, roles and resources', *Journal of Marital and Family Therapy*, 6: 286–93.

Friedman, R. (1985) 'Making family therapy easier for the therapist: burnout prevention', *Family Process*, 24: 549–53.

Fulmer, R. (1989) 'Lower income and professional families: a comparison of structure and life cycle process', in B. Carter and M. McGoldrick (eds), *The Changing Family Life Cycle*. Boston: Allyn & Bacon.

Guldner, C.A. (1978) 'Family therapy for the trainee in family therapy', *Journal of Marriage and Family Counselling*, 4: 127–32.

Gurman, A.S., Kniskern, D.P. and Pinsof, W. (1985) 'Research on the process and outcome of marital and family therapy', in S.L. Garfield and A.E. Bergin (eds), *Handbook of Psychotherapy and Behavior Exchange*, 3rd edition. New York: Wiley.

Haley, J. (1975) 'Why a mental health clinic should avoid family therapy', *Journal of Marital and Family Counselling*, 2: 3–13.

Haley, J. (1976) *Problem Solving Therapy*. New York: Harper & Row.

Hawkins, P. and Shohet, R. (1989) *Supervision in the Helping Professions*. Milton Keynes: Open University Press.

Hellman, I.D. and Morrison, T.L. (1987) 'Practice setting and type of case load as factors in psychotherapist burnout', *Psychotherapy*, 24: 427–33.

Hoffman, L. (1992) 'A reflexive stance for family therapy', in S. McNamee and K.J. Gergen (eds), *Therapy as Social Construction*. London: Sage.

Jenkins, H. (1985) 'Orthodoxy in family therapy practice as servant or tyrant', *Journal of Family Therapy*, 7: 19–30.

Kingston, P. and Smith, D. (1983) 'Preparation for live consultation and live supervision when working without a one-way screen', *Journal of Family Therapy*, 5: 219–34.

Lask, B. (1987) 'Cybernetico-epistobabble, the Emperor's new clothes and other sacred cows', *Journal of Family Therapy*, 9: 207–16.

Lask, B. (1989) 'A matter of balance', *Journal of Family Therapy*, 11: 389–92.

Lazarus, R.S. (1990) 'Theory-based stress management', *Psychological Inquiry*, 1: 3–13.

Lieberman, S. (1987) 'Going back of your own family', in A. Bentovim, G. Gorell Barnes and A. Cooklin (eds), *Family Therapy: Complementary Framework of Theory and Practice*. London: Academic Press.

Pilalis, J. (1984) 'The formalization of family therapy training – issues and implications', *Journal of Family Therapy*, 6: 35–46.

Raquepaw, J.M. and Miller, R.S. (1989) 'Psychotherapist burnout: a component analysis', *Professional Psychology: Research and Practice*, 20: 32–6.

Reder, P. and Kraemer, S. (1980) 'Dynamic aspects of professional collaboration in child guidance referral', *Journal of Adolescence*, 3: 165–73.

Rice, D. and Rice, J. (1974) 'Status and sex-roles issues in co-therapy', in A.S. Gurman and D. Rice (eds), *Couples in Conflict: New Directions in Marital Therapy*. New York: Jason Aronson.

Street, E. (1985) 'From child-focused problems to marital issues', in W. Dryden and D. Hooper (eds), *Marital Therapy in Britain*, Vol. 2: *Social Areas*. London: Harper & Row.

Street, E. (1989) 'Challenging the white knight', in W. Dryden and L. Spurling (eds), *On Becoming a Psychotherapist*. London: Tavistock/Routledge.

Street, E. (1994) *Counselling for Family Problems*. London: Sage.

Street, E. and Reimers, S. (1993) 'Family therapy services for children', in J. Carpenter and A. Treacher (eds), *Using Family Therapy in the 90s*. Oxford: Blackwell.

Treacher, A. (1989) 'Whose responsibility – a reply to Bryan Lask', *Journal of Family Therapy*, 11: 377–82.

Treacher, A. and Carpenter, J. (1993) 'User-friendly family therapy', in J. Carpenter and A. Treacher (eds), *Using Family Therapy in the 90s*. Oxford: Blackwell.

Wetchler, J.L. and Piercy, F.P. (1986) 'The marital family life of the family therapist: stressors and enhancers', *American Journal of Family Therapy*, 14: 99–108.

PART 2

THE STRESSES OF COUNSELLING IN DIFFERENT CONTEXTS

6 The Stresses of Working in a General Practice Setting

Richard House

> The more one learns of the problems of general practice, the more impressed one becomes with the immediate need for psychotherapy. (Balint, 1986: 282)

Theoretical prologue

My main concern in this chapter is to consider those setting-specific characteristics of the general practice setting which make it a source of stress *over and above* the 'normal' stresses experienced by counsellors in their work. In focusing on the environmental aspects of stress in this way, I am not assuming *either* that environmental factors are more (or less) important than personal, dispositional factors in the origins of stress, *or*, indeed, that it is somehow possible to isolate in any simple causal sense the relative contribution of environmental and dispositional factors to observed variations in counsellor stress. Rather, my focus will be *interactional*, whereby stress is viewed as a function of the interaction between the setting, on the one hand, and the way in which the counsellor subjectively experiences her or his environment, both cognitively and psychodynamically, on the other. On this view, *setting-specific* stress will be experienced to the extent that the characteristics of the setting resonate unhelpfully or pathologically with the counsellor's personality dynamics.

My approach to stress is therefore strongly psychodynamic in focus, and in what follows I will be paying much attention to the psychodynamics of stress in the general practice setting.

The general practice setting

Several distinctive features of the general practice setting are notable. First, and perhaps most obvious, the setting is explicitly *medical* in nature, with an emphasis on the so-called 'biomedical model' of diagnosis, treatment and cure – and with implications in turn for the make-up of the counsellor's caseload. GP-referred clients are probably more likely to be taking psychotropic medication of some sort, with consequent effects upon the trajectory and the success of the counselling relationship (Hammersley and Beeley, 1992). The caseload is also typically very wide-ranging (Irving, 1992: 27–8), with a huge span of presenting problems. This is important because the greater the range of presenting problems in the counsellor's caseload, the more likely it is that the counsellor will come up against difficult, personally challenging dynamics in the counselling relationship, with associated higher levels of counsellor stress. Expressed in psychodynamic terms, the probability of there being difficult countertransference experiences for the counsellor increases as the range of presenting problems widens.

It is also clear that a medical setting entails an atmosphere dominated by ill-health and disease, with all the attendant levels of fear and anxiety, whether overt or collusively denied. As Higgs and Dammers (1992: 27) write, 'Illness and anxiety are as inseparable as winter and wet weather.'

Secondly, there are diverse problems with the security of what Langs (1988) calls the 'therapeutic frame or framework', which refers to the various ways in which the counselling relationship is organized or designed, particularly with respect to the degree of safety experienced by the client (Smith, 1991: Chapter 7). It is not uncommon for the basic physical aspects of the setting to be less than secure – for example, room space, confidentiality and record-keeping – as well as there being some lack of clarity about who precisely has ultimate responsibility for the client in the general practice setting (Higgs and Dammers, 1992: 33).

Thirdly, there is typically an enormous demand for counselling in general practice which far outstrips the supply, with obvious implications for length of counselling contracts and waiting-list pressures.

Finally, the general practice setting is an *organizational* one, which is important in terms of unconscious group and organizational dynamics, and the possible effects on the well-being of practice staff – particularly in a setting in which there are strong collusive forces mobilized to deny the primitive anxieties that are inevitably present in any medical setting (Stein, 1985; Menzies Lyth, 1988).

In the next section I will describe the nature of the stresses experienced in the general practice setting, drawing upon both the literature in the field and on the results of a questionnaire survey of Norfolk surgery counsellors' experiences of stress in their work, especially carried out by the author for this chapter.[1] Sixteen completed questionnaires were received of the 22 that were distributed, and in what follows I quote anonymously from the responses to support the text discussion.

The nature of the stresses

> To write prescriptions is easy, but to come to an understanding with people is hard. (Franz Kafka, *A Country Doctor*)

I will divide the stresses experienced by general practice counsellors into six broad categories, based upon an analysis of the questionnaire responses, my reading of the literature in the field, and my own personal experiences as a general practice counsellor.

Frame insecurities of the general practice setting

The 'therapeutic frame' is important for the safety and 'holding function' of the counselling relationship. Discussions of the 'insecure' or 'deviant' frame (e.g. Smith, 1991: Chapter 7) invariably place emphasis upon its deleterious effects upon the *client*; what seems to be neglected are the effects of a deviant frame on the *counsellor* – both the direct effects upon the counsellor's working milieu, *and* indirect effects to the extent that the counsellor is affected by the client's discomfort within a deviant frame.

Smith (1991: 173) argues that the 'patient' (his term) has 'deep unconscious expectations' about a secure, safe therapeutic frame. It can be argued that there exist universal human needs for boundaries and safety within interpersonal relationships; and to the extent that the security of the frame is not 'good enough', the counsellor's own anxieties about insecure boundaries may also be triggered.

There are several ways in which the general practice frame is less than secure. Of the eleven components of the secure frame listed by Smith (1991: 174–91), at least five are compromised – total privacy, total confidentiality, consistency of the setting, the question of a fee, and the client's responsibility for termination. Hoag (1989, 1992) has given extended consideration to such general practice frame difficulties. An uncertain, unsafe therapeutic framework can also compromise the effectiveness of a counsellor's work, with the associated impact on self-esteem via doubts about professional competence and so on.

Case load particularities
Apart from the ubiquity of lengthy waiting lists, several other features of the general practice caseload contribute to general practice counsellor stress.

Type of client seen
Degree of 'damage'   Six respondents referred to the stress of having many clients with difficult presenting problems, with clients perhaps experiencing a complex combination of psychological and somatic symptoms. Some GPs also refer their so-called 'heart-sink' or 'fat envelope' patients to their surgery counsellor. One respondent listed her most stressful experience as being 'the degree of damage and deprivation and abuse suffered by the people referred for counselling'. A difficult, challenging case load will tend to increase the likelihood of stressful countertransference responses in the counsellor. In terms of object relations theory, it can be argued that clients attempt to deposit unbearable parts of themselves into the counsellor; and the more often this happens, the greater the emotional demands placed upon the counsellor. Some counsellors may also feel a professional responsibility to work with *any* clients who are patients in the practice in which they work.

Reluctant clients   Manthei and Matthews (1989: 41) have argued that 'Many counsellors, pressed by time and institutional demands, quickly become frustrated with reluctant clients.' Thus, clients taking up a 'victim' position (Hall, 1993) can easily draw counsellors into unconsciously acting out from their own internal 'rescuer' or 'persecutor', with resultant stressful effects on the counselling relationship. Reluctant clients are often very resistant to entering into a therapeutic relationship, which may lead in turn to frustration and a deskilling experience for the counsellor.

Nine respondents mentioned this as a stressful feature; four referred to clients not showing up for sessions, and six counsellors referred to clients who are less than willing to enter into a meaningful therapeutic relationship: 'A number of GP clients are there "because they were sent",' wrote one.

The phenomenon of the 'reluctant client' also interacts with the constraints of time-limited work. As Manthei and Matthews (1989: 41) write, 'Counsellors must accept the fact that these clients need more time.' Just how the counsellor can be expected to follow this advice within the context of time-limited counselling is far from clear.

'Psychosomatic' clients There is a considerable literature on psychosomatic illness (e.g. Pennebaker and Susman, 1988; McDougall, 1989), and in the general practice setting there will probably be a greater preponderance of 'somatizing' clients than in other settings.

For Alexander and Szasz (1952: 286), 'whenever [the psychological approach] attempts to penetrate behind the ego's defenses and uncover etiological factors, it is likely to activate emotional tension *and cause an exacerbation of somatic symptoms*' (my emphasis) – with the associated likelihood of client resistance to the counselling process. It is also widely recognized in the literature (see Strain, 1978: Chapter 2) that physical illness precipitates anxiety and *regression* in patients, with a greater likelihood that the patient/client will develop a very challenging transference relationship with the doctor and counsellor (Nemiah, 1961: 299; Balint, 1969: 111).

Finally, Blair (1993: 43) argues that there tends to be a bias towards the somatization of symptoms in people from lower socioeconomic classes – which leads us on to a consideration of social class.

'Social class' Seven respondents mentioned the 'working-class' nature of their caseloads. It can be argued – controversially – that more deprived clients tend *on average* (a crucial qualification) to be less willing or able to enter into a therapeutic relationship. In a much neglected paper, Bernstein (1964: 55) has argued that because of their restrictive linguistic codes and meaning elaboration, working-class people 'are likely to benefit less from therapy, to break off treatment early, whilst the therapist will tend to find the relationship unrewarding'. Blair (1993: 43) expresses similar views, claiming that working-class people tend to have a more fatalistic view regarding the aetiology of illness; this suggests a position that veers towards victimhood (Hall, 1993). Surgery counsellors may therefore find some of their work frustrating and unfulfilling, as their professional competence and sense of self-worth is challenged by occasionally encountering clients who are difficult to connect with.

Medication and counselling

Hatwell (1992: 7) writes that 'Drug prescribing can lead to some spectacular clashes', by which I take her to mean radical differences of opinion between doctors and counsellors over the efficacy and appropriateness of the use of medication for psychological and emotional difficulties.

A relatively greater proportion of GP clients will be on some form of psychotropic medication compared with patients in most other settings, and it is the very symptoms that psychotropic medication suppresses that provide the opportunity for working with the underlying problem. Medication may also prevent the client from fully experiencing the counselling relationship (Hammersley and Beeley, 1992: 162). Medication can disrupt, muddy and undermine the therapeutic process, quite possibly leading to counsellor frustration.

The referral process

Five respondents mentioned the process of referral in the context of stress, and one respondent described the GP referral process as 'a vital part of the dynamic'. I have already discussed the question of reluctant clients, at least some of whom could be categorized as clients whose appropriateness for time-limited counselling is at the very least uncertain.

First, there are clearly therapeutic-frame implications stemming from third-party (GP) referral to counselling, in terms of possible splitting of the therapeutic relationship (Pickvance, 1993). This refers to the diffusion and possible subversion of the therapeutic alliance stemming from the client's involvement in more than one therapeutic relationship in the general practice setting, with the attendant possibility of counsellor frustration. Smith (1991: 182) writes: 'To the deep unconscious system [of the client] it is vital that the analysis be restricted to two people ... with no third party involved.'

Two respondents write of GPs referring clients who either require crisis intervention, or who are in shock after a traumatic life event. One counsellor wrote: 'I am not in a position to do crisis work, but sometimes doctors panic and expect me to see people immediately.'

GPs sometimes seem to displace their own anxiety about difficult or emotionally demanding patients on to the surgery counsellor, and some GPs may occasionally refer clients more as a matter of convenience and expediency than of clinical judgement. Hatwell (1992: 7) writes bluntly: 'So why don't doctors always refer suitable cases? ... because if you are part of the Primary Care team, sometimes it is "Buggin's Turn" to work with the sad and hopeless cases who increasingly are "returned to the community".'

The dynamics of the general practice setting

Balint refers to 'the special psychological atmosphere of general practice' (Balint, 1986: Chapter 13). Sher (1992: 61) puts it much more bluntly: 'In general practice . . . there are *noxious substances about*. These noxious substances are the pain, both physical and mental, the anxiety and the stress that both the patients and the difficulty of the work bring to the situation' (his emphasis).

With regard to personal and interpersonal dynamics, there is a substantial literature on the kinds of process that are triggered in a medical setting, where ill-health and the threat of death are ongoing realities (for example Stein, 1985; Ryle, 1987). I have already referred to the question of regression in ill-health; Strain (1978: Chapter 2) and Segal (1991) describe the psychological determinants of adaptation to chronic illness. Many authors have considered the effects upon doctors stemming from the presence of illness (or fear thereof) within the clinical relationship (e.g. Balint, 1986; Dubovsky, 1981: Chapter 4; Stein, 1983, 1985; Massie *et al.*, 1989: 465–6). General practice counsellors' work is likely to be more stressful because of the powerful psychic processes activated by ill-health – for example in the areas of regressed or infantilizing helplessness and primitive death anxiety – and especially if the counsellor has particular difficulties and fears in these areas. Furthermore, such processes may well be paralleled in, and carry over into, the relationships between health-care professionals themselves (Stein, 1985).

With regard to organizational-level and interprofessional psychodynamics, I referred earlier to Menzies Lyth's work (1988; see also Jaques, 1955). Stein (1990: Chapter 4) has paid detailed attention to the question of dysfunctional group dynamics within health-care teams, and Sher (1992) reviews the psychodynamic processes operating within general practice settings: 'Counsellors and psychotherapists [within general practice] have become bearers of the unconscious system that is intended to *shield us from unhappiness*, rejection and abandonment' (Sher, 1992: 56, his emphasis). Integral to such a system is the requirement that counsellors be omniscient, and 'Counsellors and therapists themselves foster this belief and fall victim to it, often at great personal cost' (1992: 56).

Heckman (1980) found that psychotherapists employed in institutional settings reported burnout (an extreme form of stress) to a significantly greater extent than either private or group practitioners, and Farber (1990) reports similar findings.

Three distinct stressful themes were identifiable from the survey responses: interprofessional unease and conflict; remoteness of and poor communication with doctors; and staff ignorance with regard to the nature of counselling. Seven of the respondents referred to interprofessional difficulties of some sort.

The isolation of the general practice setting

Counsellors working in general medical practice often feel very isolated, given the strict confidentiality boundaries around their work, and their still ambiguous professional status. Five survey respondents explicitly mention the problem of isolation as a source of stress. One respondent who had previously worked in a team of counsellors wrote: 'I have found the relative isolation of GP counselling work quite stressful in that you have to contain a lot of feelings and thoughts about clients without the opportunity for discussion, sharing, etc.'

Issues of professionalization

Sher (1992: 60) refers to general practice counsellors as 'the most junior and unprofessionalized of the professional groups'; and Green (1993: 187) comments on 'the chaotic way that the field of counselling in general practice has developed'. Although the British Association for Counselling has recently published a set of *Guidelines for the Employment of Counsellors in General Practice* (1993), the reality on the ground is unfortunately very far from the ideal.

Empirical research has explored professional role ambiguity and inconsistency in the working environment. Status ambiguity and uncertainty can be a source of organizational stress (see Farber, 1983; Guy, 1987: 258–61), in the sense that uncertainty tends to trigger quite primitive, anxiety-provoking psychodynamics. Where professional identity is in doubt, personal identity can also easily be undermined and threatened, with all the associated anxieties that spring therefrom.

In the survey, ten respondents reported stressful experiences concerning professional issues, most commonly regarding funding uncertainty and the associated job insecurity. One respondent refers bluntly to 'the appallingly chaotic way in which counselling has been funded recently'. Two counsellors referred to the stressful nature of GP attitudes to their status: one counsellor described 'the difficulties some GPs have in accepting counsellors as colleagues and fellow professionals'.

The diverse responses that surgery counsellors have had to the setting-specific stresses described in this section will now be examined.

Counsellors' responses to the stresses

> I desperately try to find ways to ease anxiety in different ways. (A Norfolk surgery counsellor)

The psychodynamics of experienced stress
The conceptualization of stress is far from being a straightforward process (Pollack, 1988). It seems extraordinary that within the enormous literature on stress, the psychodynamics of stress is a subject which has been almost completely ignored. Some notable exceptions are the work of Fischer (1983), Margison (1987), Johnson (1991) and Firth-Cozens (e.g. 1992a). From an object relations standpoint, Segal (1985: 160) has written that 'In a work situation, whatever it is, old phantasies are evoked and worked through again' (though at least 'this time round the adult is there to help'!). Firth-Cozens has explored 'the different ways that early experience, especially family relationships, can influence later job perceptions and the experience of stress at work' (1992a: 62; see also Firth, 1985; Firth-Cozens, 1992b), and has coined the term 'psychoanalytic transference in job stress' (1992a: 61). Margison (1987: 115) briefly outlines an object relations view of stress in psychiatrists, with the psychiatrist being made susceptible because of work pressure such that highly defended areas within the psychiatrist's early object relationships are reactivated: thus, the exposure of previously split-off and unacceptable parts of the self can produce intensely shameful feelings, which is particularly difficult for professionals working in a setting 'where a "professional", competent persona is being maintained' (Margison, 1987: 115; see also Waring, 1974).

Thus, I favour a psychodynamic approach to the experience of stress, linking stress symptoms to underlying personality psychodynamics, with the characteristics of the setting affecting the level of stress to the extent that those characteristics interact unhelpfully or pathologically with the counsellor's personality dynamics. Counsellors are, of course, drawn into surgery counselling for all manner of motivations, many or even most of them unconscious (see Sussman, 1992); but from the standpoint of developmental psychology and object relations theory, it can be argued that there are certain universal developmental experiences which render all counsellors susceptible to given environmental stressors – for example, exposure to rapid environmental change and uncertainty under conditions of diminishing resources – thereby triggering acute anxiety as such change resonates unconsciously with the imprinting of pre- and perinatal experience (Wasdell, 1987).

Analysis of survey responses
I analysed responses to question 5 – 'Please describe your personal responses to the stresses you've described in your previous answer'

– along the dimensions of healthy and unhealthy responses, and dispositionally focused (including intrapsychic and self-care) and environmentally focused (including interpersonal and organizational) responses.

My procedure was, first, to list all of the different stress responses given – there were 27 in all; and the counsellors listed some 52 'instances' of a stress response (respondents gave more than one stress response in their answers to question 5). I then analysed the responses in four different ways to throw some light on the dimensions of experienced stress.

Healthy vs unhealthy

I defined 'healthy' responses as those which might be expected to reduce stress levels without a substantial (and secondarily stressful) cost being incurred by the counsellor. Typical healthy responses were seeking consultation with doctors (mentioned by five respondents), keeping tight boundaries (n = 2) and referring clients on to other agencies rather than being overwhelmed by caseload pressures (n = 2). Unhealthy responses included overidentifying with clients (n = 2) and feelings of guilt, rejection and hurt (n = 3).

Interestingly, there were 17 categories of healthy response and just 8 unhealthy ones (with 2 judged to be indeterminate); and there were 30 healthy response instances and just 10 unhealthy responses. This might suggest that the surveyed counsellors' responses to stressors are more likely to be healthy than unhealthy – after all, we might reasonably expect counsellors to be more tuned into their own stress responses and then to take positive and effective action to alleviate those stresses. Alternatively, the respondents may either be more honest about, or more conscious of, their healthy responses than they are of their unhealthy ones. This latter point is very important, because if we adopt a psychodynamic view it is clear that, by definition, respondents will not be fully conscious of all the processes involved. Such reservations should be borne in mind when attempting to draw any more general implications for coping from survey data such as these.

Dispositional vs environmental

I divided responses into those which veered towards an internal, intrapersonal (*dispositional*) response to stressors, and those which involved action in the external environment in an attempt to alleviate stress (*environmental*). Examples of dispositional responses were anger (n = 9) and self-caring activities generally; while environmental responses included creative ways of working in a time-limited framework (n = 4) and distancing from the surgery (n = 4).

Interestingly, there was an almost perfect 50:50 split between the two. Certainly in this survey it seems that, as a whole, counsellors responded to their stressful experiences with a very even mixture of dispositional and environmental responses.

Further cross-tabulations

I further divided responses into four categories: 'healthy dispositional' (HD), 'unhealthy dispositional' (UH-D), 'healthy environmental' (HE), and 'unhealthy environmental' (UH-E).

The most interesting comparison is between 'HD' and 'HE' responses, with there being over twice as many HE as HD instances (21 against 9). Totals for HD and UH-D instances were very similar. However, the number of HE instances was very high (21), while the number of UH-E instances was minimal (just 2). The implications for coping which arise from these data will be evaluated later.

Most common response categories

There were six categories of response which were mentioned at least three times, and these are described more fully below, in order of importance.

Anger This response was cited by nine respondents, over half of the total surveyed. It is revealing to look closely at the object of respondents' anger. Anger was fairly evenly divided between anger about the counsellor's personal situation (n = 5) and about their clients' plight (n = 4). In the former case, four of the five described anger related to how they were treated by the surgery, and the fifth mentioned uncertainty over funding. As for the other four respondents, it seemed that all four were identifying with their *clients'* situation – one actually wrote of 'getting very angry, over-identifying with clients who feel like "victims of the system"'.

Psychodynamically, there are probably two different psychic processes operating here. For some counsellors frustration has an inwardly oriented focus, possibly reflecting response patterns to anger adopted in their early family relationships; whereas others' anger is directed out into the environment, possibly via the process described in object relations theory as 'projective identification' – that is, projecting on to their clients the mistreated parts of themselves and then getting angry about the projection (their clients' plight).

Consultation with GPs and other staff This response was mentioned by five respondents, and seems to reflect a quite general dissatisfaction with the treatment received by surgery counsellors. Looking at the reasons given for this response, again, a mixture of responses is evident, with two counsellors seeking more GP contact because of their personal situation, and two because of their concern about clients (the other response was a mixture of both). A typical self-concerned response was trying 'to tackle doctors about the difficulties of the pressure of work'; while a typical other-directed concern was one counsellor who tries to discuss with the GP the arrangement of future specialist medical help for the client. Again, there seem to be some counsellors who 'go inwards' towards self-concern, while others 'go outwards' towards concern for clients.

Distancing from the surgery   Four respondents mentioned this response, which clearly seems to be related to setting-dynamics difficulties. One counsellor categorized as 'healthy' her 'not becoming too involved with the practice'; another wrote that 'I have tended to keep myself to myself in one surgery, where there is quite a hostile atmosphere . . . Now I cut myself off to protect myself.'

Regarding the psychodynamics of the 'consultation' and 'distancing' responses, it seems that some counsellors tend to respond to a stressor by distancing themselves, whereas others tend to engage with the environment in an attempt to alleviate the perceived source of stress. These differential responses are again most likely to be a function of the personality dynamics of the counsellors concerned.

Peer meetings and sharing   Three counsellors mentioned this response, and it is frequently mentioned in the professional self-care literature as an important antidote to occupational stress. One counsellor wrote of 'sharing experiences with other counsellors in similar *predicaments*' (my emphasis – a highly revealing choice of word, perhaps indicative of the funding anxiety current at the time of the survey). Another wrote: 'As there are two of us we meet regularly and discuss our situation.' Both of these respondents also mentioned the Norfolk Surgery Counsellors Group, a self-help group set up with the express intention of providing a supportive forum for general practice counsellors.

Creative/positive response to time-limited counselling   This involves responding proactively to an unwanted situation rather than seeing it in exclusively negative terms. One counsellor wrote quite explicitly of 'trying to look for creative responses to the time-limited framework – e.g. considering cognitive-analytic approaches to counselling [Ryle, 1989]'. Another respondent wrote: 'I actually feel strongly that with limited resources and a waiting list, 6 [sessions] is fair – I have a good knowledge of local agencies . . . . It's hard work, but I like variety and enjoy the challenge. I don't feel the only good work is long-term.' Both of these respondents were able partially to regulate their surgery caseload by 'siphoning off' some clients into the voluntary agencies for which they also work, no doubt feeling slightly less negatively about time-limited counselling as a consequence. Finally, one counsellor wrote: 'I feel sometimes that by offering 6 sessions one can do some concentrated beneficial work – it concentrates the mind for counsellor and client!'

Some counsellors, then, seem to view time-limited counselling as an *opportunity* to re-evaluate their way of working, rather than it *having* to be an unambiguously negative experience.

Supervision Three respondents mentioned the importance of their supervision in helping to relieve stress (it is perhaps surprising that only one counsellor mentioned personal therapy as a coping response). The respondents seemed to view supervision as a necessary support – somewhere to take one's stresses and moans. For at least one respondent, a significant part of his supervision time was taken up with issues related to the general practice setting, and the difficulties it raises for his surgery work. It seems plausible that those three counsellors make a particularly strong supportive use of their supervisor over and above the normally supportive function of supervision for counsellors.

The data I have discussed in this section should be regarded as indicative of how counsellors cope with the stress of working in the general practice setting, rather than as a definitive empirical study. Some interesting patterns have emerged, and these will be explored further below. The wide range of responses is striking, and it was only when the data were examined more closely that clear patterns of response began to emerge.

Suggestions for improved coping

> 'Caring for the carers' becomes particularly essential because the prevalence of ill-health and disease tends to arouse deep emotion in those striving to help. (Abel Smith *et al.*, 1989: 130)

A few remarks about the 'coping' concept are necessary, as it is crucial to specify as precisely as possible the way in which 'coping' behaviour is assumed to be produced in alleviating experienced stress.

A psychodynamic-humanistic view of coping, which I favour here, is quite different from the more common cognitive-behavioural-type approach typical of much of the stress literature. I argue here that what is crucial for successful coping is not the uncritical adoption of preconceived self-care regimes of stress reduction, but rather, that the counsellor be in a position to make self-caring decisions and choices that are appropriate to her- or himself. On this view, the reasons why a counsellor is not coping with a given stressor will in part be some function of that person's developmental history, the influence of which may well be completely ignored by the kinds of programmatic strategy commonly advocated in the coping literature.

What may be required, therefore, is a deeper level of 'organismic' holistic change, such that the underlying psychodynamics of lack of self-care or failure to cope are addressed, worked through and integrated. Only then will the counsellor be able to make an appropriate decision regarding adequate coping and self-care. To be truly authentic and not merely 'grafted on to' the personality in a mechanistic way, the specifics of a counsellor's way of coping should emerge from a more fully integrated self, from what Neumann (1971) calls 'the creative unconscious'.

It should be clear that the coping strategies found to be useful by other counsellors should not be treated mechanistically as some kind of magical formulaic solution to the stress experienced by surgery counsellors in general.

Analysis of survey responses

Respondents were asked what kinds of coping strategy surgery counsellors could embrace to mitigate their occupational stresses. Taken as a whole, respondents again preferred coping strategies with a combination of dispositional and environmental responses. For current purposes, I will divide the responses into intrapsychic; interpersonal and environmental/organizational; and self-caring strategies.

Intrapsychic strategies

Eight respondents mentioned the importance of supervision (and, in one case, personal therapy) in combating work stressors. Good-quality, frequent supervision was especially strongly emphasized by six counsellors, and it does seem that supervision is expected to take much of the strain when surgery counsellors are substantially stressed in their work. One respondent also mentioned the importance of 'confidently accepting our own professional status'.

Interpersonal and environmental/organizational strategies

The most commonly cited strategies were consultation with and 'education' of surgery staff; educating GPs about counselling; and the negotiation of clear terms, conditions and boundaries.

Staff and GP education and consultation was cited by eight respondents, and is clearly seen as a very important and necessary condition for the successful and smooth functioning of general practice counselling. One counsellor mentioned 'ensuring that all members of the team understand that counselling is different from "treating people"'; and another advocated 'meeting with surgery staff to help them have a clearer understanding of who a counsellor is and what they do'. According to Green (1990: 52), the general practice counsellor 'should attend PHCT [Primary Health Care Team] meetings or relevant practice meetings and be part of the decision-making process where appropriate'.

Another counsellor suggested the 'encourage[ment] of GP attendance at seminars with counsellors in medical settings'. One respondent referred to 'educating doctors and clients in the aims and practice of counselling so that their expectations are realistic and appropriate'. Negotiating clear terms and conditions was stressed very strongly by six respondents. One counsellor argued for 'a clear and concise description of work at the outset of working in a surgery'; and similarly, another wrote '*it is vital to sort out groundrules right from the outset*' (his emphasis suggests some retrospective learning here!). And a bit later, 'I would recommend a check-list of points that any surgery counsellor should sort out with his or her employing GPs right from the outset, rather than adopting a piecemeal approach, with all the associated uncertainties and lack of clarity.' Another respondent conveyed assertiveness tempered with realism, by being 'very clear about what I would like, and then negotiat(ing) to achieve [these aims] as far as I can within the inevitable constraints'.

Green (1990), in her feasibility study of general practice counselling in Leeds, advocates very clear lines of responsibility and accountability to the practice: 'Expectations must be made explicit to all parties and clarified as situations change and develop.' She also sets out a list of points which any contract should incorporate (Green, 1990: 49).

Finally, a related but more general point was raised by one counsellor who advocated pushing for 'proper professional recognition of [their] work within the medical profession'.

Self-care strategies

By far the most often recommended strategy (by ten respondents) was that of peer-group meetings, sharing and support in general. This is consistent with the stress literature, which has consistently found peer and social support to be important buffers against burnout in the caring professions (e.g. Maslach and Jackson, 1982:

245–6). A number of the respondents regularly attend the Norfolk Surgery Counsellors Group, with some travelling a considerable distance. It is interesting that peer support was mentioned much more often than other forms of support (for example family, friends) – clearly, quite a specific need is felt for professional peer support, which may be related to the relative isolation of the setting described earlier. One counsellor referred to 'a regular forum in which surgery counsellors can meet, share gripes, pool ideas, gain peer affirmation and support, etc.'

Earlier it was pointed out that the counsellors surveyed had a far greater propensity to go for healthy *environmental* coping strategies than they did for healthy *dispositional* ones. I would argue that to embrace environmental/organizational strategies is very likely to alleviate at least some stress; but from a psychodynamic viewpoint, it is not a sufficient condition for psychic well-being, given that an exclusive focus on environmental strategies will tend to leave untouched whatever pathological personality dynamics are being triggered by the stressors. If is often very painful, challenging and resistance-provoking to explore our deepest pathologies and difficulties – which may partly account for the respondents' seeming preference for environmental over dispositional approaches, and the notable lack of mention of personal therapy.

However, the literature on the psychodynamics of stress, alluded to earlier, makes it clear that psychodynamics may well play a much more central role than most of us care to realize and problem-focused, cognitive-behavioural-type coping strategies will tend to miss this crucial point. Thus, if, as has been found with doctors, career choice for (surgery) counsellors is to some extent 'a response to unconscious drives to compensate for childhood experiences of parental impotence, or emotional neglect' (Johnson, 1991: 317), or for any number of other unconscious reasons (Sussman, 1992), then it is clearly extremely important that counsellors pay attention to this dimension of their difficulties as well as trying to tackle the environmental stressors directly.

Discussion

I will now refer briefly to those stressors discussed earlier which have not been adequately covered to date, outlining some possible effective coping strategies. First, regarding the *security of the frame*, the more successfully the frame can be secured, then the less stress will be experienced from this source. Hoag (1992: 426–7) has convincingly shown how paying close attention to the security of the therapeutic frame in her general practice counselling work, making the boundaries as clear and as safe as possible given the constraints of the setting, resulted in a quite dramatic effect on the take-up and smooth running of the service.

With regard to *reluctant clients and inappropriate referrals*, it is important to be as open and as clear as possible with the referring GPs regarding the kinds of problem for which counselling is and is not suited. Thus, for example, clients with histories of sexual abuse, early maternal abandonment or psychotic disturbances may well be singularly inappropriate for referral to time-limited counselling: indeed, in some cases, time-limited contracts may actually be abusive to such clients. In addition, clients sometimes do not reveal (or may sometimes not even be conscious of) the root(s) of their difficulties prior to counselling, and so the major source of their problems may well not be known by the doctor at time of referral, only emerging once counselling has begun. These difficulties should allow the counsellor to make a strong case to the doctors for some degree of flexibility and professional autonomy in deciding what length of contract it is appropriate to offer different clients – though there is likely to be resistance to this where there exists the pressure of long waiting lists, and doctors have a less than informed understanding of the complex and delicate dynamics of the counselling process. If a doctor is determined to refer unsuitable clients, there is little that counsellors can do, short of making their feelings known.

When a counsellor finds her- or himself working with a reluctant client (probably in a time-limited modality), it is important that the counsellor does not take total responsibility for their client's 'stuckness' (although counsellors must, of course, also be open to exploring their own part in the dynamics of client stuckness or reluctance).

Medication is again an issue for open discussion with the referring GPs where at all possible – which might well involve a frank and sometimes conflictual exchange about the differing philosophies of the 'medical' and the 'healing' approach to psychological or emotional difficulties. If the doctor is inflexible on the issue of medication and its possible deleterious effects on the counselling process, then he or she must be made aware of the limitations that continued medication may place on the efficacy of counselling for some clients. It is important, of course, for general practice counsellors to have a reasonable working knowledge of psychotropic medication and its effects on the counselling process (Hammersley and Beeley, 1992), and for counsellors not to be rigidly and inflexibly set against the use of medication in all circumstances.

Regarding *setting dynamics*, it is totally unrealistic to hope that the various dynamics of the general practice setting can be fully brought out into the open and acknowledged (notwithstanding the excellent and pioneering work of Michael Balint and Howard Stein in this field). In part this is because the primitive anxieties that are activated in any medical setting are so profound that anyone who tries to articulate them is liable to be scapegoated and even vilified as an 'undesirable troublemaker' (compare Wasdell, 1989). Perhaps the best we can hope for is to deepen our own personal understanding of the psychodynamics of the setting (an intrapsychic strategy), and then apply this understanding in practice where the constraints and resistances are not too great as to be prohibitive (a constrained organizational strategy).

Finally, *professional issues*: the birth of a profession is inevitably a long, slow process (Charles-Edwards *et al.*, 1989), and perhaps the best general practice counsellors can hope for is that the positive results of their work will gradually come to be recognized and valued in a realistic way. This in turn will necessitate surgery counsellors taking responsibility in arguing for the (cost-) effectiveness of their work (House, forthcoming) and in embarking upon detailed quantitative and qualitative evaluation of their counselling in the general practice setting (King *et al.*, 1994). For, in the new 'audit-driven' National Health Service, competition for scarce resources is intense, and counselling must prove its worth if it is to continue to play an important and growing role in primary health care. The recently formed Norfolk Association of Professional Surgery Counsellors (of which the author was a founding member) has been set up with just these aims in mind, and there is no doubt that moving towards a more solid professional grounding for general practice counselling will greatly help to reduce the tensions and stresses of working in a field where one's professional status is often uncertain, ambiguous and insecure.

In addition, to the extent that the ethos of counselling (certainly in its humanistic manifestation) is antithetical to the 'biomedical model' of modern Western medicine (Engel, 1977), it would be naive to underestimate the resistance that is likely from within the medical profession to an approach which, if widely adopted, might substantially undermine the very assumptions on which the medicalization of human ill-health rests (House, 1994).

In closing, and to modify and extend an Alcoholics Anonymous epigram,

People should try to change the noxious (environmental) and the pathological (dispositional) things that can be changed, accept those that cannot, have the wisdom to know the difference, and be prepared to exit from the situation when all other avenues have been fully explored.

Note

1 My thanks to all those surgery counsellors who completed and returned the questionnaire.

References

Abel Smith, A., Irving, J. and Brown, P. (1989) 'Counselling in the medical context', in W. Dryden, D. Charles-Edwards and R. Woolfe (eds), *Handbook of Counselling in Britain*. London: Routledge. pp. 122–33.

Alexander, F. and Szasz, T.S. (1952) 'The psychosomatic approach in medicine', in F. Alexander and H. Ross (eds), *The Impact of Freudian Psychiatry*. Chicago: University of Chicago Press. pp. 260–91.

Balint, M. (1969) *The Basic Fault: Therapeutic Aspects of Regression*. London: Tavistock.

Balint, M. (1986) *The Doctor, His Patient and the Illness*, 2nd edition. Edinburgh: Churchill Livingstone. First published Pitman Publishing, 1964.

Bernstein, B. (1964) 'Social class, speech systems and psycho-therapy', *British Journal of Sociology*, 15 (1): 54–64.

Blair, A. (1993) 'Social class and the contextualization of illness experience', in A. Radley (ed.), *Worlds of Illness: Biographical and Cultural Perspectives on Health and Disease*. London: Routledge. pp. 27–48.

British Association for Counselling (1993) *Guidelines for the Employment of Counsellors in General Practice*. Rugby: BAC.

Charles-Edwards, D., Dryden, W. and Woolfe, R. (1989) 'Professional issues in counselling', in W. Dryden, D. Charles-Edwards and R. Woolfe (eds), *Handbook of Counselling in Britain*. London: Routledge. pp. 401–23.

Dubovsky, S.L. (1981) *Psychotherapeutics in Primary Care*. New York: Grune & Stratton.

Engel, G.L. (1977) 'The need for a new medical model: a challenge for biomedicine', *Science*, 196 (4286): 129–36.

Farber, B.A. (1983) 'Dysfunctional aspects of the psychotherapeutic role', in B.A. Farber (ed.), *Stress and Burnout in the Human Service Professions*. New York: Pergamon. pp. 97–118.

Farber, B.A. (1990) 'Burnout in psychotherapists: incidence, types, and trends', *Psychotherapy in Private Practice*, 8 (1): 35–44.

Firth, J. (1985) 'Personal meanings of occupational stress: cases from the clinic', *Journal of Occupational Psychology*, 58 (2): 139–48.

Firth-Cozens, J. (1992a) 'The role of early family experiences in the perception of organizational stress: fusing clinical and organizational perspectives', *Journal of Occupational and Organizational Psychology*, 65 (1): 61–75.

Firth-Cozens, J. (1992b) 'Why me? A case study of the process of perceived organizational stress', *Human Relations*, 45 (2): 131–41.

Fischer, H.J. (1983) 'A psychoanalytic view of burnout', in B.A. Farber (ed.), *Stress and Burnout in the Human Service Professions*. New York: Pergamon. pp. 40–5.

Green, A.J.M. (1990) *A Feasibility Study into the Use of Counsellors in Primary Health Care Teams*. Leeds: Leeds MIND (157 Woodhouse Lane, Leeds LS2 3ED).

Green, A.J.M. (1993) 'Reflections on a feasibility study into counselling in primary health care teams', *Counselling*, 4 (3): 186–7.

Guy, J.D. (1987) *The Personal Life of the Psychotherapist*. New York: Wiley.

Hall, J. (1993) *The Reluctant Adult: An Exploration of Choice*. Bridport: Prism Press.

Hammersley, D. and Beeley, L. (1992) 'The effects of medication on counselling', *Counselling*, 3 (3): 162–4.

Hatwell, V. (1992) 'Counselling in general practice', *CMS News (Quarterly Journal of the Counselling in Medical Settings Division of the BAC)*, 32 (August): 6–7.

Heckman, S.J. (1980) 'Effects of work setting, theoretical orientation, and personality on psychotherapist burnout', PhD dissertation, California School of Professional Psychology, Berkeley/Alameda.

Higgs, R. and Dammers, J. (1992) 'Ethical issues in counselling and health in primary care', *British Journal of Guidance and Counselling*, 20 (1): 27–38.

Hoag, L. (1989) 'Psychotherapy in the general practice surgery: considerations of the frame', MA dissertation, Department of Psychology, Regent's College, London.

Hoag, L. (1992) 'Psychotherapy in the general practice surgery: considerations of the frame', *British Journal of Psychotherapy*, 8 (4): 417–29.

House, R. (1994) 'Counselling in general practice – a conflict of ideologies?', *The Therapist*, 4 (1): 40–1.

House, R. (forthcoming) 'The efficacy of general practice counselling: a metacritique', *British Journal of Guidance and Counselling*.

Irving, J. (1992) 'The practice counsellor', in M. Sheldon (ed.), *Counselling in General Practice*. London: Royal College of General Practitioners. pp. 26–9.

Jaques, E. (1955) 'Social systems as a defense against persecutory and defensive anxieties', in M. Klein, P. Heimann and R.E. Money-Kyrle (eds), *New Directions in Psychoanalysis*. New York: Basic Books. pp. 478–98.

Johnson, W.D.K. (1991) 'Predisposition to emotional distress and psychiatric illness among doctors: the role of unconscious and experiential factors', *British Journal of Medical Psychology*, 64 (4): 317–29.

King, M., Broster, G., Lloyd, M. and Horder, J. (1994) 'Controlled trials in the evaluation of counselling in general practice', *British Journal of General Practice*, 44: 229–32.

Langs, R. (1988) *A Primer of Psychotherapy*. New York: Gardner Press.

McDougall, J. (1989) *Theatres of the Body: A Psychoanalytic Approach to Psychosomatic Illness*. London: Free Association Books.

Manthei, R.J.M. and Mathews, D.A.M. (1989) 'Helping the reluctant client to engage in counselling', in W. Dryden (ed.), *Key Issues for Counselling in Action*. London: Sage. pp. 37–44.

Margison, F.R. (1987) 'Stress in psychiatrists', in R. Payne and J. Firth-Cozens (eds), *Stress in Health Professionals*. Chichester: Wiley. pp. 107–24.

Maslach, C. and Jackson, S.E. (1982) 'Burnout in health professions: a social psychological analysis', in G.S. Sanders and J. Suls (eds), *Social Psychology of Health and Illness*. Hillsdale, NJ: Lawrence Erlbaum. pp. 227–51.

Massie, M.J., Holland, J.C. and Straker, N. (1989) 'Psychotherapeutic interventions', in J.C. Holland and J.H. Rowland (eds), *Handbook of Psycho-oncology: Psychological Care of the Patient with Cancer*. New York: Oxford University Press. pp. 455–69.

Menzies Lyth, I. (1988) 'The functioning of social systems as a defence against anxiety', in *Containing Anxiety in Institutions: Selected Essays*. Volume 1. London: Free Association Books. pp. 43–85.

Nemiah, J.C. (1961) *Foundations of Psychopathology*. New York: Oxford University Press.

Neumann, E. (1971) *Art and the Creative Unconscious*. Princeton, NJ: University Press.

Pennebaker, J.W. and Susman, J.R. (1988) 'Disclosure of traumas and psychosomatic processes', *Social Science and Medicine*, 26 (3): 327–32.

Pickvance, D. (1993) 'Sheffield GP counsellors' conference: The Therapeutic Triangle', *Counselling*, 4 (1): 92.

Pollack, K. (1988) 'On the nature of social stress: production of a modern mythology', *Social Science and Medicine*, 26 (3): 381–92.

Ryle, A. (1987) 'Problems of patients' dependency on doctors: discussion paper', *Journal of the Royal Society of Medicine*, 80 (1): 25–6.

Ryle, A. (1989) *Cognitive-Analytic Therapy*. Chichester: Wiley.

Segal, J. (1985) *Phantasy in Everyday Life: A Psychoanalytic Approach to Understanding Ourselves*. Harmondsworth: Penguin.

Segal, J. (1991) 'The use of the concept of unconscious phantasy in understanding reactions to chronic illness', *Counselling*, 2 (4): 146–9.

Sher, M. (1992) 'Dynamic teamwork within general medical practice', in British Association for Social Psychiatry, *Counselling in Primary Care? Conference Proceedings*. London (November). pp. 50–63.

Smith, D.L. (1991) *Hidden Conversations: An Introduction to Communicative Psychoanalysis*. London: Routledge.

Stein, H.F. (1983) 'The influence of countertransference on decision making and the clinical relationship', *Continuing Education for the Family Physician*, 18 (7): 625–30.

Stein, H.F. (1985) *The Psychodynamics of Medical Practice: Unconscious Factors in Patient Care*. Berkeley: University of California Press.

Stein, H.F. (1990) *American Medicine as Culture*. Boulder, CO: Westview Press.

Strain, J.S. (1978) *Psychological Interventions in Medical Practice*. New York: Century-Appleton-Crofts.

Sussman, M.B. (1992) *A Curious Calling: Unconscious Motivations for Practicing Psychotherapy*, Northvale, NJ: Jason Aronson.

Waring, E. (1974) 'Psychiatric illness in physicians: a review', *Comprehensive Psychiatry*, 15: 519–30.

Wasdell, D. (1987) *Response to Change*, revised edn. London: Unit for Research into Changing Institutions. First published 1981.

Wasdell, D. (1989) *Constraints Encountered in the Conduct of Psychosocial Analysis*. London: Unit for Research into Changing Institutions.

7 The Stresses of Counselling in Private Practice

Colin Feltham

Freud began his part-time private practice in 1886 and agonized over the economics involved in it. In the 1930s and 1940s the Scottish psychoanalyst Fairbairn was seeing nine or ten patients a day. We are told that

> Fairbairn was now almost whole-time in his consulting room/study in the house. The increased number of analysands, however, isolated him from 9am to 7.30pm daily except for a brief break for lunch. He was also habitually at work in his study on most nights from about 9.30 till after midnight. (Sutherland, 1989: 32)

Fairbairn was simultaneously experiencing domestic and marital stress. Psychotherapists have practised from their own homes and from treatment centres for decades. The first recorded instance of a *counsellor* in private practice in Britain is in 1956. There were about 127 such counsellors in 1979, which rose to 1,270 by 1990 and 1,924 in 1993 (Syme, 1994). By far the highest concentration is in London, followed by Surrey and other home counties. Independent practice is far better established and understood in North America than in Britain (Margenau, 1990).

What all these practitioners have in common is that they are self-employed and usually negotiate payment directly with their own clients. Without going into the debate about the real or alleged differences between counselling and psychotherapy, I believe that counsellors who engage in short-term work face very different challenges and stresses from those faced by practitioners who engage in long-term work. The present chapter focuses on the stresses experienced by counsellors who, like myself, engage in work that is often, although not necessarily, short term or temporally unpredictable in nature.

Few of us rely solely on counselling for our income. There are relatively few full-time jobs in counselling in Britain, so it seems reasonable to suppose that there is a relatively large number of counsellors who have part-time private practices, often in addition

to other part-time work or commitments. One American survey
('1985 survey report') found that the average number of client
hours worked each week by private practitioners (social workers,
psychologists, marriage and family therapists) was 28.7. As far as I
know, few counsellors in private practice in Britain can yet match
such figures.

My own experience may serve as a useful, however atypical,
illustration of how a counsellor comes to be in private practice. I
did not make a bold decision that I wanted to do it (although I did
attend a one-day workshop on 'going solo'). Rather, after a series
of less than satisfactory jobs containing elements of counselling, I
took an opportunity to become self-employed, based on a year's
contracted work which freed me to develop other work. Over the
past few years I have been involved in counselling, supervision,
training, group facilitation, conference organizing, research, writing
and diverse counselling-related activities. Counselling itself has
always been only part of my overall workload. I rarely maintain a
private caseload of more than eight clients a week and sometimes
considerably fewer. Currently I also supervise six counsellors, some
fortnightly, some monthly. I see clients in a comfortable attic room
in my home in east London. The main stresses I experience are
economic and environmental, but these in turn have problematic
effects on my family life.

The nature of the stresses

The first source of stress for the private practitioner is setting up in
business. The counsellor is confronted with many decisions about
how to begin practically (for example advertising, providing a
suitable environment, charging fees) as well as dealing with the
unfamiliar experiences of having strangers entering the home, and
having no immediate colleagues. I know one counsellor who was
able to begin counselling quickly in a group practice, who therefore
obviously did have colleagues, but he had to pay for this privilege
by surrendering 50 per cent of his fees to the practice. Most
counsellors acknowledge that it can take a considerable time (six
months, a year or several years) to establish a sustained practice,
and obviously during that time few people can rely on such
minimal and unpredictable income. There is, then, an unavoidable
transitional stress, from one professional identity to another; from
a predictable to a variable income.

It has always been acknowledged that therapeutic work makes
peculiar personal demands on practitioners, but only in the last
decade has this occupational stress and burnout been studied

seriously (Edelwich and Brodsky, 1980; Farber and Heifetz, 1982).
I intend to discuss the nature of the stress encountered by the
private practitioner under the headings of emotional and physical
stress; environmental stress; economic stress; and ethical and
ideological stress.

Emotional and physical stress

Perhaps the fact that someone telephones you at home, enters your
home regularly, in that setting discloses his or her most intimate
concerns, and pays you directly, lays the foundation for a peculiar
sense of commitment and responsibility on your part. Arguably,
this relationship is more intimate than one formed in a neutral
office setting. Like the doctor and the minister, you are visited by
people in some degree of pain or confusion who invest hope and
authority in your knowledge and skills. But unlike those situations,
nothing stands between or behind you and the client, like the NHS
or the Church. As a counsellor, you sell your psychological skills,
your willingness to listen intensely and to attempt to offer a variety
of helpful strategies in return for money. Yet you usually cannot
avoid forming quite close bonds with your clients (indeed,
Goldberg, 1992, points out that therapists are often more intimate
with clients than with their own family and friends). Being the
vendor in the 'purchase of friendship' can sometimes feel uncomfortable and even faintly immoral. A counsellor who practices
in a GP's surgery and privately tells me that he feels more stress in
his private work, where cash transactions suggest higher expectations of positive results.

The mental concentration and demand for creative thinking,
effective interventions and self-evaluation required in counselling
may not differ in private practice and in other settings. However,
when working from home you are usually much more isolated than
you would be if working in a group practice or an organization.
You cannot turn to colleagues, and the ethic of confidentiality
means that you cannot (or should not) discuss clients with your
partner or others close to you. An aura of confidentiality and
preoccupation may inadvertently surround you, which may affect
relationships with partners and children (Guy, 1987; Maeder, 1990;
Goldberg, 1992). Maeder reports that the emotional effects on the
children of psychotherapists and counsellors are frequently negative. I sometimes experience a sense of a split persona indoors: one
moment the attentive, empathic counsellor; the next the tired,
preoccupied, impatient husband and father. Sometimes I am
playing with my children when the doorbell rings, I have to stop
play abruptly and switch roles, and I know as I take the client

upstairs that my children are disappointed and bewildered. I have to shake off these feelings as I settle down to concentrate on my client. I prefer to have some minutes before each client arrives in order to compose myself, but this isn't always possible. As a self-employed counsellor, I am at home yet not at home, isolated by time-consuming counselling, writing and teaching preparation.

As a self-employed counsellor you cannot afford to take much time off from work and you cannot afford to be sick too often or for too long. I am not alone in having seen clients when I have felt physically unwell. There is a certain pressure to be emotionally and physically constant and reliable for clients. There is also the economic need to keep the fees coming in. (Goldberg's, 1992, research suggests that economic stress is ranked as the most significant concern among male psychotherapists.) This unavoidable preoccupation with the economics of private practice may have an insidious effect on the counsellor's emotional well-being. Sickness insurance for self-employed counsellors is expensive, so most counsellors rely on remaining healthy or soldiering on through their minor illnesses. The cumulative effects of denying your body's recuperative needs may eventually take their toll in the form of serious illness. It is noted by Goldberg (1992) that many psychotherapists begin to find the work much more physically tiring in their later years.

Environmental stress

Before clients arrive, you are very aware that the house should look clean, tidy and somewhat neutral. Occupants of the house keep out of the way or duck out of sight at the last minute when the doorbell rings. I am not a psychodynamic counsellor, but I believe that clients should not encounter too many signs of my domestic life. You are aware of cooking smells, children's toys and clothes lying around, the dog or cat being noisy or demanding. The bathroom and toilet must be clean and vacant, yet children (and adults) seem often to forget to take their personal effects away. I almost envy a psychotherapist I know who lives alone and whose bathroom is a model of anonymity. Matters of this kind, concerning the environmental impact on clients, are interestingly addressed by Rowan (1988).

Once inside the room, you occasionally wince and perhaps apologize as you hear the normal cries and screams of your children downstairs. Occasionally a child forgets that you're working and bursts into the room. Clients who have been seeing you for some time seem to get accustomed to these periodic, amusing, homely intrusions, but you're never sure what new clients are thinking. A majority of clients prefer to be seen in the early evening, just when your children may be having baths or going to bed. Even for those counsellors who work outside the home, clients' preferences for certain appointment times can be problematic. As Blower and Rink (1987: 11) put it, 'Most of our counselling sessions take place in the evening, which inevitably brings a clash between domestic and business interests.'

Working from home means that you probably have no secretary or colleagues and no means of screening clients before seeing them. There is some risk involved in this, and an additional risk for women and men who live alone. As well as emotional isolation, then, counsellors may experience risks to their physical safety and professional reputation that colleagues working in organizations escape.

Economic stress
I have already mentioned the difficulties involved in relying on counselling for your income. I have discussed elsewhere (Feltham, 1993) the importance of anticipating how much money you need to make, and the need to take into account the overheads of initial and continuing training, supervision, personal therapy, professional memberships, accreditation and insurance. You must anticipate cash-flow problems, sickness and its consequences, the need to provide a pension for yourself and other savings, for example for your tax bill. Following one particularly lean year, when a promised major contract failed to materialize and the British economic recession was at its height, I was forced to remortgage my house to pay tax and other debts. I was not alone in having difficulty surviving. One colleague, who had previously had part of her house structurally converted into a counselling room, gave up counselling altogether. Another terminated his private practice and became a full-time trainer. Even as I write, the national economy of Britain is far from healthy, and clients sometimes change from weekly to fortnightly sessions to reduce their spending.

Counsellors in private practice must decide on a fee scale. You may flourish economically if you are well-known and/or practise in a prestigious setting, but most counsellors charge modest fees. Ironically, counsellors who least need to make money (those, for example, with affluent partners, those who are retired and comfortably off, or reasonably well-paid academics whose jobs leave them free time) are often in a better position to charge higher fees (because they often live in more affluent neighbourhoods, in houses with spacious accommodation, and have more money and time to spend on further training and qualifications). Counsellors in disadvantaged social circumstances, however, are subject to the same stresses as other disadvantaged groups (Mirowsky and Ross, 1989). Counsellors living in London experience competition for clients, while in certain areas of the country there are very few counsellors, and I know one who is the sole counsellor in a particular rural area, who enjoys a busy practice accordingly. It is not necessarily better counsellors who charge more, but often those who 'believe in themselves' or are willing to 'chance their luck'. There are, of course, some clients who believe that they are more likely to be effectively helped by counsellors who charge high fees.

I have indicated that counsellors often have to take on a diversified workload. This sometimes means that you travel around from one location to another, constantly adjusting to different tasks. One or two colleagues have confirmed my own experience of rushing home from one 'job' to see a client and arriving just in the nick of time. A diversified workload often entails myriad loose ends which, unless you can afford secretarial support, may involve you in time-consuming and unremunerated administrative tasks. I have never rented rooms for counselling, but other counsellors tell me that such arrangements often cost far too much in relation to the number of clients seen. Another problematic feature of counselling is that clients sometimes terminate unexpectedly or simply feel satisfied with their achievements after a few sessions. Unlike psychoanalytically oriented (and some humanistic) therapy, which has created an expectation that clients will be in therapy for years, counselling is usually associated with much shorter time spans. This places considerable economic burdens on the counsellor, who must strive to maintain a reputation that in turn will support a waiting list, or constantly find new clients.

Unfortunately, the myth prevails that psychoanalysts and psychotherapists, especially those who are associated with the more prestigious training institutes, are invariably more knowledgeable and skilful. Counsellors still often tend to be perceived as a rather inferior version of psychotherapists and can have difficulty charging the level of fees their intensive work may warrant. Counsellors in private practice tend not to have the close links with training organizations that many psychotherapists have and usually do not receive referrals from such organizations. As the 'poor relations' among helping professionals, counsellors do not enjoy the prestige of psychiatrists, psychoanalysts and psychologists and usually cannot have clients referred to them whose treatment is paid by insurance companies, for example.

Ethical and ideological stress

It seems unlikely that anyone would choose this work primarily to improve their income; the primary motivations are probably the wish to engage in meaningful interpersonal work and to achieve occupational autonomy. It may therefore go against the grain for most counsellors to be economically ruthless and indifferent to issues of social ethics. It is my impression that most counsellors are politically somewhat left-wing and probably find it difficult to ignore their own altruistic leanings. In addition, they are likely to have high ethical standards and a commitment to reflecting critically on their own work. This commitment to constant self-examination may be a source of considerable stress. The isolation in which most private practitioners work – Goldberg (1992) refers to sole practice as the 'most serious peril' for therapists – deprives them of feedback on the quality of their work. Supervision notwithstanding, counsellors working alone probably often experience doubt about their performance, and may fantasize about how successful other counsellors are. This phenomenon has been called 'closet competition'.

Sometimes counsellors must decide whether to take on a client or to refer them to a more suitable counsellor or service. Counsellors are required to keep abreast of professional developments, but also to be aware of the social factors influencing clients' distress. Taken seriously, this demands that the counsellor consider the possible counterproductive features of counselling for some clients, including its economic costs (Pilgrim, 1992). Counsellors may feel uncomfortable with the implicit politics of private practice and may believe that counselling should be freely available as a right (Holmes and Lindley, 1989). They may experience tension between a 'philosophy of service' (Herron and Welt, 1992) and the pragmatics of economic survival.

Counsellors' responses to the stresses

Unhealthy responses

The largest single stress I experience is economic, and my own unhealthiest response to this is to feel angry at myself for not having foreseen the difficulties. I become resentful towards (my fantasy of) those counsellors who appear to have it easy. Having seen the rather plush houses and consulting rooms of some counsellors, it is easy for my residual working-class bile to surface. 'It's all right for them!' is then my inner response. Counselling is a game for the middle-class mafia, I tell myself. This is linked with an 'if only' inner refrain: if only I had a psychology degree, a PhD, friends in the right places, a house on the hill. I do not condemn myself for this envy and resentment, but I recognize that it is not helpful to me or to those around me. Worrying about shortage or unpredictability of income has sometimes led me to become irritable and, in the extreme, insomniac. This, of course, can result in exhaustion and in lower levels of attentiveness and creativity with clients. Other counsellors, depending on their personalities, will of course react differently (Cooper and Payne, 1991).

Knowing that *some* counsellors and trainers are doing very well out of counselling can also lead me to doubt my competency: perhaps I simply don't have what it takes, otherwise I'd be able to command the high fees and waiting lists that some do! Resentment, cynicism and self-doubt sometimes feed each other. Counsellors are not alone in experiencing the rise and fall of their fortunes and moods in this way. I have sometimes felt like a hopeful or hopeless out-of-work actor. Fortunately I have never felt seriously depressed in relation to these stresses, but we know from evidence that a proportion of therapists and mental health workers experience quite severe depression and in some cases resort to suicide. These degrees of distress are more likely to occur when the practitioner ('wounded healer') has predisposing personality characteristics, rather than directly as a result of occupational stress.

A particularly sinister unhealthy response, in my view, is the calculated holding on to clients, persuading them that they need more frequent sessions, longer in therapy, or that they need to join a group you are running. Although I have only anecdotal evidence, this seems to be by no means a rare practice. Perhaps counsellors who maximize their income in these ways do so with the best of intentions for clients, but I believe it involves a dangerous temptation. Counsellors and therapists are in a powerful position with clients and can easily persuade them of such 'needs'. Even when they are not consciously calculating how much they may get out of clients, counsellors may be unconsciously tempted to respond to their own economic insecurity by selling more of their services than are really needed.

A quite different form of unhealthy response, which has recently become all too familiar to me, is to throw yourself into work all the harder. After my worst economic trough, work began to increase, I began to say yes to everything that came my way and gradually found myself working six or seven days a week, often evenings as well as days. This may be something commonly experienced by many self-employed people: to take on all the work you can while it's there. It has sometimes meant that I've squeezed in far too many appointments. Counselling (as well as supervision and training) requires time for reflection, reading and preparation, yet when you need to chase every penny, such quiet times seem an impossible luxury. Also, when you yourself are in 'manic' or 'workaholic' mode, it is sometimes difficult to adjust within counselling sessions to clients who are moving at a very slow pace. I have also been aware of becoming at times the 'absent father', too engrossed in the 'caring business' to care for my own family. This is a painful irony, but I know from discussions with other counsellors that I am not alone in having this experience. Many examples are given by Guy (1987) and Goldberg (1992).

Healthy responses

I think it is essential that you are honest about the stresses involved in private practice. Whether with a supervisor or partner, it is sometimes necessary to offload your anxieties about money and about a too low or too high caseload, and to try to explore solutions. It can help if you have a good sense of humour and can laugh things off, or an ability to shed tears when necessary. Intense private rumination on your plight does not usually help. I have found it helpful at times to refer to rational-emotive principles (Ellis, 1988), or more broadly to stoical principles which remind me that life is not a rose garden, but is rarely as awful as it may appear in the cinema of my own troubled mind. I have learnt to some extent to regard each day as a unit of adversity or challenge ('sufficient unto the day are the evils thereof') and to meet certain obstacles when necessary, but not prematurely.

Following such cognitive strategies for healthy adaptation, I increasingly turn to problem-solving mode. What can I do about this problem? Who shall I contact to ask about more work? Which pieces of work are not paying off? What am I putting off that I would be better off facing and completing? I address these questions and take whatever actions I can. In addition, I sometimes simply take a few hours off. In that time I may go to the local gym and work out, visit a bookshop and browse, or see an old friend. I find a periodic change of mental and physical application essential for my equilibrium.

I am sometimes reminded that what I consider stresses are not necessarily perceived in the same way by others. I have mentioned the concern about cooking smells and innocently intruding children. Although I may be uneasy about these, several clients have told me how reassuring it is to be in a 'normal household'. Often this domestic reality will remind clients of scenes from their own lives. One client heard my son being scolded by his mother downstairs. 'I always hated being told off,' she said, and went on to recall and explore some very salient issues from her own childhood. As a counsellor in such a setting, you are not seen as omniscient or inscrutable but as the obviously imperfect human being you are. I believe this can be used as a healthy reminder to clients that you are not a guru and that counselling is not a ritual taking place in a vacuum.

One of the healthiest responses of all, perhaps, is to remind yourself that you have chosen self-employment for good reasons. Along with the trials and tribulations of an unpredictable income and domestic inconvenience goes the freedom of 'being your own boss'. In this sense, private practice exactly mirrors a central principle of counselling ethics – autonomy, or self-determination. There is something very liberating about not depending on a salaried job, a nine-to-five routine and a paternalistic organization. I remember how refreshing it felt to me at first, not having to wait on bosses' whims, not having to attend dreary meetings and not having to ask for time off. I also realized how much more real work I could achieve when I didn't waste half the day gossiping with colleagues and wrestling with organizational politics and rituals. Employment is usually economically safer than self-employment, but often more infantilizing. This comparison becomes all the more interesting for those counsellors who, like myself, maintain ongoing professional commitments (part-time employment or engagements which resemble salaried employment) alongside a private practice. It is a healthy response to the stress of private practice to diversify your workload, although this very diversification can also take its toll.

Suggestions for improved coping

Emotional and physical stress
Isolation, as Guy (1987) has so clearly demonstrated, is one of the main sources of stress for private practitioners. The higher your caseload, the longer you spend shut away with one other person at a time. Depending on how you structure your time, you may face a series of clients every day with very different and intense emotions, some of which may rub off on you. Can you withstand long days full of distressed clients, each arriving on the hour, for five days a week? Personally, I offer clients a full (60-minute) hour, and I always leave at least 15 minutes between appointments, and more often half an hour. In a sense this may be poor time management (insofar as time is money), but it is, for me, good stress management. I would suggest that counsellors carefully

consider strategies for managing time and allowing for rest and holiday periods.

If your problems include economic ones, you may be tempted to reduce the supervision you receive to a minimum. A disadvantage of being in private practice is that you have to pay for your own supervision, further training and conference attendance (and in addition to paying for these, you have to forfeit income during that time). The more counselling you are doing, the more supervision you need, not only in order to discuss your clients, but also to monitor your own overall stress level and coping resources. If you cannot afford frequent supervision, seek out colleagues and arrange for peer supervision or, as I have sometimes done, seek out allied professionals who are keen to develop their supervisory skills and will agree to supervise you free in return for the experience you give them. Similar considerations apply to further personal therapy, which is costly, especially if you are on a low income. Goldberg (1992) reiterates the Freudian view that personal analysis should be repeated periodically, but he also suggests that self-analysis can be a powerful tool for the therapist's self-replenishment.

Take time out to be with your loved ones. Discuss with your partner how she or he feels about your working hours and your occupational hazards. Do you appear preoccupied after seeing clients? Do you grind your teeth during your sleep and show signs of chronic anxiety over money? As well as discussing these kinds of issue, remember to allow time for the simple pleasures of life which are not related to counselling at all. Maeder (1990) notes that therapists often fail to maintain close personal friendships when they become immersed in clients' emotional turmoil and forget to nourish themselves with the lighter side of life. Sometimes counsellors have had enough of listening to clients and may, without being aware of it, avoid further interpersonal 'demands'. Ensure, however, that you keep in meaningful contact with good friends. Balance your professional commitments with recreational and physically challenging pursuits. Counselling is sedentary and should probably be balanced by physical activity like sport, dancing, yoga, meditation, massage or whatever your preference may be.

Environmental stress
If you must work from home, consider in advance the issues that arise from the location and layout of your house, as well as family considerations. Do you have a suitable private room? Can your family accommodate to clients' appointment times? Some

psychotherapy training institutes stipulate the environmental conditions that therapists must offer clients; for example that there must be a waiting room or area, a separate toilet or separate exit for clients. Indeed, it is reasonable to suppose that many counsellors do not know what they should be offering, since there are no real guidelines on the subject.

Blower and Rink (1987) recommend establishing a group practice based in hired rooms. This incurs extra costs, but provides you with colleagues, as well as a working environment which is probably safer and may also be more accessible for clients, since you can choose rooms close to public transport. In some cities there are organizations offering a comprehensive deal, where you can rent rooms on a daily or half-day basis and also buy into a receptionist's time. These arrangements are more costly and demand more organization than working from your own home, but they are worth considering for the greater peace of mind they can offer. You may also prefer to establish completely clear boundaries between work and home.

Economic stress

Calculate the lowest amount you can afford to live on. Work out realistically what all your expenses will be and hence, what you will have to charge your clients. I recommend that before anyone commits themselves to self-employed counselling, they should clarify the economic risks in their own mind. Ideally, training courses should always include training in the issues of private practice. These should always be thought out beforehand, because you need to consider whether your house is suitable, whether you live in a favourable setting, and whether you can afford the risks involved (Margenau, 1990).

I recommend that you do not rely on counselling to supply all your income, unless you have extremely good qualifications and contacts, extended contracts for work, or if you do not need to make much money. Some practitioners keep a full-time or part-time job and begin to develop a private practice 'on the side', making the transition only when they are confident that there will be sufficient work to keep them solvent. Another way to offset the insecurity of private practice is to put aside savings. Also, keep in contact with local organizations, whose staff may refer clients to you or hire you to offer supervision or training. If you are very ambitious, you may promote yourself vigorously by making professional contacts, sitting on committees, facilitating workshop events and writing. Counsellors are often reluctant to market themselves (one of Goldberg's, 1992, questionnaire respondents described the business side of being a therapist as 'loathsome') but you need to avoid thinking magically that clients will just queue at your door without some effort on your part. If you have a taste for literature on the psychology of wealth creation, many positive thinking and neurolinguisitic programming techniques are available for helping you into 'prosperity consciousness'.

Ethical and ideological stress

Consider how committed you are to the principle of private practice, as opposed to being uncertain about it politically. The pertinent political arguments are discussed by David Pilgrim in Dryden (1993). Think carefully about the kind of counselling or therapy you wish to offer and what the economic implications may be. If your aim is to provide effective, short-term counselling, which may mean purposefully discouraging clients from becoming dependent on you, then this forms an ethic which may be at odds with the more economically convenient ethos of long-term therapy. McCormick (1990) charges higher fees for sessions of (time-limited) cognitive-analytic therapy, because these often require the counsellor to put in more work than other approaches. Herron and Welt (1992) discuss the meaning of fees and attitudes towards them. Study these considerations and decide whether you need to charge more for intensive, short-term counselling than for long-term.

One compelling argument for private practice is that many clients have no comparable service available to them. Certain organizations offer free or low-cost counselling for relationship problems, alcoholism, HIV and cancer, for example, but many people fall between all such categories and find themselves on a year-long waiting list for an urgent problem. Some clients have told me how pleased they were that I could see them so promptly when the alternative was a GP who didn't want to listen or months on a waiting list. At these times I feel few qualms about taking the money and this sense of providing a timely service feels satisfying, thus reducing any ethical stress I may experience.

In conclusion

Counselling in private practice can be very stressful, for the reasons given. However, put this into perspective by remembering that millions of people probably work at far less fulfilling jobs and earn rather less too. If you are considering, but are not yet committed to, becoming a private practitioner, consult Shimberg (1975) and Falloon (1992) for practical and marketing ideas. Guy

(1987) and Goldberg (1992) demonstrate some of what may be in store for you as you become a mature practitioner. I recommend (for clients' protection) that all counsellors and therapists work within organizations for some years before launching into private practice. If you have the inclination and time for systematic analysis and problem-solving in relation to your occupational stress as a counsellor, consult Palmer and Dryden (1994). If you prefer a more transpersonal approach, Harding (1990) offers innovative and inspirational perspectives on transcending stress.

In Goldberg's (1992) survey of master psychotherapists, the 'theme of overcoming adversity' permeated many of their responses. Counsellors who wrestle with and overcome the adversities in private practice implicitly model the spirit of negotiating and overcoming stress to their clients.

Acknowledgements

I should like to thank Liz Friedrich, Clare Townsend and Gabriel Syme for sharing their experiences and knowledge. Above all, I acknowledge the greater stress that my wife, Marie, has endured and continues to endure (usually) very tolerantly.

References

'1985 survey report', *Psychotherapy Finances*, 12 (9): 1–8.

Blower, V. and Rink, V. (1987) 'Counselling in a private practice', *Counselling*, 60: 10–13.

Cooper, C. and Payne, R. (eds) (1991) *Personality and Stress*. Chichester: Wiley.

Dryden, W. (ed.) (1993) *Questions and Answers on Counselling in Action*. London: Sage.

Edelwich, J. and Brodsky, A. (1980) *Burn-Out*. New York: Human Sciences.

Ellis, A. (1988) *How to Stubbornly Refuse to Make Yourself Miserable about Anything – Yes, Anything!* Secaucus, NJ: Lyle Stuart.

Falloon, V. (1992) *How to Get More Clients*. London: Brainwave.

Farber, B.A. and Heifetz, L.J. (1982) 'The process and dimensions of burn out in psychotherapists', *Professional Psychology*, 13: 293–301.

Feltham, C. (1993) 'What are the difficulties in making a living as a counsellor?' in W. Dryden (ed.), *Questions and Answers on Counselling in Action*. London: Sage.

Goldberg, C. (1992) *The Seasoned Psychotherapist*. New York: Norton.

Guy, J.D. (1987) *The Personal Life of the Psychotherapist*. New York: Wiley.

Harding, D. (1990) *Head Off Stress*. London: Arkana.

Herron, W.G. and Welt, S.R. (1992) *Money Matters: The Fee in Psychotherapy and Psychoanalysis*. Hove: Guilford.

Holmes, J. and Lindley, R. (1989) *The Values of Psychotherapy*. Oxford: Oxford University Press.

McCormick, E. (1990) 'Cognitive-analytic therapy in private practice', in A. Ryle, *Cognitive-Analytic Therapy*. Chichester: Wiley.

Maeder, T.C. (1990) *Children of Psychiatrists and Other Psychotherapists*. New York: Harper & Row.

Margenau, E. (ed.) (1990) *The Encyclopedic Handbook of Private Practice*. New York: Gardner Press.

Mirowsky, J. and Ross, C.E. (1989) *Social Causes of Psychological Distress*. New York: Aldine de Gruyer.

Palmer, S. and Dryden, W. (1994) *Stress Counselling*. London: Sage.

Pilgrim, D. (1992) 'Psychotherapy and political evasions', in W. Dryden and C. Feltham (eds), *Psychotherapy and its Discontents*. Buckingham: Open University Press.

Rowan, J. (1988) 'The psychology of furniture', *Counselling*, 64: 21–4.

Shimberg, E. (1975) *The Handbook of Private Practice in Psychology*. New York: Brunner-Mazel.

Sutherland, J.D. (1989) *Fairbairn's Journey into the Interior*. London: Free Association Books.

Syme, G. (1994) *Counselling in Independent Practice*. Buckingham: Open University Press.

8   The Stresses of Directing a University Counselling Service

Peter Ross

Twenty years ago the director of a university counselling service in the UK probably worked on his own. He was one of about fifty such people, and mostly worked in a reactive way with individual clients. Overwhelmed by demand, the planning of service delivery was impossible. Today, the director of a university counselling service probably works at the head of a team of perhaps four to eight people. He will be one of about a hundred such people, with the number of institutions designated 'university' increasing by the day. Within the older universities, the director will most often run an independent counselling service, reporting directly to a pro-vice-chancellor. The latter, acting as dean, will be in charge of other services too; such as the library, computer centre and careers service.

In the newer universities, the director may well report to a student services manager, be part of a more integrated system, and have relatively little autonomy, even over such matters as the service budget. In these the director may have a study adviser, an overseas student adviser, a financial adviser and an educational adviser on the staff, in addition to counsellors.

In both older and newer universities, staff may be charged with responsibility for generating income from outside the university through service fees, research or consultancy. Service delivery will be a function of strategic planning, not reactive. The work of the service will include increasing amounts of group work and personal development programmes (building confidence, team leadership skills, presentation skills and so on) often in co-operation with the careers service. In addition, the service may run clinical pro-grammes focused, for example, upon stress management, eating problems or social skills. There may also be in-service training for tutors, security staff and catering staff, designed to help them cope with the large numbers of students from other cultures. There will almost always be orientation and support programmes for mature

students and other non-traditional students. The service will also
provide daily telephone back-up and consultation for the many
staff in the university who, of necessity, deal with student problems
without needing formal counselling qualifications, and offer
supervision of trainee counsellors. Many university counselling
services also provide counselling for staff, or staff and families, in
Employee Assistant Programme fashion.

The traditional function of sitting in an office waiting for clients
to turn up is long gone. Nowadays, demand almost always exceeds
staff resources. The traditional figure of 5 per cent of the student
body who use the counselling service each year is steadily
increasing. In these circumstances, the director of a university
counselling service finds herself having to devise methods to assess
who will be accepted for counselling and who will not, and
devising waiting-list management techniques. A director will, in
addition, find increasing amounts of paperwork necessary in order
to justify standards and use of resources, both of which are under
scrutiny as never before. A director will serve on numerous
committees. At Reading, for example, the director chairs the
committee which organizes the Overseas Student Welcome
Programme (reception, orientation and support of about 1,000
new overseas students a year), sits on the 'Failures' committee –
the court of last resort for those who have failed examinations –
and on the 'Special Needs' committee, which is responsible for
smoothing the transition of all disabled students into and through
the university. Many directors teach counselling, do research, and
publish as well. In short, the director of a university counselling
service serves at the head of a diversely qualified professional team
which is constantly under pressure from the demands of a huge
and complex organization. The potential for stress can readily be
seen to be great.

The nature of the stresses

Research has been published on the stresses of most groups of
health professionals (Payne and Firth-Cozens, 1987). There is no
published research on the stresses of directors of university
counselling services. This discussion must therefore draw upon
related studies which, while providing useful pointers on director
stress, provide few grounds for firm conclusions. The job of
director falls into two clear but closely related elements – that of
counsellor and that of manager. Both elements are subject to
stress. It is important to be clear that much of the attraction of
such a job is the challenge and excitement of the personal and

technical demands. Only when the demands are experienced as consistent overdemands to which personal adaptations are not readily and flexibly made, do we experience 'stress'. If the overdemand is experienced over a long period we may experience 'burnout'. Maslach and Jackson (1981) defined this in terms of emotional exhaustion, a negative and cynical perception of clients (labelled 'depersonalization') and depression-bordering feelings of failure. It follows that what one director may experience as excitement, another may experience as despairing exhaustion, and that perception is critical to coping.

As far as the counsellor element of the job of director is concerned, no studies of counsellor stress in the UK had been made until Hope (1985) undertook a pioneering study of student counsellors. It is important to be clear that this was not a study of directors, but of student counsellors in general. He found no evidence of burnout, but some evidence of stress, with 14 per cent of the 185 counsellor sample feeling overworked nearly all the time, and a further 25 per cent feeling overworked often. Of the 185 counsellors, 8 counselled face to face for 30 or more hours a week and an astonishing 15 did so for 45 or more hours a week. In the last three or four years the rapid expansion of student numbers in UK universities has not been accompanied by a commensurate expansion of counselling resources. It is not an accident that only in this period have most services generated a 'waiting list' for counselling. No doubt a replication of this research would now yield significant evidence of stress symptoms – headaches, fatigue, irritability, physical tension, minor aches and pains, absentmindedness, indecisiveness, poor concentration, wanting to get away from others, loss of confidence, agitation – reported in small measure by Hope.

The perceived triggers for stress among counsellors as reported by Hope were: difficult relationships with colleagues; too many clients; the special demands of clients who are suicidal, depressed, panicky and so on; lack of clerical and secretarial support; the 'top-up' demands from other roles such as teaching and committee work; institutional problems such as politics and split site working; unsympathetic attitudes and unrealistic expectations from senior managers; inadequate time for training, conferences, or even keeping up with the literature; constant exposure to unhappiness; and the unpredictability of exposure on the front line of primary care.

About a third of the time of a university counsellor is spent on clinical work very similar to that of a clinical psychologist. American studies (Thoreson and Skorina, 1986) suggest that psychologists suffer stress levels at least as high as those of the general population. No studies on stress in UK clinical psychologists appeared until Cushway (1992) examined 287 clinical trainees. Although factors specific to trainees were found, general factors such as poor supervision, lack of feedback and support, conflicting ideology and fear of disapproval from superiors reflect findings from similar studies.

We can expect with some confidence then that the director of a counselling service in her role as counsellor will share most if not all of the perceived triggers for stress. But what of the director in her role as manager?

A director has to manage other counsellors and their caseloads, manage other professionals such as advisers, argue for resources, defend a budget against competing department heads, negotiate policy with management committees, develop and set objectives together with strategies for monitoring achievement of those objectives, negotiate for and select new staff, write job descriptions and large numbers of reports. Some examples may clarify these tasks. Within the last few years the University of Reading Counselling Service has had two major investigations by the University Council into its need for resources. Its functions and relationships with other internal services have also been examined. These investigations have involved extensive consultation and negotiation in committee together with draft after draft of complex reports on cost-effectiveness. The quality of such reports may determine whether the service continues to be funded at all, or is dramatically altered in nature. Within the last year, inspectors from the Higher Education Funding Council and the Higher Education Quality Council (division of Quality Audit), have looked at the quality of systems and standards the counselling service adopts and how it knows whether it meets these standards or not, as well as inspecting the actual quality of the output according to external criteria. Procedure manuals on everything from complaints to initial assessment, client files and confidentiality were written to near British Standard 5750, for the purpose. As these quality inspection reports are made public, their outcome naturally matters very much to an institution and there is considerable pressure, both self and other imposed, to 'get it right'! It should be borne in mind that inspections occur with little warning, and the extensive paperwork is involved against a background of ever-rising waiting lists. A 'good' inspector's report will influence favourably the atmosphere surrounding subsequent submissions for resources. A 'bad' inspector's report will 'let down' the institution, to say the least. Refusal to see 'urgent' clients while writing such material may bring even greater trouble in the short run. The temptation for directors is to work longer and longer hours, knowing full well that tired and irritable counsellors are unlikely to do good work. Given that directors were full-time counsellors before they began to manage too, one would expect them to be particularly aware of such ambiguities. Kelloway and Barling (1991) have shown that role ambiguity and role conflict are involved in emotional exhaustion and depersonalization.

Myers and McCaulley (1985) researched the personality characteristics of health professionals. They divided their subjects into 'thinking' and 'feeling' types, and discovered that those attracted to health fields such as counselling represented a disproportionate number of feeling to thinking types: the ratio was 80/20. By the same measure, managers represent a disproportionate number of 'thinking' to 'feeling' types: 80/20. Directors who go from counselling a suicidal student in one hour to chairing a large committee in the next are very aware of the need to 'change gear', and how difficult it is. The role of chairperson often requires a degree of deliberate distancing from feeling, which is usually incongruent with the role of counsellor.

Naisberg-Fenning *et al.* (1991) showed that psychiatrists who had high levels of repressive ability showed less stress and burnout than others. It has long been known that people whose arousal levels are easily inhibited, who repress things easily, are better at coping with invasive surgery and disorders like severe burns and polio (Cohen and Lazarus, 1973; Hamburg and Adams, 1967). There is evidence then that personality characteristics are relevant to the level of stress experienced as well as the ability deliberately to alter one's perceptions. There is also evidence from the same sources that trainees and others whose levels of sensitivity, empathy, anxiety and dependent need to please are high, are particularly prone to stress and burnout.

Maslach (1982) and Naisberg-Fenning *et al.* (1991) found that health professionals tend to show less stress and burnout with age and tenure. No doubt those findings would also be true of directors of counselling services they reflect less direct involvement with clients, more control over one's environment with seniority, and an increase in learned coping mechanisms with experience. The latter may represent a more internal locus of control, and is very important for stress control. Cooper and Baglioni (1988) have proposed a comprehensive theory to explain the link between environmental stresses and mental health. In stress studies, two personality characteristics have been seen as important mediators. The first, known as 'locus of control', relates to individuals who see their actions as being either largely irrelevant to outcome (who are said to have an external locus of control); or individuals who perceive events as being substantially influenceable by them (who are said to have an internal locus of control). Most studies show that the greater the perception of control, the lower the experience of stress. It must be clear that directors, most of whom will have experienced extensive personal psychotherapy and will on a daily basis help individuals gain more control over their lives, will themselves have a tendency towards an internal locus of control by virtue of their training. The second personality characteristic identified in the literature as an important mediator of stress is 'Type A'; often stereotyped as the competitive, ambitious, hard-driving and obsessive executive. Directors of counselling services show ambition in their wish to take charge, compete with others in a university for resources and recognition, and are often hard-driving initiators of private counselling clinics and publishing programmes. Opportunities for financial success in the field are greater than they used to be. We could well conclude that some external locus of control is also relevant to many directors of counselling services. When Rees and Cooper (1992) examined stress patterns among 1,176 health professionals including 147 psychologists, counsellors and members of other professions allied to medicine, they found evidence for a tendency towards internal locus of control. By implication, counsellors probably have some inbuilt inoculation against stress compared with non-health-care workers. There is no evidence to suggest that this applies to directors of counselling services. Indeed, as we have seen, there is reason to doubt it until more evidence is available. Having examined environmental stresses, symptoms of stress and mediators of stress, it is now possible to turn to directors' responses.

Directors' responses to stress

As already noted, there are no direct studies of the way directors of counselling services respond to stress. However, as far as the counsellor part of their role is concerned, Hope (1985) discovered that the most popular form of coping was talking, in the form of discussion with colleagues, partners, friends, in personal therapy and supervision and so on. Some 72 per cent of the women counsellors and 50 per cent of the male counsellors listed talk as their first preference. Relaxation techniques such as meditation, yoga, autogenics or prayer were listed as personally useful by 49 per cent of the men and 55 per cent of the women. Some 47 per cent of the men and 22 per cent of the women rated physical exercise as useful. Other coping activities were social contact, music, gardening, DIY, smoking, drinking and reading.

Studies of stress among successful managers (Quick *et al.*, 1990) show that although mediating factors are often idiosyncratic, managers resistant to stress most often actively control it by giving and getting good social support. This implies the ability to form good relationships, the very core of counselling training. The studies also show that successful managers often 'cut off' by reading widely outside their field. Personal experience suggests that directors of university counselling services do just the same.

There exists an organization called the Heads of University Counselling Services Group, a section of the Association for Student Counselling. It meets formally once a term but in addition small groups meet to work on common problems. This group of some 100 people, with about 50 very actively involved, combines a commonality of interest with the closeness of knowing people and their work over many years. The group is a closely knit network for support, exchange of information and policy development. Indeed, even the experiences gained from an audit inspection of one university counselling service are immediately available to others. Social activities are a riot of cathartic laughter. In short, a director has only to lift the telephone to find all the support that could be needed.

This group, and the wider Association for Student Counselling, comprising almost all student counsellors in the UK and Ireland, forms a powerful peer reference group. This has important stress reduction implications, all a function of the power of a peer reference group to enhance self-esteem. It has long been known that self-esteem is a powerful stress inoculator. Di Matteo *et al.* (1993) recently found, for example, that dentists' emotional well-being and lack of stress was best predicted by their feelings of being respected and having prestige. Similarly, being respected by management as having a central function rather than being organizationally marginalized is important to counsellors. In recent years one of the most common themes of conversation at meetings and conferences of university counsellors is that of 'the waiting list'. The theme is elaborated to the contrast between the obvious valuing of counselling and respect for counsellors by clients, who clamour to attend, and the lack of valuing implied by management who do not provide adequate resources to meet the demand. Another contrast is with industry. In recent years Employee Assistance Programme schemes have mushroomed. Industrial journals regularly extol the virtues of EAPs and senior managers regularly boast about how cost-effective they are. Not being valued by one's own university management can be balanced against respect and support from peers and colleagues. Indirect valuing by outside sources such as industry and commerce may also enhance self-esteem. The 'locus of control' literature makes it clear that it is all too easy to give one's self-esteem away.

For example, if a particular vice-chancellor does not value counselling, the director of a counselling service may be susceptible to feelings of devaluation. However, most directors have a lengthy training which makes available to them a clear internal locus of control, and great tolerance of ambiguity. A director will use this to make his feelings explicit if necessary: 'He does not value me, but I do, peers do, clients do, and even if my service is temporarily stopped in its tracks, I will work my way around my vice-chancellor through committees and network support.' Many directors have been or are also in private practice and are very aware of the positive feedback from clients and those who refer them. Far from being a source of stress, as it may be for inexperienced counsellors, most directors seem to view being in private practice as a relatively simple, supportive and positive experience by contrast to the everyday complexities of organiz-ational life. Directors who teach, research and publish similarly have alternative peer reference groups and feedback from them is readily available. It is therefore not difficult for a director, familiar with the theory of locus of control, to deliberately and explicitly use her knowledge to reinforce her perception that she has it within her power to control, or at least seriously to influence in the long run, a large part of her professional life and that of her counselling service.

Unlike most industrial and commercial management where stress is imposed by project schedules, a director of a university counselling service works within an academic year, and the terms, or increasingly semesters, within which an academic year is divided. Workload varies with term and vacation periods. This used to make a lot more difference than it does nowadays. Now fewer home students actually go home due to family break-up from the highest divorce rate in Europe; and more postgraduate, international, mature and part-time students continue to work and reside in universities even in 'vacations'. However, there is certainly less client demand out of term. This momentary 'breathing space' enables a director to attend to non-client demands, such as budget submissions, planning meetings and report writing.

No studies of how counsellor stress varies over an academic year have been done but teacher stress appears to vary (Kinnunen and

Leskinen, 1989) particularly within unique school environments. No doubt directors' stress varies with semester variations and unique university cultures. However general stress points appear to be

The very beginning of the year (October) when large numbers of homesick and disorientated students line up to be seen. At the same time brief information speeches have to be given repeatedly to different groups of new students and new tutors. New full and part-time staff of one's own have to be settled in at the same time.

The month of December, when students become aware that a real home is not available to them for Christmas celebrations, yet all around it appears that their peers are busily planning vacation pursuits.

The month of January, when admissions to hospital for depression traditionally rise and suicide figures temporarily leap. January also adds as clients all those who thought university would be a new start but, after a term, have discovered that their relationships with others are just as problematic as before university, and are driven to do something about it.

The pre-summer examination period when 'urgent' arrivals, distraught with panic, must be seen despite long waiting lists.

At such times weekend recovery periods provide respite. However, as Kinnunen and Leskinen have shown, during prolonged periods of excess demand 'recovery' ceases to take place among teachers, over a mere weekend. No doubt this is also true of directors of university counselling services.

In every large organization long-simmering issues and themes emerge from groups and committees with no prior warning to others not directly involved. These matters then become urgent. Senior managers request detailed written input on such matters by a short deadline, which, to a director with a packed and committed diary for weeks ahead, looks impossible without cancelling significant client space. Cancellation may upset clients, colleagues who have to bear additional pressures, tutors who complain their tutees are not being seen, or medical staff awaiting an assessment. Quite apart from this, there is the director's own exasperation at yet another blow to a carefully planned professional programme with clients. Few directors fail to use time management techniques to plan work, meet known deadlines, and leave 'blank' space in a diary for the as yet unknown events which it can readily be predicted will need a rapid response. Regardless of what strategies one uses for planning ahead, it is very difficult to preserve such spaces in a diary without feeling 'uncaring' and appearing 'uncaring' in the face of the need to hand. 'Cognitive' techniques are often employed for this reason.

The 'manager' talks to the 'counsellor' role: 'We're all in the same boat. My medical colleagues will not permit "emergency" time to be pre-booked. Such time can only be filled on the day. I have to do the same. People will just have to talk to their tutors or hall wardens, or doctors, or friends, or anyone. I have to have priorities. I have to have boundaries. If needs are not met, that's tough. I can only use the resources I've got.' While such self-talk helps, it does so partly as a result of distancing self from feeling. Every manager in every organization has to tolerate such ambiguities.

All universities are increasing the use of part-time staff in all areas of their operations. Despite the understandable logic of holding down staff costs – with no pensions or out-of-term salaries to pay – the very act of employing part-time staff reduces traditional ways in which all managers, including directors, have managed their stress. Delegation, for example, has always been used not only to reduce stress, but to train others. It is not easy to do this when staff often are not in the office to handle queries. To work longer hours oneself is always tempting as the easier solution. This temptation is untenable in the long term, and must usually be resisted.

Suggestions for improved coping

Most counsellors have regular supervision, or consultative support, for their clinical load. Directors of university counselling services do so; it is not only supportive and enriching but a requirement for professional membership of the British Association for Counselling. Industry and commerce have long recognized a similar need for consultative support. In that context it is called 'management consultancy'. It provides managers with an outsider with whom they can reflect upon structure and process, preventing them from becoming locked into a restraining way of looking at problems by feeding in new ideas and questioning established ones.

Universities are reluctant to fund the considerable expense of employing management consultants even when the need is recognized. However, failing this, regular supervision for directors can be extended from focusing upon clinical issues to management issues as well. The management issues which could be reflected upon with possible benefit are numerous. The British government has recently issues an 'Education Charter' which attempts to clarify what students should expect from university services. While a student should expect a reply to a letter within 10 days, it is not at all clear what a student should expect as a reasonable wait before counselling begins. Nor is it clear what implications this may have for specifications of the boundaries of client catchment populations. Formulating possible policy options for management could greatly benefit from consultative support. This helps to reduce stress, even if the everyday tensions inherent in any waiting list remain.

The same is true of formulating policy, and implementing it, on computerizing client databases. Some information is available through the Association for Student Counselling Research Committee. However, unique circumstances need unique solutions, and few directors of university counselling services are either computer literate enough, or indeed have sufficient time, to design and implement adequate solutions on their own.

Another management issue to which attention needs to be paid on a regular basis is the increasing risk of legal action against counsellors. Services which have implemented quality systems will have complaint procedures. Complaints will be against individual counsellors as well as the organization. They may involve, for example, allegations of damage due to neglect in terminating counselling; or alleged neglect leading to a suicide attempt or suicide. An increase in general knowledge and education, awareness of legal opportunity, and a growing emphasis on 'rights' as defined in government charters all lead to a higher risk of complaints. Management has to be focused not only on early monitoring of possible problematic cases but on procedures designed to be defensive. The most important is an adequate procedure for the detailed assessment of cases in the first place. Consultative support, both clinical and legal, can greatly reduce stress in a director by increasing confidence that everything that can be done to reduce risk is being done.

Counselling is an occupation where the risks of client suicide, for example, are high and even a poor strategic judgement on the part of the counsellor can lead to increased difficulty and suffering for the client, the client's friends and family, employer, and even the counsellor. Years of personal observation indicate that poor judgements are most often made during periods of tiredness and emotional vulnerability. To be able to take responsibility for such actions without destructive self-blame is an important stress coping method, for the next client awaits. In a study of young doctors, also well trained and selected for empathy, transparency and self-criticism, Firth-Cozens (1992) found that no objective measure of workload, such as number of extra patients, featured as a good predictor of stress. Dispositional factors, such as capacity for self-criticism, did.

An important characteristic of well trained and experienced counsellors is the fine-tuned capacity to reflect, if necessary critically, upon oneself and one's performance. There is a fine line between honest critical reflection and self-blame, especially for a director who like any good manager takes the view that, whatever the problem, 'the buck stops here'. A director can greatly improve not only their own coping capacity, but that of the team by encouraging an atmosphere of transparency among the counselling team. The director benefits from support from colleagues which discourages self-blame while encouraging the taking of responsibility. The director of a counselling service is quite rightly expected to see the more difficult cases, and is expected to sort out difficulties – clinical, organizational and 'political' – which arise from the work of other counsellors. The director is quite rightly expected to make unenviable judgements, for example about which needy client will be accepted for counselling and which will not. There are seldom 'good' solutions to such problems only 'less bad' ones. Mutual empathy among the counselling team on these matters can greatly reduce the stress of the whole team.

Apart from these factors the most important way to reduce stress appears to be to bring about change in organizational structure and culture. Does it really benefit a university to reduce direct costs by increasing the number of part-timers but in so doing also increasing the stress levels of directors by making delegation almost impossible? Does it make sense to put academic staff under so much pressure to raise contract income that tutorial staff are less available to students and, when the counselling service then becomes overwhelmed by the consequent demand, fail to put substitute resources into counselling?

Organizational attention is now turning to focus on 'quality'. The systems thinking that underlies organizational approaches to quality demands that resources are specified at the same time as objectives are defined, because if they are not, adequate feedback loops will soon expose the gap. The director of a university counselling service has a wonderful opportunity to influence not only counselling service structures but the structure of the entire welfare system. This influence can reduce the potential of the structure for triggering stress in everyone, including all those who work in the counselling service, not least the director. The heads of University Counselling Services group is already hard at work on this task, and the Committee of Vice-Chancellors and Principals of the Universities of the UK (CVCP) expect to publish the results, as quality benchmarks, in 1995.

However carefully an organization is structured, the inherent paradoxes of life together with the imponderables of Murphy's Law and the uniqueness of human behaviour will continue to shine through. For this reason the anti-stress weapon of last resort for directors must remain humour and laughter. Lefcourt and Martin (1986), pioneers of the use of humour as an antidote to stress, remain a fertile source of perspective for the director under siege from stress.

References

Cohen, F. and Lazarus, R.S. (1973) 'Active coping processes, coping dispositions and recovery from surgery', *Psychosomatic Medicine*, 35: 357–9.

Cooper, C.L. and Baglioni, A.J. (1988) 'A structural model approach towards the development of a theory of the link between stress and mental health', *British Journal of Medical Psychology*, 61: 87–102.

Cushway, D. (1992) 'Stress in clinical psychology trainees', *British Journal of Clinical Psychology*, 31: 169–79.

Di Matteo, M.R., Shugars, D.A. and Hays, R.D. (1993) 'Occupational stress, life stress and mental health among dentists', *Journal of Occupational and Organizational Psychology*, 66: 153–62.

Firth-Cozens, J. (1992) 'The role of early family experiences in the perception of organizational stress: fusing clinical and organizational perspectives', *Journal of Occupational and Organizational Psychology*, 65: 61–75.

Hamburg, D.A. and Adams, J.E. (1967) 'A perspective on coping behavior: seeking and utilizing information on major transitions', *Archives of General Psychiatry*, 17: 277–84.

Hope, D. (1985) 'Counsellor stress and burnout', MA thesis, University of Reading.

Kelloway, E.K. and Barling, J. (1991) 'Job characteristics, role stress and mental health', *Journal of Occupational Psychology*, 64: 291–304.

Kinnunen, U. and Leskinen, E. (1989) 'Teacher stress during a school year: covariance and mean structure analysis', *Journal of Occupational Psychology*, 62: 111–22.

Lefcourt, H.M. and Martin, R.A. (1986) *Humor and Life Stress: Antidote to Adversity.* New York: Springer-Verlag.

Maslach, C. (1982) *Burn-out – The Cost of Caring.* Englewood Cliffs, NJ: Prentice-Hall.

Maslach, C. and Jackson, S.E. (1981) 'The measurement of experienced burnout', *Journal of Occupational Behaviour*, 2: 99–113.

Myers, I. and McCaulley, A. (1985) *A Guide to the Development and Use of the Myers–Briggs Type Indicator.* Palo Alto: Consulting Psychologists Press.

Naisberg-Fenning, S., Fenning, S., Keinan, G. and Elizur, A. (1991) 'Personality characteristics and proneness to burnout: a study among psychiatrists', *Stress Medicine*, 7: 201–5.

Payne, R. and Firth-Cozens, J. (1987) *Stress in Health Professionals*. Chichester: Wiley.

Quick, J.C., Nelson, D.L. and Quick, J.D. (1990) *Stress and Challenge at the Top: The Paradox of the Successful Executive*. Chichester: Wiley.

Rees, D. and Cooper, C.L. (1992) 'Occupational stress in health service workers in the UK', *Stress Medicine*, 8: 79–90.

Thoreson, R.W. and Skorina, J.K. (1986) 'Alcohol abuse among psychologists', in R. Kilburg, P.E. Nathan and R.W. Thoreson (eds), *Professionals in Distress*. New York: American Psychological Association.

9 The Stresses of Running a Stress Management Centre

Stephen Palmer

The published literature on the topic of running stress management centres is limited although a number of articles do give some insight (Palmer, 1992a, 1993a). The author is currently founder director of a stress centre.

During the 1980s interest in stress and its management grew, with a plethora of articles being published on stress in mass readership magazines and newspapers. In addition, radio and television programmes included interviews with 'stress experts'. The scene was set for an independent stress centre to be established which concentrated on six distinct areas:

stress counselling, stress management and psychotherapy for individuals;

training of health professionals in the field of stress management, stress counselling and psychotherapy;

industrial stress management consultancy;

clinical, counselling and industrial stress research;

publication of books, articles, manuals, audio cassettes and leaflets on stress management and other relevant health-related topics;

a mail-order section marketing suitable goods for sale for the individual and for organizations (books, manuals, cassettes, videos, biofeedback machines and so on).

The Centre was established in 1987 in south-east London. The director decided that it would be totally self-financing, due to his previous negative experience of running voluntary organizations on local government and European Community grants. Income would be obtained from the six key areas listed above.

This chapter will highlight the stress-related problems for all of the staff involved in the Centre's daily affairs, not just the director or the counsellors. The next section provides some information about organizational structure, the staff and consultants.

The Centre's director has ultimate control over the different strands of the organization although on a day-to-day basis different staff may be responsible for training, counselling, co-ordinating the counselling service, administration, book-keeping, sales and purchases. The director has to respond to advice from the Centre's Honorary Advisory Board and the six external course-accrediting bodies. The director needs and has skills in management, financial accounting and public relations as well as in counselling and training.

The training staff are self-employed consultants who are counsellors and trainers with industrial experience. These trainers are usually head-hunted, as the combination of counselling and industrial training experience is not always easy to find among job applicants. The trainers are also selected according to the articles, journals and books they have written or edited. Each is a specialist in at least one approach to counselling and psychotherapy.

The counselling team consists of a counselling co-ordinator, trainee placements and experienced counsellors. The latter usually have a psychiatric training or a psychology degree and post graduate qualifications in counselling or psychotherapy, preferably both. In recent years, if trainees on placement show good clinical acumen they are invited to extend their contract after their period of training has ceased. They are also encouraged to publish articles on their research.

The nature of the stresses

The administrator
The administrator has a number of important duties, including the following:

administration of the training courses;

production of course certificates;

dealing with general and specific enquiries from potential and existing individual and organizational clients;

invoicing and chasing up unpaid debts;

payment of wages to staff;

liaising with staff, trainers, students and external course-accrediting bodies;

supporting the director with secretarial back-up.

Due to the large number of short- and long-term courses the Centre regularly holds, the administrator has to deal with a great deal of mundane paperwork. Course supervision dates have to be negotiated with the trainers and supervisors according to their own availability and the availability of rooms. The training rooms also serve as counselling rooms and this can limit the time slots available for each activity. The Centre is often open from 9 a.m. to 9 p.m. seven days a week to enable all of the activities to take place.

In particular, the Diploma in Stress Management programme is a flexible, open-ended modular course. At any one time, this course may have up to 100 students enrolled on it who need to be sent regular course information. Students often apply to undertake a one- or two-day module at short notice. The administrator then has to provide students with the necessary course details and relevant books prior to the course in a very short space of time. She is also very aware of the need to fill vacant places on any course and is reluctant to turn away last-minute applicants.

The administrator is not expected to have counselling or psychotherapy qualifications, yet is regularly asked specific questions by students and potential clients about issues related to training and accreditation which are beyond her remit. This can prove frustrating both for her and for the enquirer.

With the recession, bad debts and returned cheques are an another concern. The administrator may know the debtor personally, which can be an additional stressor.

The counsellors
The experienced counsellors and therapists at the Centre are usually trained in multimodal, behavioural, cognitive-behavioural and rational-emotive behavioural approaches. The emphasis is on a multimodal approach to counselling, therapy and stress management (see Palmer, 1992b). They have also been trained in basic counselling skills. The clients may be referred by general practitioners, hospitals, industry, other counsellors and national registers. In addition, clients may have seen advertisements or articles about the Centre and may refer themselves.

The concept of stress management or stress counselling is often perceived differently by clients and health professionals. Thus there may be a mismatch between what the clients, counsellors and other professionals involved believe the clients will receive. Usually, the counsellor will have limited knowledge of the client's clinical or medical history. In some cases, prior knowledge can be a hindrance as a client may have been misdiagnosed by her doctor, therapist or psychiatrist.

The client is usually keen to start therapy immediately whereas the counsellor may need to spend a number of sessions on assessment. This tension is greatest with clients who are experiencing extreme levels of stress and anxiety. In some cases the counsellor needs to decide whether immediate crisis intervention or other suitable methods are necessary. Some clients feel so overwhelmed by their experiences that they are depressed, with suicidal ideation. The counsellor has to assess the risk of the client taking her own or another's life. If the risk appears to be high then the counsellor needs to ensure that the client receives psychiatric care. The client in her depressed state may have no wish to be helped and the counsellor must deal with this issue before the client decides to leave the session.

In our experience some groups of people are more prone to suffer from stress than others. Clients with disorders such as passive-aggressive, manic-depressive, paranoid, obsessive-compulsive, and borderline personality are more easily distressed by negative life events and daily frustrations. The counsellor may be attempting to help clients who may have long-term, sometimes undiagnosed, intractable problems and whose personalities may sabotage a good working relationship. In the initial stages of stress counselling, these disorders may not always be apparent. Sometimes they are noticed as the client's relationship with the counsellor deteriorates. As the client's underlying schemata are gradually revealed and his behaviour analysed, a diagnosis can be tentatively made.

Stress counselling and stress management can be a psycho-educational active-directive approach, which may not always be what the client desires. The client may wish to spend much of the counselling session discussing her childhood rather than dealing with her current problems. This often occurs if the client has previously received other forms of counselling elsewhere. Although the client's childhood and current problems may be interrelated she may be reluctant to undertake homework assignments such as the completion of dysfunctional thought forms. Other clients may not wish to undertake any self-help assignments for a variety of reasons: for example because it reminds them of school, they cannot see the point, or they fear failure. The counsellor must successfully challenge these reasons if any or further progress is to be made. This is not necessarily easy and may take a fair amount of patience on the part of the counsellor.

Each year the Centre offers a small number of trainee counsellors the opportunity of a placement. In addition to the more usual stressors that the experienced counsellors and therapists encounter, trainees have their own concerns about their performance and about being out of their depth (see Jensen in Chapter 12). They are always on an advanced counselling training programme at Diploma or MSc level, normally at another establishment, so they have the requirements of their course to fulfil as well as the application of their existing skills to stress counselling. They may experience conflict between the active-directive nature of stress counselling and the approach they had previously learnt on a basic counselling course.

The counselling co-ordinator

The counselling co-ordinator, the first person clients speak to, has to assess the nature and severity of their problems. She explains to the potential client the approach the Centre normally uses. If the person does not agree with the approach then he may be referred elsewhere. If a suitable counsellor has an available time slot that the client can regularly make then an appointment is arranged. However, this is not always straightforward: different counsellors may have specialisms such as phobias or obsessive-compulsive disorder whereas other counsellors may not wish to see clients with certain problems. The term 'stress centre' implies so many different things to so many people that the Centre's counsellors are likely to see clients with a wide variety of diverse stress- and non-stress-related issues. The client may also have requested a counsellor of a particular sex and age range, and the counselling co-ordinator may sometimes experience difficulty in matching the client's wishes to any available counsellor.

The trainers

The trainees on the stress management programme may be health professionals, counsellors and psychologists as well as trainers, health educators, welfare and personnel professionals. Therefore the Centre's trainers need to be experienced at working in clinical and industrial settings. When running these courses the trainer needs to give examples of the application of stress management to both of these fields of work. Another concern is pitching the input at the right level for the mixed-experienced and mixed-ability groups. Also, as the programme is modular, each student may have attended the courses in a different order and may lack an understanding of some of the course concepts. All these factors place demands upon the trainers if they wish to be an effective resource.

The counselling and psychotherapy courses place certain pressures upon the student, including the learning of new skills, many hours of reading, supervision, written work and assessment. The trainer may receive unconstructive comments that can reflect a student's anxiety. The trainer may also be involved in supervising a number of the students, which needs clear boundary setting in the trainer's mind. The trainers need to liaise regularly with the Centre's director about students, course content and assessment. Books often go out of print and this causes much aggravation for the trainer and the students.

The training rooms are not ideally suited to the hot summer weather that Britain has recently experienced. At times this can make teaching and learning difficult.

The director

Generally, the major problem for the principal or director of small organizations is having to wear many different hats. This can lead to role conflict and role ambiguity. The Centre is no exception. The main roles the director has are:

financial accounting;

managing staff;

public relations;

supervising when necessary;

serving as caretaker of building when necessary;

directing courses;

training;

designing new courses;

writing, editing and publishing relevant course texts;

dealing with students' difficulties;

serving as industrial consultant/trainer when necessary.

Each of the above roles has its own stresses. However, the main problems revolve around work overload and deadlines, which are frequently cited as some of the major sources of executive stress (Cooper, 1984). Not surprisingly the director may exhibit Type A behaviour such as impatience and polyphasic activity (see Friedman and Ulmer, 1985) and this can occasionally lead to friction with staff which later needs to be resolved. An 'open door' policy with staff can also add to the workload. Working at weekends in the Centre either as a 'caretaker' or as a trainer is an additional source of stress, as it conflicts with family and social activities.

The director has a large amount of administrative work that

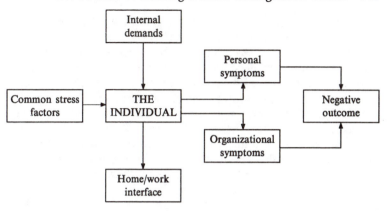

Figure 1 *The relationship between stress factors, the individual and the symptoms (Palmer, 1993c: 2)*

regularly needs attention. To ensure that high standards are maintained on the courses, the director is usually involved in marking examination papers and journals, and as the Centre runs an increasing number of courses, this can take up a considerable amount of time.

The individual and organizational responses to stress

Figure 1 represents the relationships between the more usual common organizational stress factors and the symptoms of the individual and organization. The common stress factors include organizational structure and climate, career development, relationships at work, role in the organization, the environment, interface between the internal demands of the individual and the organization, and the home/work interface.

The common stress factors, in addition to the issues described in the previous section, can lead to a number of healthy or unhealthy responses to stress by staff:

Unhealthy	*Healthy*
Depression	Sadness
Anxiety	Concern
Guilt	Remorse
Damning anger	Non-damning anger
Shame/embarrassment	Regret
Hurt	Disappointment

Some of the behavioural responses include aggressive/passive behaviour, avoidance, checking behaviour, increased alcohol/caffeine intake, Type A behaviour, interpersonal difficulties and poor time management. Initially, it is probably easier for other staff to notice changed behaviour than it is for the individual. However, with unhealthy physiological responses to stress the individual becomes aware of these almost immediately although he may not see the link with stress. These effects include allergies, angina, asthma, backache, cardiac arrest, neckache, diarrhoea, dyspepsia, heartburn, high blood pressure, migraines, tension, palpitations and ulcers. Some of these disorders can be fatal, and one stress consultant did die of coronary heart disease although the exact cause cannot be definitely related to stress.

Challenge can be healthy, but unfortunately too much or too little pressure can lead to stress-related diseases and serious cardiac problems can go unnoticed. The symptoms are pertinent to individuals under stress and each member of the Centre's staff is likely to suffer from one or more of the symptoms at some time. Some symptoms may be specific to the role. For example, staff under pressures of time and deadlines, such as the director or the administrator, may exhibit Type A behaviour, for example anticipating what others are going to say, having no time for pleasantries with others, walking/eating/talking fast, emphatic speech, pushing self and others and generally being impatient. In the short term, such behaviour can be considered as an adaptive coping strategy, but if Type A behaviour is maintained over a prolonged period then this appears to increase the risk of coronary heart disease. Type A behaviour can also lead to interpersonal problems in the workplace as the person concentrates exclusively on their job and neglects interpersonal relationships. Simple pleasantries such as 'Good morning', are overlooked in the rush to complete work. Such behaviour may trigger irrational beliefs (Dryden, 1990) among staff; for example: 'If I am not recognized by significant others, as I should be, then I am worthless.' This does not help the work situation.

As the amount of general paperwork for the director and the administrator can be high, a secondary unhealthy response that can be exhibited is a lack of creativity when attempting to problem-solve or in creating new courses. The resolution of specific problems is easier when more time is available. Since stress management and counselling is in vogue at the moment, the director may receive a large amount of correspondence from researchers, practitioners, the media and from stressed individuals, in Britain and overseas. An unhealthy response to this can be a lack of prioritizing and poor time management.

A counsellor suffering from stress may leave insufficient time to prepare their counselling sessions and this can reduce their therapeutic effectiveness. Understandably, the counsellor experiencing travelling difficulties may not arrive at the Centre in sufficient time to prepare a client's notes, the tape recorder or the room. Counsellors and trainees on placement who are very busy elsewhere due to a high workload or busy social commitments may also arrive at the Centre with little time to spare. In both cases, this can affect their counselling. They may even arrive late for supervision. In addition, when under stress the counsellor may use inappropriate self-disclosure in the counselling session, be unaware that her own agenda is affecting the dialogue with the client, lack concentration, use basic counselling skills poorly and become generally forgetful (forgetting to record the counselling session, forgetting the client's name, and so on). As a stress centre is referred clients with extremely high levels of stress and anxiety, the less experienced counsellor or trainee may initially feel anxious or overwhelmed by clients' problems. Counsellors have to accurately assess the risk of self-harm of clients who have suicidal ideation. This is a responsibility which should not be avoided and may need immediate action by the counsellor. Although a healthy response to this would be concern, many counsellors experience unhealthy anxiety, which can interfere with their judgement and counselling skills.

If clients are stressed and also have personality disorders, the relationship with the counsellor can be very difficult. The client may not appear very co-operative and transference and counter-transference issues may enter the therapeutic relationship at an early stage of counselling. The client may make negative comments about the counsellor's competence. The counsellor may think that she is being undermined and is likely to experience anxiety about her work, and anger towards her client. Subsequently, the counsellor's self-esteem or level of self-acceptance may be lowered. All of this can have a negative effect on the therapeutic alliance. If this happens, the relationship with the counsellor can be perceived by the client as an additional burden in his life. The psycho-educational approach may raise issues of 'power and control' with the client, which may lead to more 'conflict' in the counselling session.

The counselling co-ordinator's main emotional responses to the demands of the job are concern to ensure that the client has been referred to the most suitable counsellor or referred elsewhere, if necessary. However, organizing the best match can be frustrating.

Unfortunately, the most suitable counsellor may not be available at the time the client can come to the Centre for counselling.

Trainers are usually kept busy with their own workload elsewhere. Although this is seldom a problem, the design of new courses and their implementation at the Centre can be an extra initial strain until the course is up and running. Liaising with the director and the administrator over dates and other course-related issues can be mildly frustrating if answers are not immediately available. It can be difficult for the trainer to meet the needs of every group member, due to their differing professional backgrounds and mixed learning abilities. Three clear telltale signs that a trainer is suffering from stress are irritability, inappropriate self-disclosure to students and not keeping to the agreed agenda.

All staff would prefer better environmental conditions at the Centre. As a result of the rapid growth in work the accommodation has not kept pace with requirements for more rooms. This can be frustrating for staff, counsellors and trainers.

An organization can have a healthy or an unhealthy response to stress. In a stress centre some of the signs to look out for are communication breakdown, faulty decision-making, high staff turnover, staff burnout, high absenteeism, lowered efficiency/morale and lowered motivation. Organizational well-being is normally apparent in organizations that do not have these unhealthy responses. However, there are indicators of a healthy response to pressure. Two crucially important healthy responses are rapid adaptability and flexibility to changing financial challenges. This ensures growth and medium to high performance. Another healthy organizational response is regular staff training, which is so often overlooked in British industry. This direct investment in staff not only maintains morale but increases overall staff and organizational efficiency and helps with staff retention.

Suggestions for improved coping for staff

This section will be broken down into four key areas: intrapsychic, interpersonal, environmental/organizational and self-care factors. Although there will be an overlap when looking at coping strategies for staff, the different issues that may arise for the counsellors or the administrative staff are highlighted.

Improving intrapsychic coping
Intrapsychic stress-related issues include the individual's perceptions and beliefs. When considering improving coping strategies

(apart from resigning from the job) this is one area where members of staff at a stress centre can take positive action to overcome or reduce their levels of stress. Some of the options are attending suitable courses (multimodal, cognitive-behavioural, rational-emotive, behavioural); reading relevant literature (e.g. Burns, 1989; Dryden, 1990; Ellis and Dryden, 1987); or receiving counselling, thereby having unrealistic perceptions, expectations of self and others and beliefs challenged. Palmer (1993b) noted six work-related absolutist internal demands that lead to intrapsychic and interpersonal stress:

I/others must perform well at all times.

I/others must always reach deadlines.

I/others must be perfect.

The organization must treat me fairly at all times.

I should get what I want otherwise I can't stand it.

Significant others must appreciate my work, otherwise I am worthless.

If these internal demands (see Figure 1) or evaluative beliefs (see Dryden and Gordon, 1990) are adequately disputed and subsequently relinquished by the person then her level of stress is likely to be reduced when working at a stress centre (or in any other work context). The common disputes that can be used to challenge these beliefs are:

logical (is this belief logical?);

empirical (where is the evidence for the belief?);

pragmatic (where is it going to get you if you continue to hold on to this belief?)

Although the previously mentioned beliefs may apply to all staff there are specific evaluative beliefs that the counsellors and trainers may hold which can be very disabling. These are (see Ellis, 1983):

I have to be successful with all my clients practically all of the time.

I must be an outstanding therapist, clearly better than other therapists that I know or hear about.

I have to be greatly respected and loved by all my clients.

Since I am doing my best and working so hard as a therapist, my clients should be equally hard-working and responsible, should listen to me carefully and should always push themselves to change.

Because I'm a person in my own right, I must be able to enjoy myself during therapy sessions and to use these sessions to solve my personal problems as much as to help my clients with their difficulties.

Not only do these internal demands and beliefs contribute to intrapsychic stress, they also help to reduce the counsellor's effectiveness in stress counselling or stress management. For example, the counsellor may 'back off from encouraging clients to change' (Dryden and Gordon, 1990: 48). When working with clients suffering from personality disorders the counsellor who is expecting to make great therapeutic gains may become very disappointed or angry if these gains do not occur. If we take the example of the belief: 'I must be an outstanding therapist', the counsellor can consider the three common disputes:

Logical: Although it is strongly preferable to be an outstanding therapist, how does it logically follow that I *must* be one? ANSWER: It does not logically follow.

Empirical: There is plenty of evidence that I strongly desire to be an outstanding therapist but where is the evidence that I *must* be an outstanding therapist? or, Where is it written that I *must* be an outstanding therapist? ANSWER: There is no evidence anywhere, nor is it written anywhere (apart from inside my own head) that I *must* be an outstanding therapist.

Pragmatic: If I carry on holding on to the belief that I *must* be an outstanding therapist, where is it going to get me? ANSWER: whether my clients improve or do not improve, either way I will remain anxious and paradoxically my anxiety will reduce my effectiveness. This is exactly what I don't want.

Once the counsellor has disputed her unhelpful beliefs then she can develop a more helpful coping statement, as follows:

Coping statement: Although it is strongly preferable and desirable to be an outstanding therapist I don't have to be one. I'll just do my best whenever I can.

One of the best methods of alleviating a counsellor's anxiety about a difficult or distressed client is adequate supervision. Hence, at the Centre, a supervisor is normally available on the telephone to discuss important problems that may arise in between the usual supervision consultations. In supervision any blocks to effective counselling such as unhelpful internal demands or beliefs can be pointed out by the supervisor and examined. Trainers also receive supervision to maintain their effectiveness.

Improving interpersonal relationships

To improve interpersonal relationships in the workplace, and in particular clear communication between staff, assertion and communication skills are useful. These can be learnt on a suitable training course, and attendance on such a course could be recommended to all new staff who appear to have a deficit in these skills. Regular meetings between the director, the administrator and the counselling co-ordinator are essential to agree policies and disseminate information to other staff and students.

Counsellors and trainees on placement who may have deficits in specific interpersonal skills usually receive assertion and communication skills training, especially if their counselling is adversely affected. Some may require personal therapy if they hold back from challenging clients due to fear of being rejected. This can be discussed with their supervisor.

To reduce interpersonal conflict that may arise from staff members exhibiting Type A behaviour, a reduction in workload may be beneficial. This would be in addition to adequate disputation by their counsellor, or sometimes colleagues, of any unnecessary internal demands they may hold.

A number of organizational methods of preventive stress management may be used (see Quick and Quick, 1984). These include team building, social support, role analysis and goal setting. Briefly, team building is a method to resolve interpersonal conflict by confronting issues and coming to a group resolution. Social support of colleagues and friends generally helps to buffer the effect of stressors. Role analysis is undertaken to clarify an employee's work role and thereby reduce stress caused by role ambiguity and role conflict. Goal setting concentrates specifically on the relationship between the individual and her line manager so that they know each other's objectives.

Improving coping by making environmental/organizational interventions

The best environmental intervention that could be made is for the Centre to acquire a new, purpose-built set of offices located in an area with good transport facilities. In a recession, this may not be practicable. However, the existing building could be improved by better air-conditioning units. An alternative is to have a separate training establishment located in central London, without moving the administration, mail order and counselling departments.

The Centre's staff can share some of the workload of the director by being available at a number of the weekend events in any one year. In addition, the director can reduce a number of his commitments such as counselling, teaching and supervising to allow more time to complete the paperwork. A fair amount of non-essential correspondence could be returned to the author with a polite standard letter stating that the Centre is not in a position to provide answers to the enquiry. It is probable over the next few years, with the advent of national vocational qualifications and course recognition, that the director may spend even more time on correspondence and at meetings. Reduction of the workload will become imperative.

If the modular Diploma in Stress Management course was changed to a standard fixed-term course then the extra workload and associated difficulties this course gives both the administration and teaching staff would diminish.

Enhancing self-care

Individual methods for managing work and personal demands can be considered from three different levels (see Quick and Quick, 1984: 217):

primary prevention (stressor directed);

secondary prevention (response directed);

tertiary prevention (symptom directed).

At the primary prevention level the individual can attempt to manage her personal perceptions of stress (for example change her internal demands, reduce Type A behaviour) manage her personal work environment (time management, assertion training, overload avoidance and so on) and manage her lifestyle (for example keeping a balanced lifestyle and a suitable diet).

At the secondary level the individual can use relaxation training (the relaxation response, hypnosis, biofeedback training), use physical outlets (safe aerobic exercise, sports, yoga, walking), and emotional outlets (talking and writing their stress out, for example). Finally, at the tertiary level, counselling and medical help may be necessary.

Probably one of the most important self-care techniques is for all Centre staff to attempt to keep events in perspective. Seldom are things 'really awful', 'unbearable', or 'the end of the world'. Although this works at an intrapsychic level, it is probably one of the most useful methods of reducing or managing stress if running or working in a stress centre.

References

Burns, D.D. (1989) *The Feeling Good Handbook*. New York: William Morrow.

Cooper, C.L. (1984) 'Executive stress: a ten country comparison', *Human Resource Management*, 23: 395–407.

Dryden, W. (1990) *Rational-Emotive Counselling in Action*. London: Sage.

Dryden, W. and Gordon, J. (1990) *What is Rational-Emotive Therapy?* Loughton: Gale Centre Publications.

Ellis, A. (1983) 'How to deal with your most difficult client: you', *Journal of Rational-Emotive Therapy*, 1 (1): 3–8.

Ellis, A. and Dryden, W. (1987) *The Practice of Rational-Emotive Therapy*. New York: Springer.

Friedman, M. and Ulmer, D. (1985) *Treating Type A Behaviour and Your Heart*. London: Michael Joseph.

Palmer, S. (1992a) 'Stress management interventions: mission impossible', *Counselling News*, September (7): 12–15.

Palmer, S. (1992b) 'Multimodal assessment and therapy: a systematic, technically eclectic approach to counselling, psychotherapy and stress management', *Counselling: Journal of the British Association for Counselling*, 3 (4): 220–4.

Palmer, S. (1993a) 'A day in the life of Stephen Palmer', *Counselling: Journal of the British Association for Counselling*, 4 (2): 90.

Palmer, S. (1993b) 'Occupational stress: its causes and alleviation', in W. Dekker (ed.), *Chief Executive International*. London: Sterling Publications.

Palmer, S. (1993c) 'Organisational stress: symptoms, causes and reduction', *Newsletter of the Society of Public Health*, London: Society of Public Health.

Quick, J.C. and Quick, J.D. (1984) *Organizational Stress and Preventive Management*. New York: McGraw-Hill.

PART 3

THE STRESSES OF COUNSELLOR EDUCATION

10 The Stresses of Training Counsellors

John McLeod

The expansion of counselling as an emerging profession over the last 20 years has been accompanied by a dramatic growth in the number and variety of counsellor training courses in existence. Training courses range in length from brief 20-hour introductory counselling skills modules to professional courses encompassing two years or more of intensive study, practical work and personal development. Many courses are located in independent institutes, colleges and universities that share a primary training or educational function. Other courses, by contrast, take place in voluntary agencies such as Relate, whose main purpose is the delivery of services to clients. A significant feature of recent debates over counsellor training has been the attempt to bring some order to a fragmented and largely unregulated sphere of activity. For example, both the British Association for Counselling (BAC) and the Counselling Psychology Division of the British Psychological Society have published criteria for the recognition of training courses. There is a large measure of consensus that courses should include substantial inputs in the areas of theory, skills development, appropriately supervised practical work with clients, professional issues and work on self (Dryden and Thorne, 1991).

The stage of development of counselling as a profession in Britain has important implications for those responsible for running courses. Very few counselling trainers have undergone courses in training methods and techniques. Although there exists a body of mainly American literature (see Baker *et al.*, 1990) concerned with the evaluation of well-established training method-ologies such as interpersonal process recall (Kagan, 1984), microskills training (Ivey and Galvin, 1984) or human resources development (Cash, 1984), few British courses operate at this level of technical sophistication. The emergent nature of counselling has also meant that, at least in some parts of the country, there are relatively few quality internships or placement opportunities available to trainees. Most of the British university-based courses have been running for less than ten years, with staff who are often struggling to demonstrate the academic respectability of their discipline within a sceptical college environment.

The complexity of counselling courses also represents a significant level of challenge for tutors and trainers. Compared to many other types of training, there is a much broader range of learning objectives. Counsellors should be people who are well informed, skilled, yet also sensitively self-aware. There are major difficulties in defining and assessing such a broad range of competencies and in deciding whether a trainee has in the end achieved the objectives of the course (McLeod, 1992).

Given these sources of both institutional and operational pressure, it would seem reasonable to assume that the role of counsellor trainer or educator is associated with high levels of stress. However, despite the existence of a host of studies of stress and burnout in allied professions such as teaching, psychology and counselling itself, there do not appear to be any published studies of trainer stress. This finding is surprising, given the statement in the BAC code of ethics for trainers that:

> trainers have a responsibility to themselves and to their trainees to maintain their own effectiveness, resilience and ability to work with trainees. They are expected to monitor their own personal functioning and to seek help and/or withdraw from training, whether temporarily or permanently, when their personal resources are sufficiently depleted to require this. (BAC, 1993: 2).

This passage is a clear acknowledgement by the lead professional body of the potential for stress-induced 'depletion of personal resources' in the role of trainer.

For the purpose of this chapter, a small-scale survey of counselling trainers was carried out. Thirty colleagues employed as counsellor trainers and educators were invited to complete an open-ended questionnaire asking them to write about their experiences of stress, the impact this stress has had on them, and their modes of coping. Twenty-seven of these trainers returned questionnaires, most of them writing about their experiences in great detail. The frankness and openness of these accounts reinforces a sense of authenticity of the material being disclosed. Twelve of the respondents were men, and fifteen women. Ages ranged from 38 to 63 years, with a mean of 45.7 years. Their experience as trainers ranged from 1 to 24 years, with a mean of 9.5 years. Only 10 of the 27 described themselves as full-time or near full-time trainers, with the majority combining the trainer/tutor role with that of counsellor, priest, lecturer or researcher. Most worked for at least part of the time in college or university settings, with a smaller number carrying out training in independent institutes, voluntary agencies or freelance. In orientation, these trainers were fairly evenly divided between those espousing a psychodynamic approach, and those using a humanistic or person-centred model. There were no avowedly cognitive, systemic or behavioural practitioners in this sample.

The questionnaire data were subjected to a grounded theory analysis (Strauss and Corbin, 1990), a research technique which is designed to allow the identification of categories and themes within the material. The rationale behind this methodology is that of developing models that are firmly based or 'grounded' in the reality of what people experience. A first draft of the researcher's analysis of the data was sent to a selection of informants for comment. This strategy was used as a way of determining the validity and generalizability of the themes identified by the researcher. The feedback and suggestions gathered through this process of 'negotiating accounts' have been incorporated into this report.

The nature of the stresses experienced by counselling trainers

In response to a question inviting a brief account of what they found *most* stressful in their role as trainer, this group of informants generated a wide variety of categories, reflecting the multidimensional nature of their work.

Relationships with students/trainees
The type of stress most often mentioned by trainers was associated with different aspects of their relationships with trainees. Within this broad classification, a number of discrete sources of stress could be identified. Issues arising from the evaluation of students were mentioned by many trainers. Specifically, the strain of dealing with situations where a decision was made to fail a trainee had a

strong impact not only on the tutor or trainer, but on his or her relationships with other trainees and with colleagues. At these moments of assessment 'crisis', the tension between the facilitative/nurturing and assessment/judgemental sides of the role of trainer can trigger high levels of anxiety, guilt and self-doubt, as well as avoidant defensive manoeuvres.

Another form of stress in relation to students or trainees originated in the extent to which the emphasis on experiential work and self-awareness in counselling courses resulted in course members projecting strong feelings on to trainers. Staff can be idealized as all-knowing experts, and at other times attacked for their insensitivity or other shortcomings. Although there may occasionally be some reality base for these feelings, stimulated by the actual behaviour of the trainer, it is also true that the trainer–trainee relationship is often used by trainees as a vehicle for personal learning and growth. One trainer, comparing the experience of being a counselling tutor with that of teaching on other courses, wrote that 'students often practise the counselling ethos of open expression of feeling towards the trainer, feelings which are often angry or critical . . . on a non-counselling course, the expression of such feelings would be seen as inadmissible'.

Trainees who represent very different value systems can be stressful for trainers. In some training settings, there may be unwilling course members who have been instructed by their employers to attend, and who may use the arena of the course to engage in what one trainer labelled 'destructive undermining'. At other times, there may be trainees who express racist or sexist attitudes and behaviour, or challenge the alleged racism or sexism of the trainer. In a counselling relationship, there are possibilities for exploring the origins of these attitudes, forming an alliance with other parts of the client, or referring on the person to another therapist. These strategies are much more difficult in the environment of a training course, where time pressures may make it impossible to spend the amount of time with an individual student or trainee necessary to carry out productive work in this area. The relationship between trainer and trainee is not a therapy contract, and intervening in depth to begin to resolve the personal conflicts and problems of trainees can raise a host of ethical and boundary-management issues.

A stressful aspect of relationships with trainees that was mentioned by only a few trainers, but is nevertheless of interest, is the sense of being exposed and vulnerable. The counselling trainer is a role model for trainees, and is being observed closely by students or trainees. One experienced trainer wrote that 'it is a

considerable stress being on public display all the time . . .
counselling is a subject related to all that is most personal [and] it
is therefore very difficult to have a private life insulated from one's
public reputation'. Another stressor that came up infrequently, but
is of significance, is the feeling in the trainer of contributing to the
distress felt by trainees: 'training is such a vulnerable time for the
students; I see them experiencing crises in their personal lives and
watch their pain and I sometimes *almost* feel responsible for it, as
if I'm causing it . . . at worst I feel like some kind of sadistic
voyeur'.

Underlying these observations appeared to run a fundamental
dilemma for trainers, concerning the kind of relationship they
should have with trainees and students. One of the research
participants wrote of the stressfulness of 'achieving the appropriate
balance between personal involvement and detachment'. Others
wrote of some very practical ways in which this balance might be
tested. For example, could a trainee become a friend? Should offers
of lucrative work in the sponsoring organization of a trainee be
taken up?

Relationships with colleagues

The importance of having good relationships with supportive co-
workers was presented by most trainers as a major means of
coping with the stress of their job. Poor relationships with
colleagues were reported as a significant source of stress. One of
the simple ways in which this stressor manifested itself was the
absence of colleagues. Some trainers wrote about the pressure and
isolation they felt when running courses alone in 'alien environments'. More common, though, was the experience of having
personal or professional differences with a colleague, and as a
consequence not being able to rely on that person for help in
dealing with demands from students or employers. One trainer
observed that:

> Sometimes, especially on long courses, the effort I put into trying to
> make an unhealthy co-trainer relationship work greatly outweighs the
> effort I put into other aspects of course work. This is at times, literally
> painful and very draining. It must also have a detrimental effect on the
> students' experience – if I'm so busy trying to 'paper over the cracks',
> the process gets clearly replicated amongst them, too.

There is a suggestion at the end of this quote of the existence of a
parallel process (McNeill and Worthen, 1989) which many tutors
believe exerts a powerful influence in counselling training courses.
According to this theory, the dynamic and process of the student

group is mirrored in the staff group. Similarly, the process of the staff group may be reflected in what is happening in the student group. Examples of this parallel process would include groups of students appearing to attempt to 'split' a staff team into 'good' and 'bad' members, or the reproduction of anger avoidance in the staff group in the emerging norms of the student group. The prevalence of these processes is a factor in the importance that many trainers place on the maintenance of strong co-worker relationships, and the distress that can result when these relationships are in trouble.

Organizational pressures
The organizational setting in which training takes place is a source of stress for many trainers. There were many references to the stress caused by inadequate resourcing of courses: too many students, too few staff, inappropriate rooms, lack of video facilities, lack of time for preparation. In addition to these resource problems, a number of trainers described tensions associated with the contrast between the values of the host organization, which were seen as being 'academic', 'profit-oriented' or concerned with 'cost-effectiveness', and the values seen as intrinsic to counselling, such as respect for the person and professional integrity.

Work overload
Several of the trainers who participated in the study drew attention to the multi-task nature of their role, and the dangers of overload and burnout. One informant depicted a typical working day, which included researching background literature in the library, working on administrative and secretarial tasks, preparing the teaching room, welcoming students and running a workshop, acting as coffee bar attendant during the break, then clearing up afterwards. Most of the trainers in the sample gave substantial proportions of their time to maintaining a client caseload. Those working free-lance or employed on part-time contracts reported needing to take on increasing volumes of work in order to achieve a decent standard of living. The demands of liaison with professional bodies such as the British Association for Counselling, or with other training institutes, were also mentioned as adding to the workload by some research participants.

Other sources of stress
The categories of relationships with trainees, relationships with colleagues, organizational pressure, and workload, represent themes that appeared often in the research material. There were also a number of stressors which were acknowledged by smaller

subgroups of trainers, but which were nevertheless seen as significant by them.

Some trainers identified self-induced pressure or stress connected with doubting their own personal competence in this field, or capacity to be 'good enough' for trainees. Informants mentioned 'feeling inadequate', 'not knowing enough' or 'feeling I should know everything'. There were some references to the inadequacy of payment for training work, through either low pay or job insecurity. Some trainers discussed the stress and boredom of using the same introductory exercises, and running the same courses time after time. Finally, some trainers noted that, because of their prominent position in local networks, they had difficulty in finding personal therapy or supervision that was sufficiently 'safe'. For these trainers, it was essential that their therapist or supervisor was someone with whom they could have an unambiguous working alliance. Their problem was that the people in their geographical area they perceived as potentially competent supervisors or therapists were all individuals with whom they had other, different professional links, thus leading to the possible dangers of becoming enmeshed in a stultifying 'dual relationship' (Pope, 1991).

Trainers' responses to the stresses

Trainers respond to these stressors in a variety of ways. Their responses can be broadly divided into reactions indicative of negative effects, and those reflecting attempts at positive coping. There were two types of reaction to stress reported most frequently: illness and isolation.

Illness
In the questionnaire, trainers wrote about many ways in which their health and sense of well-being were affected by the pressures of the job. The intensity of these 'illnesses' ranged across a continuum from temporary fatigue at one end to, at the other extreme breakdowns in health requiring medical treatment and time off work. The types of symptom reported were characteristic stress responses: tiredness, anxiety, irritation, sleep disturbances, depression, mood swings, unhealthy eating, headaches, flu symptoms and high blood pressure. Because of the open-ended, qualitative nature of this study, it is not possible to estimate the prevalence of each of these symptoms in this sample of trainers. However, it was clear that the single most widely experienced physical reaction to the pressures of being a trainer was the feeling of being 'emotionally drained'.

Isolation

The other negative or maladaptive response to stress mentioned by many of the participants in the study was that of withdrawal. Several of the trainers observed that they were aware of letting themselves become more isolated and remote at times of pressure. One trainer wrote that when the workload became overwhelming, she found herself 'falling back on the neutrality and status of the teacher' rather than continuing to work with students in an experiential mode. This sense of defending against demands by becoming emotionally more distant from trainees was a significant theme for several informants. Other trainers acknowledged that they would have phases of cynicism and disenchantment with the world of counselling: 'feeling like giving it all up and becoming a hermit'. Isolation was also attributed to difficulties in securing appropriate support: 'since one is expected to be the source of wisdom on matters of human functioning, it can be very difficult to get any real support when one is not functioning well oneself'. A very acute feeling of isolation was captured by one respondent who saw himself as a 'misfit', not really at ease or accepted in any place. The isolation of the work was exacerbated by the fact that several of the trainers were in effect lone representatives of their discipline within academic departments dominated by other professional groups.

Illness and isolation emerged very clearly as themes. It is perhaps worth noting that several significant types of stress response discussed in other reviews of professional stress (Kilburg *et al.* 1987) were *not* reported by these trainers. For example, none of the trainers reported that their work precipitated drug or alcohol misuse, marital or relationship difficulties, or 'forbidden-zone' (Rutter, 1989) sexual relationships. Whether these phenomena are genuinely not present in British counselling trainers, or whether they would be uncovered by a more sensitive research method (such as in-depth interviews) is a matter for further study.

In contrast to the relatively sparse set of categories found in relation to negative effects of stress, the trainers reported a larger number of different modes of positive coping.

Social support

Social support was the form of coping mentioned most often. Effective support was sought in a variety of ways. Informal conversations with colleagues were highly valued. Many trainers organized more formal sessions with their supervisor, or set up regular debriefing meetings with co-workers. Other forms of support that were cited included staff meetings, using a course consultant, personal therapy, attending conferences, family life, and the availability of effective and reliable secretarial assistance. These forms of stress management functioned both to combat isolation and also to offload the accumulated emotional burdens of the work.

Other forms of coping

Several of the trainers wrote that they used *time management* as a strategy for coping with the demands of their role. Examples of this approach were planning ahead, doing less, limiting time spent at work, and setting specific times for availability to students. Another type of coping that similarly depends on boundary management was *separating work from home life*. Some trainers observed that it is was important to them to have a life outside, and separate from, the world of counselling. For a few, this separation could be achieved only by travelling abroad. The application of counselling methods in their own lives was apparent in the claim made by some of the research participants that they used *cognitive restructuring* to deal with stress, for example by identifying irrational fears, defusing grandiose expectations and generally gaining a more grounded perspective on any problems or worries. A few informants reported that, for them, a useful way of dealing with stress was *writing*, for example keeping detailed notes of sessions. Other means of coping that were mentioned less often were physical exercise, religion, political action within the organization, and keeping up to date with developments in the literature.

DeLongis *et al.* (1982) have proposed that the amount of stress experienced by a person can be understood in terms of the balance between *hassles* and *uplifts* in their life. Hassles are defined as everyday pressures and irritations that cause frustration and worry. Uplifts, by contrast, are everyday events that bring meaning, satisfaction and enjoyment. In the questionnaire used in this study, trainers were asked to write about the uplifts, or sources of satisfaction, in their work. Four main categories of uplift emerged from analysis of this material: contact, learning, the development of trainees and self-delight. Good contact and the establishment of satisfying, authentic relationships with colleagues and trainees was a source of satisfaction reported by most of the trainers. Several mentioned the fun, humour and energy that could flow from the work. Others referred to a sense of affirmation from being appreciated by others and being a member of an effective team. Another uplift recorded by several trainers was the learning potential of the job. Both colleagues and trainees could be sources of learning, and the process of dialogue occurring in training was seen as helping to sharpen ideas and concepts. Many of the trainers wrote about the satisfactions associated with participating in the development of trainees, for example watching them become more effective therapists, seeing them get jobs and publish articles. Meeting trainees who had graduated years before, and learning of their subsequent career achievements, was another source of satisfaction in this category. The final type of uplift reported can be described as 'self-delight' (Gustafson, 1992). One trainer wrote of 'experiencing my own spontaneity and creativity' through the work. Others wrote of their 'sense of rightness' at having work which allowed them to express their values and beliefs in a constructive manner. Throughout all the writing on uplifts and satisfaction, there emerged time and again the sense of 'privilege' in fulfilling the role of trainer.

Suggestions for improved coping

The findings of this small-scale survey of counselling trainers and tutors have a number of implications for the organization of counselling training courses, and the role of the trainer. It is clear that the organizational context of training has a significant impact on the training process itself, at least as experienced by trainers. It would appear sensible, therefore, to recommend that those running training courses should give as much attention to the creation of an appropriate setting for the courses as to other issues such as selection of trainees, choice of workshop materials and experiential exercises, and assessment of learning. The informants who contributed to this study seem to be suggesting that an important facet of the role of the trainer is the work he or she does to maintain the boundary between the course and its organizational milieu. This role is possibly less important when training is carried out in counselling agencies in which there is a consonance of values between the agency and the training course. It is, however, acutely significant in settings such as educational institutions or in freelance work, where there may exist serious tensions between the ethos and norms of a course and those espoused by its host organization.

Another implication of these findings relates to the necessity for peer support. It is stressful for counselling tutors or trainers to work alone. It is also stressful to work with colleagues who do not share core values and beliefs, or who have not been chosen as co-workers. The stress of training counsellors can be reduced by ensuring that training is delivered by a cohesive, supportive team. The use of an external consultant to act as a sounding board and facilitator to a staff team is a strategy that has been successfully employed by some groups of trainers to deal with stressful situations.

Looking at the sources of stress as a whole, it is evident that much of the pressure in the role of trainer arises from the complexity of the job. A trainer needs to be competent at imparting knowledge and skills, facilitating the process of a group, being aware of sometimes painful and difficult developmental processes in trainees, giving feedback, negotiating with placement and internship agencies, and much else besides. A work role of this level of complexity requires effective training and supervision. At the moment, however, there are few opportunities for 'training to be a trainer', and only limited recognition of the value of 'training supervision'. Undoubtedly these activities will become more widely available as counselling becomes more professionalized and evolves a secure institutional base and career structure.

The longing for support and networking in trainers is mirrored by an appreciation of the tendency to become isolated. Trainees and students can make use of an extensive peer group, but the trainer is excluded from this source of support. Skovholt and Ronnestad (1992) have suggested that professional isolation is an important issue for many older counsellors and therapists. They argue that, as the counsellor or therapist gets older, the pool of potential 'professional elders' is diminished by retirement, death or geographical distance. For a trainer, the situation is even more difficult, since he or she is likely to become the 'professional elder' for an ever-expanding number of former trainees and students as time goes on. In this role, older and more experienced trainers may find it increasingly hard to find a group in which they can express their vulnerability, uncertainty and need for support.

Personal reflections

In qualitative research of this kind, an important touchstone of authenticity and validity must always be the degree of reflexivity demonstrated by the researcher. In qualitative studies the researcher is not a detached observer of others, but is to a large extent learning through participating in the lives of informants, using his or her capacity for empathy to gain as deep an appreciation as possible of the patterns and meanings in these lives. In this study, I have up to now presented a report of my analysis of the accounts that others have given of the stresses of being counselling trainers. I will now attempt to reflect on the experiences and assumptions that have shaped my reading of their contributions.

I completed my own questionnaire before I sent it out to research participants, so that I could mark up some of the stresses as I saw them without being influenced by what others had written. At one point I had planned in fact to send my own account of my personal experience of stress to research participants along with the questionnaire, so that the disclosure would not be all one way. However, although this would probably have been a useful thing to do, in the end I found it personally too threatening to expose myself in this way, and retreated behind a more conventional research strategy of sending just the questionnaire and a friendly letter. But I can see that behind all this was a reluctance to let anyone else know just how stressful I have at times found the work to be. And I sensed this too in some of the questionnaire responses. Some informants hinted at the depths of their worries and fears. Others emphasized the confidentiality of what they were writing. So for me, as for others, there is a strong thread of 'I should be able to cope', and 'There is something wrong with me if I can't cope.'

When I was invited to write this chapter, my main reason for accepting the task was that for me being a counselling trainer has been a highly stressful endeavour, in all the ways that have already been described in the analysis of the questionnaire replies. I wanted to gain a better understanding of my feelings about being a trainer, and find out how other people in similar positions coped. The accumulation of different pressures – from students, colleagues, the institution, the standards I set myself – have left me at times feeling exhausted and utterly drained. I would describe myself as a private person, and so it is hard for me to know how to deal with being known to so many people, each of them wanting to see how I do things, and learn what I think about things. Many of these people, moreover, seem to define me as a person they imagine or want me to be, rather than as a person I recognize as myself. I have undergone several disorienting experiences, mainly in large groups, of course members around me speculating about my motives and reasons, with me sitting there wondering who they are talking about. I also see myself as a critical person, in some ways still a rebellious adolescent, and as a result it does not sit easy continually to be careful about what I say to students or colleagues, in the knowledge (or fantasy) that a playful or spontaneous remark may be wounding or hurtful to people who have invested a great deal in my approval and support. I have had to rein in my Scots humour in this job.

Another very powerful set of pressures arises from my role as director of the programme, and feeling myself acting as a buffer between the course members and the university. I believe that the kind of emotional and experiential learning that is a necessary component of counsellor training and education requires a group culture which is distinctively different from that existing in the academy as a whole. It often feels an unremitting and unrewarding struggle to ensure there are enough staff to run the course properly, enough properly equipped and furnished rooms to keep everyone happy, and enough contact hours to satisfy the BAC. As a person-centred practitioner, I want course members to identify their own learning objectives and work towards them at their own pace, but I also need to reconcile these values with the very real needs for order and predictability generated by a large bureaucratic institution. I feel anger when students say that they have to jump through academic hoops to get their Master's degree, but I understand what they mean. For me, a lot of this boundary management between the course and the university entails a sense of risk and threat. Frequently I imagine there would be hell to pay if the administration knew what we were really up to. Alongside these anxieties, however, there is also a sense of pride in contributing to the creation of one of the few places in the academy that promotes deep personal learning, and visibly engages the energies of students.

I would also like to reinforce the points made by many of the research participants concerning the importance of the staff group. I strongly believe that the emotional demands of counselling course members are too great to be sustained by an individual trainer. Or, at any rate, by this individual trainer. I would say that, unless a trainer is willing to adopt a highly remote and detached style, it is all but impossible to avoid becoming enmeshed in problematic relationships with some members of a training group. The trainees need to have other trainers or tutors to whom they can turn in such circumstances, and so do trainers. However, the way counselling courses are organized in most colleges can make it hard to evolve a cohesive staff team. Typically, a programme can only afford to resource one or two full-time posts, with much of the teaching being done by part-time sessional staff, usually on short-term contracts. Often, as in my own staff group the tenured positions are filled by men while the sessional or part-time (and underpaid) staff are women. There can be major issues around power and control that need to be addressed if a good working group can be established.

Conclusions

The limitations of the material discussed in this chapter must be acknowledged. It is based on a sample of only 27 trainers, who certainly will not be representative of the range of experience, work setting and theoretical orientation existing in British counsellor training as a whole. Also, although these informants on the whole completed the questionnaire with great thoroughness, there are many issues which cannot be adequately explored through the medium of an open-ended questionnaire. It would be of great interest, for example, to assess levels of 'burnout' (Maslach and Jackson, 1981) in trainers, to be able to compare their scores with those obtained by other professional groups, and examine differences in burnout associated with different training environments. It would also be valuable to use in-depth interviews to gain a deeper understanding of the dynamics of stress, and to give participants opportunities to disclose information that might be too delicate to commit to paper. Nevertheless, the survey has yielded the beginning outline of what is a complex picture of stress and coping in counselling trainers. It is my hope that this chapter will precipitate further research and dialogue on the topic. The consequences of trainer stress can be immense. An impaired or burnt-out trainer may effectively inhibit the development of trainees, with subsequent negative effects on many clients. The ongoing professionalization of counsellor training, and increasing location in universities, are likely to multiply the pressures felt by trainers.

Perhaps the most significant benefit to be gained from reflecting on the stresses of training counsellors is the realization that, in general, the same kinds of pressure are experienced by virtually everyone in the field. One wise veteran of the training world commented in her questionnaire that 'because of the individual nature of our work, we . . . are often guilty of over-personalizing issues which are actually part of our common world'. An appreciation that much of the stress is part of a 'common world' may contribute to the creation of suitable collective action, in the form of networks, writing, supervision, conferences and the like, that may most effectively combat the emotional exhaustion, isolation and illness that sometimes come with the job.

References

Baker, S.B., Daniels, T.G. and Greeley, A.T. (1990) 'Systematic training of graduate-level counsellors: narrative and meta-analytic reviews of three programmes', *Counseling Psychologist*, 18: 355–421.

British Association for Counselling (BAC) (1993) *Code of Ethics and Practice for Trainers in Counselling and in Counselling Skills*. Rugby: BAC.

Cash, R.W. (1984) 'The Human Resources Development model', in D. Larson (ed.), *Teaching Psychological Skills: Models for Giving Psychology Away*. Monterey, CA: Brooks/Cole.

DeLongis, A., Coyne, J.G., Daklof, S. and Lazarus, R.S. (1982) 'Relationships of daily hassles, uplifts, and major life events to health status', *Health Psychology*, 1: 119–36.

Dryden, W. and Thorne, B. (eds) (1991) *Training and Supervision for Counselling in Action*. London: Sage.

Gustafson, J.P. (1992) *Self-delight in a Harsh World: the Main Stories of Individual, Marital and Family Psychotherapy*. New York: W.W. Norton.

Ivey, A.E. and Galvin, M. (1984) 'Micro-counselling: a metamodel for counselling, therapy, business and medical interviews', in D. Larson (ed.), *Teaching Psychological Skills: Models for Giving Psychology Away*. Monterey, CA: Brooks/Cole.

Kagan, N. (1984) 'Interpersonal process recall: basic methods and recent research', in D. Larson (ed.), *Teaching Psychological Skills: Models for Giving Psychology Away*. Monterey, CA: Brooks/Cole.

Kilburg, R., Nathan, P. and Soresen, R.W. (eds) (1987) *Professionals in Distress: Issues, Syndromes and Solutions in Psychology*. Washington, DC: American Psychological Association.

McLeod, J. (1992) 'What do we know about how best to assess counsellor competence?', *Counselling Psychology Quarterly*, 5: 359–72.

McNeill, B.W. and Worthen, V. (1989) 'The parallel process in psychotherapy supervision', *Professional Psychology: Research and Practice*, 20: 329–33.

Maslach, C. and Jackson, S.E. (1981) 'The measurement of experienced burnout', *Journal of Occupational Behavior*, 2: 99–113.

Pope, K.S. (1991) 'Dual relationships in psychotherapy', *Ethics and Behavior*, 1: 21–34.

Rutter, P. (1989) *Sex in the Forbidden Zone*. London: Mandala.

Skovholt, T.M. and Ronnestad, M.H. (1992) *The Evolving Professional Self: Stages and Themes in Therapist and Counsellor Development*. Chichester: Wiley.

Strauss, A. and Corbin, J. (1990) *Basics of Qualitative Research: Grounded Theory, Procedures and Techniques*. London: Sage.

11 The Stresses of Supervising Counsellors

Michael Carroll

Borders and Leddick (1987: 2) highlight the responsibilities of counselling supervisors and focus on areas of potential stress:

> You (the supervisor) are responsible for both a counselor and that counselor's clients, for the counselor's learning and the client's welfare. You will be teacher, counselor, consultant, administrator, and evaluator. You will be challenged to translate your counseling methods into supervision interventions appropriate to your supervisee's needs, learning style, and ability level. You will be called on to be sensitive to the dynamics of both the counselor–client relationship and the supervisor–supervisee relationship.

This is an awesome list of requirements: who would want to be a supervisor with such a personal and professional agenda? And just in case you are tempted to apply for the job then perhaps Robiner and Schofield (1990: 297–8) will put you off as a prospective candidate for ever:

> although . . . more than two thirds of counseling psychologists provide clinical supervision . . . few supervisors (less than 10–15%) actually have attended formal courses in supervision . . . most lack training in supervision . . . little is known about how supervisors assume the supervisory role . . . the full extent of supervisors' responsibility and legal liabilities are not necessarily evident to supervisees or supervisors, and standardized rating scales for assessing supervisees and supervision are wanting . . . there is no solid theoretical basis, standard literature . . . or syllabus for supervision.

Yet despite the limitations within the literature and the paucity of research, supervision is fast moving from the periphery of counselling training to centre stage: no longer is it a luxurious option for either trainees or qualified counsellors. The past five years have witnessed an enormous growth in the awareness of supervision as a key feature in counselling provision. Codes of Ethics and Practice are integrating supervision into training and ongoing work with clients as a requirement (BAC, 1990). A number of training courses on supervision have emerged recently in

Britain, and somewhere in the region of 40 supervisors have been accredited by the British Association for Counselling. Research in this area has continued to develop, particularly in the US (Holloway, 1992) but also in Britain (Carroll, 1993).

Counselling supervision is a professional relationship where supervisees, either individually or in small groups, are enabled to reflect on their work with clients. From the viewpoint of the counselling profession supervision is a 'quality-control' provision where the welfare of the client is protected, and where trainees are gradually introduced into the counselling profession. From the perspective of supervisees, supervision offers a forum of support and challenge where they learn how to work more effectively with counselling clients. Clients, also, are assured by supervision, realizing that it offers a further level of accountability and expertise so that they get the best service possible. Bernard and Goodyear offer an up-to-date and probably widely acceptable definition of supervision: 'Supervision is a means of transmitting the skills, knowledge, and attitudes of a particular profession to the next generation in that profession. It also is an essential means of ensuring that clients receive a certain minimum quality of care while trainees work with them to gain their skills' (1992: 2).

But supervision is not just provided for trainee counsellors. Experienced counsellors also need provision for reviewing their client work, for continuing their development, and for monitoring their own reactions to particular clients and client groups (BAC, 1990).

The nature of stresses in supervising counsellors

What are the demands and responsibilities of counselling supervisors? This section will review three areas of possible stress: stresses arising from within supervisors themselves, those that emerge from the supervisory relationship, and a third set of stressors extraneous to the participants.

Stressors from within the supervisor

The beginning-supervisor
Moving from being a counsellor to becoming a supervisor is perhaps the first stress facing the unsuspecting beginning-supervisor. Most supervisors have no training in supervision when they accept their first supervisee. Zinkin (1989: 19) has complained about this 'but nobody trains the supervisors. Unlike practically any job I can think of supervisors are chosen without any

convincing demonstration that they can do the job.' Somewhere in the 'great unspoken' is a myth that good counsellors automatically make good supervisors. We know this is not the case because supervision is more of an educational methodology than is counselling. And this can be the first stress for the supervisor, what Bernard has called 'a basic tension underlying this shift from psychotherapy to education that is often unaddressed' (n.d.: 2).

Entering the supervision field for the first time can bring with it many unanswered questions: what are the roles, tasks and functions of supervision? what contracts should be negotiated with supervisees? how should evaluation take place and when? Questions also arise over how best to use group supervision and/ or what supervision strategies to employ.

Using counselling-bound models of supervision

There is a tendency for supervisors who have inherited this role to supervise in much the same way as they engage in counselling. The literature has called these 'counselling-bound models of supervision' (Holloway, 1992). The strength of supervisors who adhere strongly to such models is the congruence between counselling and supervision and the strong 'modelling' value. However, the weakness has been that there is a reluctance to include theory, skills, knowledge from other schools of counselling and indeed from other professions. So, for example, many psychodynamic supervisors will not use experiential teaching methods (for example skills training, role-play, psychodrama) as part of supervisory learning, while some devoted humanistic supervisors will refuse to involve themselves with purely didactic teaching. The stance may be based on strongly held principles of learning or may be an inability and lack of skill within other areas. Either way, it results in a narrow focus of teaching/learning methods. Villas-Boas Bowen exemplifies this from a person-centred approach:

> As early as 1956, Rogers has begun to apply these same principles of therapist–client interaction to the supervisor–supervisee relationship. Rogers (1956) stated that by providing the supervisee with an accepting, empathic, and genuine atmosphere, the supervisor would not only model how to create those conditions but would also offer an atmosphere in which the supervisor might freely explore the feelings, blocks, and difficulties which emerge while learning to become a therapist. (1986: 292)

In the above quotation counselling and supervision approaches are similar. A particular stress arises for supervisors when their supervisees ask for other methods of teaching not part of, or sometimes not congruent with, the counselling orientation of the supervisor.

Many supervisors are not teachers and so are unable to make judgements about the learning needs of their supervisees or how to assess their learning objectives. Some, because they have had no training as teachers or trainers, have only a few methodologies in their teaching repertoire. They begin to feel stressed if demands are made to integrate other teaching methods with which they are not familiar.

What are supervisors' responsibilities?

Confusion over their responsibilities towards supervisees can be a major source of stress for supervisors. There seems to be little agreement about what exactly comprises the responsibilities of supervisors. Some insist that supervision must be confidential to allow freedom for the supervisees to present their cases; others see evaluation and formal feedback as an essential ingredient in supervision, especially where supervisees are in training. Some supervisors see their primary role as teaching and intervene very didactically to educate the counsellor into the counselling profession; others refuse to involve themselves in formal instruction. One school of thought sees supervisors helping the supervisee deal with their reactions to clients; others consider such issues should be sent to personal therapy.

Supervisors are faced with decisions about how to implement supervision and whether or not they are skilled in different areas; for example will supervision take place in a group or individually? Will supervisees practise from within one orientation rather than across orientations? What style of supervision will supervisors adopt? Will they supervise beginning-counsellors and/or those who are experienced? Are there client problem areas where supervisors feel competent and/or experienced? Will supervisors and supervisees choose each other or be selected by others? Supervisors feel stressed when pushed beyond where they are comfortable, and external circumstances often demand that they move into unchosen areas, for example that they work in group supervision rather than individual, that supervisees are delegated to them rather than either participant having a choice.

On being an expert

Being expected to be an expert can be a stress placed on supervisors by self and/or by others. What will supervisors do if the counsellor brings clients with problems about which they have no knowledge or expertise? When will supervisors intervene directly in the external world of the supervisee, if ever? What happens if supervisors are asked to supervise a counsellor from a counselling orientation different from their own, maybe even one with which they have major disagreement? Should supervisors engage in group or individual supervision? If in groups, will they use the process in the group to facilitate learning or not? How will counsellors be evaluated? What will supervisors do if they are worried about the professional work of the counsellor and suspect the client is not getting a good service? Are there times when supervisors should advise the counsellor to give up this profession? A whole array of expectations about knowledge, skills, insights and interventions leaves insecure supervisors feeling vulnerable with constant anxiety that they will be 'caught out' and found wanting.

Stressors arising from within the supervisory relationship

Supervision as counselling

Supervision can become a form of counselling with supervisees. This is viewed by supervisees as the most objectionable aspect of supervision (Rosenblatt and Mayer, 1975) and is stressful for both participants. Supervisees react very strongly to having supervision concentrate on their personal defects rather than on their professional development. Since supervision inevitably must consider the personal reactions of the supervisees and help them deal with these effectively, this can create a quandary for supervisors. On the one hand they need to help supervisees deal with what is happening to them as a result of working with clients while on the other hand they must now allow this to become personal therapy.

Stress in supervisory relationships emerges when counsellors consider that their clients are being 'vicariously' counselled by their supervisors. This can happen when supervisors adopt an authoritarian style. At the same time, supervisors need to know that clients are not being harmed. How do they monitor this? Do they rely solely on verbal reports from supervisees, knowing these are highly subjective and may not accurately reflect what happens in that private domain between counsellor and client? Should supervisors ask for tapes of the counselling sessions as an insurance against poor practice? Supervisors can be caught between the need to trust the supervisee and the need to ensure that the client is not being harmed.

Evaluating supervisees

The most potent area of stress for supervisors is the evaluation of supervisees (Bradley, 1989). The more negative the feedback the more stressful it is for supervisors and supervisees. So anxiety-provoking is it for supervisees that Chrzanowski (1984) said that some of his students confessed to falsifying and censoring material in supervision for fear of being negatively evaluated. Assessing supervisees demands critical evaluation of their abilities as counsellors. Supervisors are aware of their power in this domain: a poor evaluation can dramatically affect the future career of a supervisee. And yet supervisors are all too aware that the protection and welfare of clients are key factors in supervision. Evaluation is necessary but can also adversely affect the relationship between supervisors and supervisees, especially where there is a difference of opinion on supervisees' abilities.

Stressors from outside

Balancing the supervisory systems

Dodds (1986) considers conflict areas between supervisors, the agencies in which supervisees work, and the training courses on which supervisees are participants, pointing out that 'there may be agency or institutional obstacles that hamper their fully performing in those roles (supervisor and supervisee)' (1986: 299). Training agencies will undoubtedly want supervisors to be part of the assessment team reporting back on supervisee progress. The agency in which supervisees see their clients may nor may not be interested in supervision. Rarely are clear boundaries and working relationships articulated between the two. Supervisors are unclear at times about their role and whether or not they should intervene, for example if inappropriate referrals are being made, if agency politics is interfering with client work or if unethical situations seem to pertain. Caught between the supervisee and the other concerned agencies, supervisors may feel stressed about involvement and boundaries.

Conclusion

There are a number of sources from which stress can emerge to dog the lives of supervisors: expectations from self and others, factors within supervisors, issues emerging from the supervisor–supervisee relationship, and finally stress-points extraneous to the relationship or the personalities of the participants, such as training courses or the counselling agencies in which supervisees see clients.

Supervisors' responses to stresses

Supervisors respond to stresses in many ways, some healthy and some unhealthy. Like all professionals, they are faced with either denying that stress exists (and paying the price), recognizing the stress and doing nothing about it, or accepting and managing stress.

Reacting to stressors from within the supervisor

The beginning-supervisor

Reacting to the insecurity of taking on a new job with minimal preparation, many supervisors supervise in the manner in which they were supervised or according to their particular counselling orientation. The danger of the first approach is that it passes on the defects in former supervision to oncoming generations. Some beginning supervisors treat supervision in a less than professional way, seeing it as a cosy chat over a cup of coffee with the initiative often left to the supervisees. Some do not work out detailed contracts with supervisees; these need to include learning objectives, areas for development, various roles and responsibilities.

Other supervisors, knowing they expect to begin supervision, either involve themselves in training courses in supervision or engage in their own supervision (supervision of supervision). This allows them to build up the skills and knowledge to process their work and give theoretical underpinning to what they are doing.

Counselling-bound models of supervision

Some supervisors use 'counselling-bound' models as ways of hiding their own limitations as supervisors. Such models of supervision rarely allow influence from other teaching approaches or indeed from other professions. Educational theory can contribute many learning insights of great use to supervisors, pointing out the strengths and weaknesses of different teaching methods, for example active and passive learning, the use of groups, experiential learning, when to use straight didactic input, the value of handouts and so on. Supervision which closes itself to these influences may be unnecessarily narrow in its loyalty to a counselling orientation. On the other hand, for those who wish to learn from within one counselling orientation, and see themselves practising solely from within it, supervision from within that particular counselling school offers a concentrated form of education.

There is a further danger of the supervisor taking authoritarian stances and insisting that the counselling work be done 'this way', which often equates to the way it is done by supervisors themselves.

Supervisor responsibilities

Confused with an array of responsibilities, supervisors sometimes resort to 'doing what I am comfortable doing', that is, focusing on the teaching or counselling or consulting role of supervision to the exclusion of other roles. This results in a very limited number of responses from supervisors, which often do not meet the learning needs of their supervisees. Furthermore, such supervisors do little to increase the number of supervisory tasks they are able to perform and can offer limited help to developing supervisees.

On being the expert

Sometimes supervisors live up to the role of being 'the expert' and fudge their areas of vulnerability. Supervisees indicate that they find it helpful when supervisors share their own casework with them, and are helped by supervisors who even share their clinical failures. However, supervisors often feel they should hide their mistakes, and keep their own work out of the supervision room. Others are more honest and share with their supervisee areas in which they have no expertise, sometimes at the beginning of supervision. This can reduce their stress and allow them freedom to admit when they are confronting counselling situations to which they cannot speak.

Reactions to stressors from within the supervisory relationship

Evaluation

Some supervisors refuse to evaluate the client work of supervisees, or set up self-evaluation as the only method of feedback to supervisees. This can be a way of avoiding their own responsibility to assess, either formally or informally. Others evaluate very subjectively without making any attempt to provide external norms against which counsellors know they are being assessed. A further way of dealing with the stress of evaluation, especially if the judgements are negative, is to write reports that are not shared with supervisees. Here, supervisors send supervisory reports that are seen only by training course personnel. Perhaps the most destructive way of managing stress in evaluation is to collude with supervisees in the view that there is nothing negative in their work. Supervisors who are afraid of conflict, or afraid of not being liked, or anxious about evaluating in case it has deleterious effects on the career of their supervisees, will often revert to 'the halo effect', seeing all good and no harm.

Providing structure

Supervisors sometimes allow supervisees to find their own way in presenting clients without providing any structure or guidelines to help. Others suggest helpful ways to prepare for supervision (Inskipp and Proctor, n.d.). The latter is perhaps the healthiest way of dealing with the stress of supervisees using their time to best advantage. Leaving the whole presentation issue completely in the hands of supervisees asks for trouble, unless these supervisees are particularly experienced.

Overstructuring the supervisory process can be the response to some supervisors who need to control the relationship or who are unable to allow flexibility within the arrangements. Such rigidity, emerging from supervisors' own needs or anxieties, can limit supervisees' creativity or ability to find their own way of working as counsellors.

Helping supervisees learn

Helping supervisees articulate their methods of learning (for example, I learn best experientially rather than through a lecture) allows the supervisor to gear interventions accordingly; less frustration for supervisees and less stress for supervisors is often the result. However, some supervisors ignore learning needs and supervise to their own strengths. Ignorance of developmental models of supervision means that supervisors have to 'pitch' their interventions to the developmental needs of supervisees by chance rather than by design. Sufficient has been written on these models (Stoltenberg and Delworth, 1987; Skovholt and Ronnestad, 1992) to supply a good background and knowledge to help congruence of learning needs and educational responses.

Relationship issues

In denying what is happening, even that they are stressed, supervisors revert to 'playing games'. Hawthorne (1975: 180–1) depicts a number of these:

> They won't let me (blaming the agency or the training course for limitations in the supervision);
>
> Poor me (how do you expect me to be excellent with all these demands on me?);
>
> I'm really one of you (approval seeking);

One more question deserves another (afraid to answer questions and face one's own vulnerabilities);

Remember who is boss (retaining power);

I'll tell on you (threat to reveal weaknesses to others);

Father/mother knows best (do it my way);

I'm only trying to help (justifying and unable to deal with conflict);

I wonder why you really asked that question? (counselling the supervisee or implying hidden motivation).

Dealing with stressors from outside

The supervisory systems
Keeping clear boundaries between the interested parties involved in the counselling process (the agency in which trainees see clients, the training institution where the counsellor is a student, supervisees, and clients) is difficult. Working with each of the above, as well as with all of them, demands negotiation and clear contracts. Some supervisors, because of complexities, refuse to involve themselves and confine their supervisory work to a few chosen areas.

Conclusion

Briefly there are a number of ways in which supervisors deal with their stress. Some confront it openly and manage it by further training, involving themselves in their own ongoing supervision, by working through stress when it arises within supervision sessions. This seems to me to be the healthy way of managing stress. For those not able, for whatever reason, to be open to the stresses, unhealthy methods enter the fray. Denial can easily take over, relationships are mishandled, and both supervisors and supervisees end up as losers.

Suggestions for improved coping

Three areas will be considered as ways of helping supervisors deal more effectively with the stresses of counselling supervisees: (1) training in supervision; (2) knowledge of the stages that supervisors go through; and (3) the setting up of structures where supervisors look after themselves.

Training in supervision

The single, most powerful item for improved coping for supervisors in dealing with the stresses of the job is, in my view, training in supervision. We have moved past the era when counselling supervision is an inherited task that comes with counselling experience. Training in supervision is no longer an option that may or may not be accepted. Supervisors should see such training as an ethical requirement of the job. The 1993 *Ethical Guidelines for Counseling Supervisors* from the Association for Counselor Education and Supervision (USA) is in no doubt about its importance:

> Supervisors should have had training in supervision prior to initiating their role as supervisors. Supervisors should pursue professional and personal continuing education activities such as advanced courses, seminars and professional conferences, on a regular and on-going basis. These activities should include both counseling and supervision topics and skills. (ACES, 1993: Section 2.01/2.02)

The BAC *Code of Ethics and Practice* is no less demanding. In the section on 'Issues of Competence' it stresses the requirement for supervisors to engage in 'specific training in the development of supervision skills. . . . monitor[ing] their supervision work . . . monitor[ing] the limits of their competence . . . evaluating their supervision work' (BAC, 1990: Section B.3).

A number of sources have outlined curricula for training supervisors (Bradley, 1989; Clarkson and Gilbert, 1991; American Association for Counseling and Development, 1988; Hawkins and Shohet, 1989). A model curriculum for counselling supervision training would include, in my view, four domains: knowledge about supervision, isolating and practising the skills involved in being a supervisor, understanding and implementing the tasks of supervision, and being supervised for the supervision work one is doing.

Knowledge about supervision

This section of training would include knowledge about supervision, presentation of different supervision models, review of the ethical and professional issues involved in supervision and consideration of the developmental models of supervision.

There are a number of up-to-date texts that outline models, review research in supervision and apply supervision to different contexts (Bradley, 1989; Bernard and Goodyear, 1992; Borders and Leddick, 1987; Hawkins and Shohet, 1989; Holloway, 1992, in press; Houston, 1990).

Practising the skills of supervision

Participants on a training course for supervisors would work together (in role-play) to practise the different skills of supervision. There are a number of guidelines in most of the specific areas:

setting up a supervisory contract (Borders and Leddick, 1987);

helping the supervisee prepare for supervision (Inskipp and Proctor, n.d.);

methods of supervisory intervention (Borders and Leddick, 1987);

determining the focus of supervision (Hawkins and Shohet, 1989);

learning how to evaluate supervision, and supervisees, and self as supervisor (Borders and Leddick, 1987; Bradley, 1989);

using group and individual supervision (Houston, 1990);

experimenting with different methods of supervision, and with different styles (Cherniss and Egnatios, 1977).

Throughout the training course participants would take turns in a variety of roles: supervisor/supervisee/observer and in a number of settings: individual, group, peer supervision.

Understanding and implementing the roles of supervision

This section of the training course would isolate the tasks of supervision and help supervisors learn how to set up and maintain a supervisory relationship which involves a number of roles. These roles would include the following:

Setting up a learning supervisory relationship A number of key questions would be raised and discussed here: what is the nature of the supervisory relationship? How does it compare and contrast with the counselling relationship? What elements need to be negotiated and how might the relationship change over the course of supervision? Holloway emphasizes the importance of the relationship within supervision:

The provision of an opportunity for empowerment is a difficult and challenging task for supervisors not only because they must confront their own narcissistic needs and issues of self-aggrandizement, but they also must distinguish between their responsibility to maximize the trainee's unique professional resources and the demands of the profession to evaluate the competence of the supervisee. Is it possible to empower within the context of evaluation? Can supervision be a kind of mutually involving experience, a collaborative effort that provides such an opportunity for empowerment and still maintain a professional gatekeeping role? It is my view that the supervisory relationship is the critical factor in the success of the supervision to provide an opportunity for an empowering environment. (in press: 13)

The teaching task of supervision Supervisors would consider what teaching means in the context of supervision and how best to instruct, coach and set up appropriate learning experiences for supervisees. They would experiment with various teaching methodologies ranging from direct information-giving to setting up experiential learning to further the skill and knowledge of supervisees.

The counselling task of supervision Although supervision is not counselling or therapy, it includes an element of helping supervisees deal with the personal issues emerging from their work with clients. Supervisors would be encouraged to struggle with the interface between supervision and counselling. The following questions would need to be explored in the training course. When is it appropriate to suggest that supervisees engage in their personal therapy? When would supervisors leave aside some time to deal with personal issues in the life of supervisees? How might they negotiate the boundaries between the two roles?

The consulting task of supervision Supervisors implementing this task would be encouraged to review the various systems involved: understanding what is happening to clients; focusing on the relationship between clients and supervisees; considering what is happening to the supervisee; and spending time on the relationship between supervisor and supervisee as a monitor for what is happening between counsellor and client (the parallel process). Each of these domains demands knowledge and skills.

The evaluation task of supervision Here the whole area of counsellor evaluation and appropriate methodologies for assessing the various elements in supervision would be reviewed; for example assessing the developmental level of supervisees when they first arrive for supervision; how to give ongoing feedback as a learning process; how to evaluate formally and write up supervisory reports; how to help supervisees assess supervision and their supervisors.

Bernard and Goodyear have sketched an outline of 'favorable conditions for evaluation' (1992: 106) which comprise the following recommendations: (a) remembering that supervision is an unequal relationship; (b) clarifying the role of supervisors in evaluation and how the valuation reports will be used; (c) addressing defensiveness openly; (d) spelling out evaluation procedures in advance; (e) making evaluation a mutual and a continuous process; (f) creating sufficient flexibility so that 'down time' will not jeopardize summative evaluation; (g) knowing that the administrative structure will support the supervisor's evaluation and also provide a supportive structure if supervisees consider they have been evaluated unfairly or incompletely; (h) avoiding making 'stars' of supervisees; (i) inviting supervisees to evaluate their supervisors and supervision; (j) monitoring the supervisory relationship; (k) not engaging in supervision as supervisors if this is not an 'enjoyed' task.

Monitoring the professional/ethical dimensions of client work   This 'gatekeeping' role concentrates on helping supervisees sensitize themselves to the complexities of the counselling relationship and the various ethical issues, problems and dilemmas emerging. The supervisory training would tackle questions such as : is it the task of supervisors to teach ethical and professional codes, or how to make ethical decisions, or simply to monitor these and address them as they arise? And how is this done?

Reviewing the administrative aspects of client work   This task concentrates on the 'surrounds' of the counselling work. How will supervisors help supervisees manage counselling within contexts that may help or hinder the therapeutic work? Will supervisors intervene in training courses or the counselling agencies if this is appropriate?

Research (Carroll, 1993) has pointed out that supervisors often adhere to a few of these roles/tasks rather than develop a portfolio or range of options that cover all seven. I am arguing here for the ability to utilize any of the seven tasks when appropriate for the learning of supervisees. Flexibility within supervisors creates more learning opportunities for supervisees.

Supervision for supervisors

This is best carried out in group supervision and allows supervisors to review their own work and learn from their experience and that of others. By placing themselves within this context, supervisors can attain the support they need to continue working at what can be a difficult job. Since modelling plays no small part in the supervisory experience (Holloway, in press), it seems important that supervisors provide a forum for reflection, support and challenge for their own work in much the same way as they ask supervisees to subject their work to examination.

Knowledge of the stages that supervisors go through

Although little research has been conducted on the stages supervisors go through as they move from beginners to experienced workers, there are two models that can help supervisors anticipate these stages. Alonso (1983) depicts the life-chart of supervisors in a matrix relating supervisor issues (self and identity, interpersonal, and sociopolitical) to three developmental stages (novice, mid-career and late-career supervisors). Hess (1986) has a simpler format which reviews three stages of supervisor development:

Stage 1 revolves around the beginning supervisor who is working through issues such as role, structuring and implementing supervision, how to work with supervisee resistance, anxiety about appropriate interventions, and stress around knowledge of models and research.

Stage 2 sees supervisors move beyond the novice stage to that of exploration. Here supervisors concentrate on working with their impact on supervisees, and build up their knowledge of supervision models and interventions. Pitfalls and weaknesses at this stage include restricting supervision to the use of one role rather than the ability to utilize a number of different roles, and being too intrusive.

Stage 3 confirms supervisors in their identity as competent supervisors. Supervision is exciting and interesting, there is less worry about relationships, supervisors share more on all fronts, and the key focus is on supervisees' agendas.

Knowledge of such stages can help supervisors monitor their own work. It can also help them anticipate the future and be somewhat prepared for what is to come.

Supervisors looking after themselves

There is no doubt that a major method of dealing with stress, both personal and professional, is a balanced lifestyle. Hawkins and Shohet (1989) include a chapter entitled 'Getting the support and supervision you need'. Here they review the support systems in a supervisor's life, how to recognize stress and the signs and symptoms of stress, elements of burnout and how to anticipate it, and they look at blocks to supervision which may delay getting the support needed to engage in difficult work. Other factors involved are time management, recognizing limitations and working within them, saying no to extra work, and carrying caseloads and commitments that are realistic. The latter will obviously differ from individual to individual: some carry large client loads with little apparent stress, others have clear cut-off points beyond which they become overstressed.

Looking after oneself demands setting and maintaining leisure time, study opportunities, involvement in ongoing training and workshops, and even time to write about experiences. A healthy lifestyle is essential in dealing with stress.

Conclusion

Supervision is a stressful activity with physical and emotional demands on both supervisors and supervisees. Recognizing and understanding the stresses is a good way of beginning to manage them. Not to manage stress is to be managed by it.

Stress is not, of itself, negative. Eustress (positive stress) has been distinguished from distress (negative stress). Positive stress challenges us to move beyond our boundaries and to create new methods of tackling old problems. It triggers our creativity, demanding we face ourselves and our work. For supervisors who are 'stressed' because of their theoretical or practical limitations, the challenge is clear. Can they look at theories and models of supervision, of tasks and interventions, at supervisory relationships, and discover new ways of being supervisors? Being able to listen to the messages of stress can result in new learning for more efficient and more effective supervision.

References

Alonso, A. (1983) 'A developmental theory of psychodynamic supervision', *The Clinical Supervisor*, 1 (3): 23–36.

American Association for Counseling and Development (1988) *Standards for Counseling Supervisors*. Virginia: AACD.

Association for Counselor Education and Supervision (1993) *Ethical Guidelines for Counseling Supervisors*. Virginia: ACES.

Bernard, J. (n.d.) *Clinical Supervision: Impending Issues*. Connecticut: Fairfield University.

Bernard, J. and Goodyear, R. (1992) *Fundamentals of Clinical Supervision*. Boston: Allyn & Bacon.

Borders, L.D. and Leddick, G.R. (1987) *Handbook of Counseling Supervision*. Virginia: ACES.

Bradley, L. (1989) *Counselor Supervision: Principles, Process, and Practice*. Muncie, IN: Accelerated Development.

British Association for Counselling (1990) *Code of Ethics and Practice for the Supervision of Counsellors*. Rugby: BAC.

Carroll, M. (1993) *The Generic Tasks of Supervision*. London: Roehampton Institute.

Cherniss, C. and Egnatios, E. (1977) 'Styles of clinical supervision in community mental health programs', *Journal of Consulting and Clinical Psychology*, 45: 1195–6.

Chrzanowski, G. (1984) 'Can psychoanalysis be taught?', in L. Caligor, P.M. Bromberg and J.D. Meltzer (eds), *Clinical Perspectives on the Supervision of Psychoanalysis and Psychotherapy*. New York: Plenum Press.

Clarkson, P. and Gilbert, M. (1991) 'Training counsellor trainers and supervisors', in W. Dryden and B. Thorne (eds), *Training and Supervision for Counselling in Action*. London: Sage.

Dodds, J.B. (1986) 'Supervision of psychology trainees in field placements', *Professional Psychology: Research and Practice*, 17 (4): 296–300.

Hawkins, P. and Shohet, R. (1989) *Supervision in the Helping Professions*. Milton Keynes: Open University Press.

Hawthorne, L. (1975) 'Games supervisors play', *Social Work*, 20: 179–83.

Hess, A.K. (1986) 'Growth in supervision: stages of supervisee and supervisor development', *The Clinical Supervisor*, 4 (2): 51–67.

Holloway, E. (1992) 'Supervision: a way of teaching and learning', in S.D. Brown and R.W. Lent (eds), *Handbook of Counseling Psychology*, 2nd edition. New York: Wiley.

Holloway, E. (in press) *The Strategic Approach to Supervision*. Newbury Park, CA: Sage.

Houston, G. (1990) *Supervision and Counselling*. London: Rochester Foundation.

Inskipp, F. and Proctor, B. (n.d.) *Skills for Supervising and Being Supervised*. East Sussex: Alexia Publications.

Robiner, W.N. and Schofield, W. (1990) 'References on supervision in clinical and counseling psychology', in *Professional Psychology: Research and Practice*. New York: Wiley.

Rogers, C.R. (1956) 'Training individuals to engage in the therapeutic process', in C.R. Struther (ed.), *Psychology and Mental health*. Washington, DC: American Psychological Association.

Rosenblatt, A. and Mayer, J.E. (1975) 'Objectionable supervisor styles: students' views', *Social Work*. 20: 184–8.

Skovholt, T.M. and Ronnestad, M.H. (1992) *The Evolving Professional Self: Stages and Themes in Therapist and Counselor Development*. New York: Wiley.

Stoltenberg, C.D. and Delworth, U. (1987) *Supervising Counselors and Therapists*. San Francisco: Jossey-Bass.

Villas-Boas Bowen, M. (1986) 'Personality differences and person-centred supervision', *Person-Centred Review*, 1 (3): 291–309.

Zinkin, L. (1989) 'The impossible profession', in *Clinical Supervision: Issues and Techniques* (papers from public conference, April 1988). London: Jungian Training Committee.

12 The Stresses of Counsellors in Training

Katrine H. Jensen

In this chapter the stresses unique to counsellors undergoing formal training will be explored. I use the term 'formal training' as a means of distinguishing between the vast array of training courses on offer. A training course can last two days, six months or five years. It is hoped that counsellors or aspiring counsellors will choose a course to meet their professional needs, whether they are seeking to update or refresh their skills or to embark on a core training course leading to a qualification considered sufficient to denote competency to practise. An evening class of one year's duration in counselling skills undertaken by youth and community workers is not formal training sufficient to practise as a counsellor, but will enhance the counselling role component of their work. Although valued, this type of training will not be addressed in this chapter, nor will brief training courses undertaken by experienced counsellors. These are considered to be professional development rather than formal training.

This chapter, then, will have as its central focus those who embark on a formal training course run by a recognized body, which will either qualify their current professional work or will enable them to gain work as a competent, qualified counsellor. It should be of sufficient duration to allow for extensive study of theory, include a practice element, provide for skill augmentation and have a personal development component.

In Britain today there is no standardized route into counselling, so there is no standardized recognition of training courses with regard to professional competency. As the profession is not, as yet, regulated by government charter, it is quite possible for anyone to set up as a counsellor trainer and offer courses. Obviously the various schools of counselling/psychotherapy profess to maintain professional standards of competency and the British Association for Counselling has started a recognition procedure for both counsellors and training courses, but these efforts remain patchy and are not uniformly applied. Until there is a licensing procedure for all those calling themselves counsellors and offering counselling courses, the profession is open to abusive practices.

The question of whether a training course is recognized or not by any of the various counselling and psychotherapy bodies as sufficient for the participants to be considered 'qualified to practise' remains contentious. It does, however, have some relevance in this context as the training chosen by a practising counsellor, or a would-be counsellor, is going to take into account not only the orientation, the cost and the duration, but also whether it is recognized or not, and whether it can be regarded as a sufficient qualification to practise. The conditions under which counsellors choose a training course have been outlined. In the next section I will look at the actual stresses counsellors encounter once in training.

The nature of the stresses

The stresses of a counsellor in training can be viewed as a multiple demand difficulty, where the demands of the training course requirements themselves are combined with occupational demands, be they related or not, and the demands of the counsellor's private life. The task for the counsellor is how to prioritize and manage each of them to a satisfactory level. I will now look in detail at the variety of stresses a counsellor in training can experience, depending on their circumstances.

Counsellors in training who are in full-time private practice

These counsellors are already trying to deal with the normal stressors of practising counselling: isolation, emotional depletion, caseload management, financial insecurity, conflictual/aggressive clients, boredom, continual restraint and fatigue (Kottler, 1986), as well as striving to maintain a satisfying and stimulating private life which is viewed as essential in the prevention of 'burnout' (Maslach, 1982). For counsellors to function effectively, a rewarding personal and social life is necessary to counter the side effects of practising counselling (Chessick, 1978; Freudenburger and Robbins, 1979). However, maintaining an intimate relationships takes time, effort and a lot of practice. It can be seen as a demand in itself, having to consider and care for another when one can scarcely recognize one's own needs. Relationship responsibilities in the form of children, financial difficulties or domestic problems all add to the stress experienced. As professionals, such counsellors would be attending regular supervision, possibly individual therapy and will probably be affiliated to some kind of professional body which will have its own meetings or attendance requirements. If training requirements are now added to this delicate balance, it can easily be upset. Each course has its own requirements, but most have theory, skills, practice and personal development components. Counsellors must not only attend the necessary hours, but also produce course assignments, prepare projects, practise as necessary and develop self-awareness through personal therapy or experiential exercises.

The demands already being felt by counsellors are now further compounded. During a training course the requirements for academic presentations, mastery of subjects not related to counselling (such as computers/statistics) and self-exposure through oral presentations and peer assessment can leave counsellors feeling deskilled, inadequate and demoralized. Their response to these developments is a challenge in itself. The necessity of self-examination and evaluation of current practice with regard to adaptation to include new learning places counsellors under considerable further pressure.

The financial costs for counsellors in training, if not met by an external source, include course fees and expenses, loss of earnings, and possibly childminder fees. The personal costs include a loss of social leisure time, additional burden on partners and/or family and possibly a reduced capacity for intimate interaction. The need to balance training needs, work schedules and domestic responsibilities often results in counsellors having to cut corners in order to meet commitments. This potential diminishing of quality in relationships, both personal and professional, can result in counsellors feeling dissatisfied with their performance. After all, there are only so many hours in the day and only so much quality concentration in any one counsellor.

Counsellors in training who practise full-time in an employed post

Here, counsellors will have to deal with the culture of the organization, which can be dysfunctional (the self-martyrdom ethos) and which may be positively hostile to their training needs, viewing 'qualifications' as a threat to the status quo or a first step to leaving the organization. Such organizations can be obstructive and attempt to sabotage the efforts of counsellors to meet training course requirements. Such hostility can be a reaction to feared new knowledge, or working practices that could be in opposition to current, accepted cultural norms in the organization. Alternatively the organization can be proactive and supportive, giving training days, paying fees and giving study time. It is also possible for an organization to espouse a belief in the value of training while, at the same time, exhibiting a passive stance, not openly discouraging, yet failing to encourage by expecting counsellors to attend training and study in their own time and still meet all work commitments. In this instance, training is accepted as long as it does not get in the way of counsellors' 'normal work' and no support is given to overcome the difficulties of combining training demands with work demands, for example team meetings, out-of-hours meetings, being on call and on-line managerial supervision.

Counsellors in training who work in allied fields

In the community mental health field, one can find support workers, outreach workers, unqualified residential social workers and general mental health workers, all of whom use counselling skills in relating to clients, yet are not practising counsellors. If such workers decide to move into counselling as a professional activity as part of their career development, or as a career change, they will face the task of combining their work commitments with a training course requirement that will also include a practice element. In this case the demands of the practice placement(s), with the associated travelling, team meetings and in-house training, are added to the stress load. There is a greater possibility of employers being hostile to such workers' aspirations to become counsellors in training, as the training can be viewed as pre-empting departure since it is not strictly relevant to, or applicable in, the current work situation. This scenario combines the worst of the conflicting demands: working full time in an unrelated but allied field, including all the demands that mental health work entails, coupled to a training course that requires regular attendance, an independent practice placement, supervision for the placement, private studying time for assignments, presentations and research projects and a possible requirement to embark on personal therapy and, with that, to examine oneself maybe for the first time. This alone would be difficult, particularly for inexperienced counsellors who are also having to face self-doubt, private fears and inadequacies with regard to their counselling abilities, but also to be expected to maintain a varied and stimulating social life and satisfy domestic responsibilities and intimate relationship expectations can produce demands which appear overwhelming and impossible to meet by all but the most determined.

Full-time counsellors in training

Here I mean counsellors who follow a course that meets at least two and a half days a week. With this, working full-time becomes an impossibility and so funding becomes paramount, whether in the form of a grant, a loan or an award. The high cost of training courses, the necessary expenses (for example in personal therapy) incurred and the duration, combined with the difficulties of earning a living, mean that such courses tend to attract those who can afford to take a year off from working, or those who can bear being unemployed or who have a secondary source of income. This helps to explain why counselling is a middle-class occupation. The necessary financial outlay inhibits individuals who are on a low or limited income, as is often the case in the caring professions as a whole. To commit oneself to paying course fees, supervision fees, therapy fees and travel and other expenses related to training, for an extended period of one to three years, requires a solvent financial position or a profound determination. For those who give up work to train and attempt to live on benefits, loans and/or savings, the struggle just to survive can erode the pleasures of exploring counselling as a vocational pursuit. It is also worth commenting on the resentments between differing types of counsellor in the counselling field, as these can also act as a further obstacle for counsellors in training. Counsellors who practise privately or who work for an employer can be very resentful of volunteer counsellors attending a placement, viewing them as undermining the field's professional status and the earning power of counsellors as a body and bringing the profession into disrepute by their ignorance of what constitutes counselling. As such, counsellors in training who attend placements in preference to setting themselves up in private practice (with all the difficulties this involves) can be treated with disrespect by their colleagues and their opinions devalued at the placement if paid counsellors are employed. This can add to the self-doubt and crises of confidence often experienced by novice counsellors in training.

What I have attempted to do here is to give an outline of the types of stress counsellors in training can encounter, while also taking into account the diversity of circumstances in which counsellors attempt to train. It is not a definitive account of all counsellors in training, as the variations are endless. However, I hope I have conveyed the difficulties, the demands (financial, emotional and personal), the divided loyalties and the relentless pressure which the majority of counsellors encounter when they embark upon a training course. The effect of these stressors on the quality of counselling offered by a counsellor can only be speculated upon. It is known that 'stressed out' counsellors deliver a reduced service (Hershenson and Power, 1987). Therefore, it rests with counsellors in training, while in the counselling room, to cope with the external and internal demands they are experiencing. Their failure to do so results in further stress as they face personal fears of incompetence. Although I can find no relevant research on the failure or 'drop-out' rates of counsellors in professional training, it would be unusual if the considerable demands engendered by embarking on such a training course did not result in some casualties.

Having looked at the variety of stresses encountered by counsellors in training, I will now examine how counsellors in training respond to them.

Counsellors' responses to the additional stresses of training

How counsellors respond to the additional demands of training depends largely on their personalities (Guy, 1987) and on their individual circumstances and available resources. I have conducted some research which has given an outline of typical stress response patterns of counsellors in training (Jensen, 1993). The main aims of this study were to discover what main sources of support were utilized and how much they were valued by counsellors. The majority of counsellor participants in the study were undertaking formal training in counselling leading to a qualification. It was found that there was a diverse and multifaceted network of support resources available and that each counsellor in training used elements of it with informed discretion, depending on their circumstances. The support resources noted can be divided into external and internal locations. From the results of the study, the external sources of support indicated were: colleagues, individual therapy, independent supervision, associates, friends, family (including partners) and workshops. Internal sources of support were: self-awareness, self-help, prayer and alternative medicine. Various social activities were also seen as sources of support. These included participation in a professional association, voluntary work, social groups, spiritual groups and sports.

For those with partners it was found that almost half perceived their partnership to be their greatest source of support in coping with day-to-day stresses. In fact, even for those without partners, having one was seen as a potential source of support. The value given to this 'partner support' was 'very important'. Such support took the form of listening, tolerating, non-sexual contact, consideration and being made to feel important. The findings concerning the value of a partner confirms Chessick's (1978) assertion quoted in Guy (1987) that 'mature love relationships' are a necessity for counsellors, a theme echoed by Dryden and Spurling's (1989) compilation of ten therapists, many of whom cited their partners as their mainstay of support. Despite this valuing of a partner, marital discord is as high among counsellors as other sections of the population (Guy, 1987) a resultant factor, perhaps, of the stresses encountered by counsellors. Looking at the whole network of support resources available, outlined in the study, it was found that 80 per cent or more of the participants felt that support was obtained from friends, colleagues, individual therapy, self-awareness and managerial/independent supervision, which is confirmed by the findings of Manthei (1987). But, although support was derived from these sources, the value placed upon them was not always proportional. For example, 80 per cent gave 'colleagues' as a source of support, but only 30 per cent named them as their 'greatest' source of support. Overall, after partners came therapy and friends in joint second place, with a combined 48 per cent naming these as their greatest source of support. These findings are consistent with what has been suggested by Guy (1987), that understanding from family and friends and social interaction can have a holding capacity for distressed counsellors, and by Freudenberger and Robbins (1979) (quoted in Guy, 1987), that the private lives and relationships of counsellors should be valued as priority needs. The naming of 'family/partner', 'friends' and 'therapy' as both obtained and valued sources of support suggests that in these areas there is a good match between what types of support are wanted and what types of support are received by counsellors in training.

This network of support resources relied upon by counsellors is not exhaustive. Included in the questionnaire was the question 'Ideally, how would you like to be supported?' This was intended to tease out any deficiencies in the support needs of counsellors covered by the other questions and to highlight in what form support is wanted. The results were that 47 per cent wanted a partner's support, 25 per cent wanted support from friends, 25 per cent wanted managerial or colleague support and 23 per cent wanted supervisory/therapist support. These results can be understood to mean that counsellors wanted some or more support from each source. Other, less 'ideal' sources cited were 'higher incomes', 'more inner resources/coping strategies' and 'more family support'. When asked, 'How do you compensate for not receiving this support?', 39 per cent of the sample relied on inner strengths and 25 per cent used their friends more. Other coping mechanisms given included: reliance on therapist/supervisor, increased involvement in leisure activities, using food as a substitute, working harder and relying on a partner or family more. Some of these responses can be seen as detrimental to the overall well-being of counsellors – for example overworking and comfort eating – and some suggest increased dependence and a reliance on a possibly strained relationship within the family. The emphasis on inner coping resources might suggest the isolation and withdrawn stance of many counsellors. Very few counsellors named client affirmations, that is, clients' expressions of appreciation of the counselling received, as a source of support. Only a few gave diverse work roles, for example counsellor/teacher, as a source of support, which is surprising, given the findings of Dryden and Spurling (1989) where a diverse work schedule and client affirmations were given as a sustaining force. This could be due to the circumstances in which counsellors in training practise, or, perhaps, the stage they have reached in their professional careers.

Included in the study was a measure of substance use. The results yielded 72 per cent who used food for comfort, 75 per cent who drank alcohol and 38 per cent who used painkillers. These findings could be interpreted as an indication of the degree of counsellors' distress. There was only minimal use of prescribed sedatives, sleeping pills and antidepressants (15 per cent in total), but if this is added to the 14 per cent who use non-prescription drugs, then 29 per cent – over a quarter – of the counsellor participants were taking mood-altering substances, to greater or lesser degrees, to alleviate something they were experiencing. Include the 75 per cent who drink alcohol – assuming that there are some who use alcohol and one or more mood-altering substance – and the picture suggests that a majority of counsellors in training are taking something to affect their mood.

There is distress among counsellors in training, the reasons for which have already been outlined. Responses to this distress can be healthy or unhealthy but must be viewed in the context of the individual counsellor. Choices are only choices if one feels able to actualize them freely. Counsellors in training are hindered by time constraints, financial constraints, unhealthy working practices and conflictual demands for excellence. It is an extraordinary load, yet one which these counsellors are often expected to carry without compromise. Many counsellors in training find themselves in conflict with employers, tutors, family, dependants and partners in their efforts to satisfy all demands. For many there is a residual anger at the unrealistic expectations of others and of themselves, which, unfortunately, only adds to their distress. Dissatisfaction with their possible diminished professional performance, with lack of time for adequate study and with reduced capacity for meaningful intimate relations, all compound the counsellors' difficulties. Their reliance on internal coping mechanisms to mitigate this pressure, confirmed by Beck (1987) – which include cognitive reframing, modified coping strategies and the moderation of the physiological stress response, combined with spiritual beliefs, meditation and self-awareness – places the emphasis firmly on the need for counsellors in training to be vigilant for signs of stress, to be proactive in maintaining their well-being, and to establish boundaries both in the working environment and in their personal lives. For someone experiencing distress, this can sound a bit like 'it's your responsibility not to get stressed, but if you do it is also your responsibility to do something about it'.

In this section I have looked at the varied sources of support utilized and valued by counsellors and the behaviours, both social and personal, they display in response to stress. In the next section I will examine what changes could be made to lessen the demands made upon counsellors in training and also what counsellors themselves can do to cope better with the stresses they encounter.

Suggestions for improved coping

There is an abundance (Norcross *et al.* 1986) of researched suggestions into how counsellors can improve their coping responses, most of which can be utilized by counsellors in training.

With regard to the intimate and social dimension, they could prioritize their private lives and relationships (Freudenburger and Robbins, 1979, cited in Guy, 1987), seek out mature love relationships (Chessick, 1978, cited in Guy, 1987), maintain a variety of social contacts and relationships (Guy, 1987), develop outside interests (Corey, 1986, cited in Kottler, 1986), share their emotions (Beck, 1987) and find understanding friends and a loving family (Guy, 1987). On a professional level they can make use of colleagues and set personal limits with clients and organizations (Corey, 1986, cited in Kottler, 1986). They can also use supervision more and increase professional involvement so as to affect the structure of service provision (Guy, 1987) and be assertive about caseloads and role ambiguities, confronting the source of stress where possible (Manthei, 1987). With reference to internal resources that can be better utilized for self-care purposes, counsellors can benefit from individual therapy (Guy, 1987), take responsibility for personal growth outside the organization and have multiple measures of success (Corey, 1986, cited in Kottler, 1986). Counsellors can also practise diagnosing their sources of stress and cognitive reframing of that stress. They can adapt their coping responses to be more flexible (Beck, 1987), or they could take heed of the therapists in Dryden and Spurling's (1989) publication and develop a diverse work schedule.

I would venture to suggest that most counsellors in training do attempt to have an effective and adaptive response to stress in all of the dimensions outlined. Most counsellors in training undergo personal or group therapy, have a supervisor as a requirement of practising and do attempt to develop a social life, given the time constraints, while practising assertiveness in the workplace or placement and consideration in intimate relationships, to the best of their abilities. But the results from Jensen (1993) suggest that these responses are insufficient in themselves to mediate the stresses felt by counsellors in training and the results also give recognition to the demands and limitations of personal adaptation. There is, perhaps, an essential part to be played by training institutions, employers and placement organizers in reducing unnecessary demands on counsellors in training.

Perhaps one should concentrate on preventing stress, as Guy (1987) suggests, but then even when coping well, we do not always know why. Depression, recognized or not, among counsellors in training is, I would suggest, more common than one would suspect. The constant emphasis on self-knowledge, self-awareness and introspective understanding does rather take the joy and spontaneity out of interpersonal relationships, leaving one self-conscious and hypersensitive. The necessity to maintain boundaries with colleagues, employers, friends, family and associates who seek informal but expert counselling on issues too close to the counsellors' interests, can easily be eroded when counsellors feel isolated, alone and hurting within. When others' and their own expectations of what constitutes a counsellor result in counsellors trying to be all-giving, understanding and accepting with expression of necessary selfishness subdued, they can find themselves playing an intolerable, suffocating role, unable to express effectively anger, resentment and, perhaps, despair at the futility of their caring. Such can be the lot and limitations of counsellors.

What can others do to help? As suggested previously, there is a part for others to play. Training organizations can help by being more flexible in the types of course on offer, by reducing fees and unnecessary expenses, by giving concessionary rates to allied professionals on low incomes, by tailoring courses more closely to the counselling experiences of counsellors, by locating and subsidizing personal therapists where individual therapy is a necessary component of the course, by providing free supervision of caseloads and crèches for those with childcare responsibilities and by allowing more varied means of paying fees (for example monthly). Most of these proactive measures of support presume that training organizations have financial resources available which, sadly, most do not.

Awareness of the differing individual circumstances of counsellors in training, as opposed to the presumption that they are a homogeneous group with the same needs, abilities and constraints, would, with the other suggestions, go some way towards providing the active support that such counsellors need. Many of the financial and attendance requirements set by training organizations appear to be specifically designed to block potential applicants who need to earn a living wage while training and who have no financial resources to call upon. This economic 'weeding out' may be costing the profession its potentially best practitioners – those who have diverse experiences of life and who have entered into counselling as 'survivors' of their experiences. As individual counsellors in training need to recognize their limits and maintain their boundaries where personal time is concerned, so tutors too need to be realistic in setting reading lists, assignments and research projects, so that precious time is not wasted in fruitless endeavours.

Placement co-ordinators can also help with regard to extra-curricular activities and their expectations of volunteer or part-paid counsellors in training to attend every placement event as a show of commitment to the organization. Counsellors show their commitment in the quality of their work with clients and not in their availability to attend fund-raising events. Very few counsellors in training who are on placements are only attending a training course. It would also be a supportive sign if the time that counsellors in training do give to the placement is valued and acknowledged openly; instead the idea is often conveyed that counsellors in training should be grateful to be allowed to practise there.

Employers can be supportive by offering day release, study leave, help with fees and an attitude that suggests that they have the welfare and professional development of the counsellors at heart. Obstructing the aspirations of would-be counsellors will not prevent them from leaving and can in fact speed up the decision to take flight for something better. An employer or organization that holds and supports counsellors in training will tend to be rewarded by increased loyalty and deepening commitment. The scope for employers to value and use the learning the counsellor in training brings to the workplace, and to integrate it into good working practices, can be of benefit to the whole organization as well as reaffirming the counsellor's position and good judgement in deciding to further their professional development.

This brings us to the cultural devaluing of those who are learning. Being referred to as a student, apprentice or trainee has connotations of inexperience, incompetence and naivety. While these could be applied to some individual counsellors, the vast majority do not deserve this disrespect to their endeavours. Friends, family, colleagues and partners can all help counsellors in training by being aware of what they expect from them and whether this is realistic, and by showing toleration, even when the counsellors themselves are unable to do so. Exercising tact and discretion when pointing out omissions and being concerned about stress signs can aid counsellors in training to take stock of what is happening and act appropriately. Critical comments and thought-less demands can result in further withdrawal from being able to address the problem.

Finally, counsellors in training should learn from others how they cope with the demands being made upon them and competitive one-upmanship should be confronted as pernicious and contrary to open expression and mutual learning. The compromise made by balancing excessive demands, personal needs, commit-ments, responsibilities, doubts, guilt and divided loyalties is a skilled art. It requires practice and an openness to try experiential methods alien to, or in conflict with, one's own self-concept.

For those counsellors in training who appear to be able to limit the effects of multiple and conflicting demands, one mainstay might be their ability to resolve the dilemma by finding acceptable compromises which minimize guilt and feelings of failure, a form of cognitive/emotional negotiation with oneself. Accepting the reality that not all demands can be met with an equal quality of performance at all times, counsellors in training must prioritize. There is also a need to recognize that performing to the very best of one's ability at all times can be impossible and a waste of personal resources. At times just satisfying one particular demand allows unused resources to be allocated to other areas. One example of this for counsellors in training is the production of a course assignment of a standard which is adequate to meet the requirements but takes less time than the best possible effort. This leaves more time for a personal or work commitment. This concept of giving less than maximum effort to any one task or demand utilizes the question 'It might not be perfect, but is it good enough?' It is an approach which can be unacceptable to those with rigid expectations of performance and to those who cannot negotiate feelings of guilt, or accept disapproval or disappointment from others.

In achieving our goals, we struggle to overcome such adverse circumstances, and in this endeavour, we truly come to know ourselves.

References

Beck, D.F. (1987) 'Counselor burnout in family service agencies', *Social Casework: The Journal of Contemporary Social Work*, 68: 3–15.

Chessick, R.D. (1978) 'The sad soul of the psychiatrist', *Bulletin of the Minninger Clinic*, 42: 1–9.

Corey, G. (1986) *Theory and Practice of Counselling and Psychotherapy*, 3rd edition. Monterey, CA: Brooks/Cole.

Dryden, W. and Spurling, L. (eds) (1989) *On Becoming a Psychotherapist*. London: Tavistock/Routledge.

Freudenburger, H.J. and Robbins, A. (1979) 'The hazards of being a psychoanalyst', *Psychoanalytic Review*, 66: 275–95.

Gladding, S.T. (1991) 'Counselor Self-Abuse', *Journal of Mental Health Counseling*, 13: 414–19.

Guy, J.D. (1987) *The Personal Life of the Psychotherapist*. New York: Wiley.

Hershenson, D.B. and Power, P.W. (1987) *Mental Health Counseling: Theory and Practice*. New York: Pergamon Press.

Jensen, K.H. (1993) 'A study of the sources of counsellor support', MSc research, Roehampton Institute.

Jupp, J.J. and Shaul, V. (1991) 'Burn-out in student counsellors', *Counselling Psychology Quarterly*, 4: 157–67.

Kottler, J.A. (1986) *On Being a Therapist*. San Francisco: Jossey-Bass.

Manthei, R.J. (1987) 'School counsellors and job-related stress', *New Zealand Journal of Educational Studies*, 22: 187–200.

Maslach, C. (1982) *Burn-out, the Cost of Caring*. Englewood Cliffs, NJ: Prentice-Hall.

Norcross, J.C., DiClemente, C.C. and Prochaska, J.O. (1986) 'Self-change of psychological distress: laypersons' vs psychologists' coping strategies', *Journal of Clinical Psychology*, 42: 834–40.

About the Editor

Windy Dryden is Professor of Counselling at Goldsmiths College, University of London. He has authored or edited over 75 books including *Rational-Emotive Counselling in Action* (Sage Publications, 1990) and *Daring to be Myself: A Case of Rational-Emotive Therapy*, written with Joseph Yankura (Open University Press, 1992). In addition, he edits 12 book series in the area of counselling and psychotherapy including the *Whurr Dictionary Series* (Whurr Publishers) and *Developing Counselling* (Sage Publications). His major interests are in rational emotive behaviour therapy, eclecticism and integration in psychotherapy and, increasingly, writing short, accessible self-help books for the general public. His latest in this genre is *Ten Steps to Positive Living* (Sheldon, 1994).

About the Contributors

Tim Bond is Staff Tutor in Counselling at the Department of Adult and Continuing Education, University of Durham and is Chair of the British Association for Counselling (BAC). He has written three books including a report sponsored by the Department of Health, *HIV Counselling* (BAC, 1991) and *Standards and Ethics for Counselling in Action* (Sage Publications, 1993). He has co-authored reports on role differentiation and ethical standards for advice, guidance and counselling for the Department of Employment, as well as many articles. His major interests include counselling in health settings, group dynamics and the ethics of the caring professions.

Joan L. Brady is a Doctoral Candidate in Clinical Psychology at Rosemead School of Psychology, Biola University, and a research assistant to James Guy in his programmatic research on the impact of conducting therapy on psychotherapists. She is also a therapist at the Biola Counseling Center and an adjunct Professor for the University. She resides in La Habra, California, with her husband, Mark.

Michael Carroll is Director of Studies in Psychology and Counselling at Roehampton Institute, London, where he directs and teaches on the MSc in Psychological Counselling. He has run a youth counselling service for one of the London boroughs, and has been involved in counselling training and supervision for a number of years. His current interests are counselling in organizations and workplace counselling, and he has recently taught one of the first Diplomas in Counselling at Work. His main research interest revolves around counselling supervision and he is engaged in writing a book on the subject.

Kate Coppenhall works as a Counsellor, Trainer and Supervisor within the voluntary and private sectors. The subject of her PhD research is the impact of work with survivors of childhood sexual abuse upon the person of the therapist. Within the nursing press her published works reflect her previous career as a health worker. In addition to her work with survivors of sexual abuse, her major interests are the counsellor-practitioner as researcher and the use of psychodrama and sociodrama to explore personal, relational and societal issues connected with childhood sexual abuse.

Colin Feltham is Course Consultant for the Thameslink Counselling Diploma, a course accredited by the University of East London. He is also a Regional Consultant for Mentors Counselling Consultants, a specialist employee counselling consultancy. He has written and edited a number of books with Windy Dryden, including *Brief Counselling* (Open University Press, 1992), the *Dictionary of Counselling* (Whurr Publishers, 1993) and *Developing Counsellor Supervision* (Sage Publications, 1994). His interests include time-limited counselling, and the interface between professionalism and critiques of counselling.

James D. Guy is Vice-President for University Services and Professor of Psychology at Biola University, La Mirada, California. He has authored over 50 professional articles and one book, *The Personal Life of the Psychotherapist* (Wiley, 1987), on the relationship between the professional role and personal life of mental health professionals. Dr Guy is a Diplomate in Clinical Psychology of the American Board of Professional Psychology and a Fellow of the American Psychological Association.

Francis C. Healy is Research Assistant to John Norcross in the Psychology Department at the University of Scranton, where he received his baccalaureate with high honours. His major interests, including psychotherapist stress, child therapy, and parent–child interactions, lie in clinical psychology, but stretch into the cognitive sciences as well.

Richard House is a professional GP counsellor in Norwich and a group facilitator. He is currently undergoing further training in body-oriented psychotherapy and studying for an MA in the Philosophy of Mind at the University of East Anglia. He has published several articles on the dynamics of the accreditation process and the ideological tensions of GP counselling. His philosophy is humanistic and integrative, with special interests in questions of free will, determinism and the nature of (psycho)therapeutic change; pre- and perinatal psychology and primal integration; group and organizational dynamics; and evolutionary psychiatry and the psychodynamics of social systems and human survival.

Katrine H. Jensen has been counselling for five years and is currently working with individuals, couples and as a group facilitator. She is a consultant supervisor and has run workshops on stress management. Katrine has specialized in difficult bereavements and those with chronic mental distress. Originally from a background in community mental health, she worked with individuals who had 'challenging behaviours'. While working with them in developing their communication skills and their ability to identify and constructively express their emotions, her desire to further this role, as a counsellor, emerged. She trained at the Roehampton Institute, London, obtaining an MSc in Psychological Counselling.

John McLeod is Director of the Centre for Counselling Studies at Keele University. He is a person-centred counsellor with research interests in the fields of counsellor training, the social and organizational context of counselling and therapeutic process. His recent book, *An Introduction to Counselling* (Open University Press, 1993) explores the nature and development of current theory and practice in counselling.

John C. Norcross is Professor and former Chair of Psychology at the University of Scranton and a clinical psychologist in independent practice. Author of more than 100 scholarly articles, Dr Norcross has written or edited nine books, the most recent being the *Handbook of Psychotherapy Integration*, with Marvin Goldfried (Basic Books, 1993), *An Insider's Guide to Graduate Programs in Clinical Psychology*, with Tracy Mayne and Michael Sayette (Guilford Press, 1994) and the third edition of *Systems of Psychotherapy: A Transtheoretical Analysis*, with James Prochaska (Brooks/Cole, 1994).

Stephen Palmer is Director of the Centre for Stress Management, London, and an Honorary Visiting Lecturer in Psychology at Goldsmiths College, University of London. He has written over 50 articles and a number of books and training manuals on stress management and counselling. He is currently writing with Windy Dryden *Counselling for Stress Problems* (Sage Publications). He is Managing Editor of *Counselling*, Editor of *Counselling Psychology Review* and Co-editor of *The Rational Emotive Behaviour Therapist*. His major interests are in multimodal therapy and rational emotive behaviour therapy, and their application to group stress management in counselling and industrial settings.

Peter Ross is Director of the University of Reading Counselling Service. Trained as both an occupational psychologist and a psychotherapist, he is the author of numerous chapters and journal papers as well as popular magazine articles. His main interests are in the psychology of beliefs systems (especially in religion, hypnosis and meditation) and in the management of counselling and psychotherapy services. He is currently working on editing a CVCP (committee of vice-chancellors and principals of the universities of the UK) volume on benchmark quality standards for university counselling services and on refining a client problem coding system for the Association for Student Counselling.

Julia Segal is a Counsellor at the CMH Multiple Sclerosis Unit, Central Middlesex Hospital, London. She is the author of three books: *Phantasy in Everyday Life* (Penguin, 1985), *Melanie Klein* (Sage Publications, 1992) and *My Mum Needs Me: Helping Children with Ill or Disabled Parents* (Penguin, 1993). Strongly influenced by the work of Melanie Klein, she writes and teaches at present mostly in the fields of disability and illness.

Eddy Street is a Consultant Clinical Psychologist in the health service in Cardiff. He is also a visiting member of staff at the Family Institute, Cardiff. He is author of *Counselling for Family Problems* (Sage Publications, 1994), co-editor, with Windy Dryden, of *Family Therapy in Britain* (Open University Press, 1988) and has written over 30 chapters and articles. His major interests are in working systemically with children and families, particularly those with genetic and handicapping conditions.

Index

Compiled by Jackie McDermott